# Living Divorced

## THE DIARY OF A PASTOR'S DAUGHTER-IN-LAW

## Lillian Nowlin-Hunt

TRILOGY CHRISTIAN PUBLISHERS

*TUSTIN, CA*

Trilogy Christian Publishers
A Wholly Owned Subsidiary of Trinity Broadcasting Network
2442 Michelle Drive
Tustin, CA 92780

*Living Divorced*

Trilogy Christian Publishers A Wholly Owned Subsidiary of Trinity Broadcasting Network

2442 Michelle Drive Tustin, CA 92780

Unless otherwise indicated, all scripture quotations are from the King James Version of the Bible. Public domain.

Rights Department, 2442 Michelle Drive, Tustin, CA 92780.

Trilogy Christian Publishing/TBN and colophon are trademarks of Trinity Broadcasting Network.

Cover design by: Jeff Summers

For information about special discounts for bulk purchases, please contact Trilogy Christian Publishing.

Manufactured in the United States of America

10 9 8 7 6 5 4 3 2 1

Library of Congress Cataloging-in-Publication Data is available.

ISBN: 978-1-63769-892-1

E-ISBN: 978-1-63769-893-8

# Endorsements

Wow. *Living Divorced* is a must read. To know that I lived through these occurrences, reading this memoir has literally enraptured my memories into amazement, and made my survival surreal. That's how worthy this book is..."

- Pastor Kenneth Hunt

A unique contribution to the growing memoir genre, Lillian Nowlin-Hunt's masterful storytelling takes you on a journey through her life as a woman, mother, wife, and Christian. In a moment her personal story is heart wrenching, and the next inspiring. Nowlin-Hunt's ability to make her life experiences relatable to the masses will leave you empowered and confident through her vulnerable, and authentic writing."

-Four Pillars Press Publishing
*www.fourpillarspress.net*

"Reading Lillian Nowlin-Hunt's words feels like you're listening to your best friend share their day. Except this friend's life is truly stranger, and more inspiring than fiction! A relatable memoir, Nowlin-Hunt lays her life bare to encourage us that we too can live empowered, and authentic lives."

- Nakeia Councils Daniels, Editor FPPP

# Contents

# Divorce

So I think I should just leave and divorce my husband. If I walk away now, I am sure I could find Mr. MarcTrain, and maybe he will take me back. The way he showed me and told me he loved me back then, if he has just a pea size of that love left, I have something to run back to. Yes. I know his mom loves me because she has already shown love to me and the family that has developed through this marriage, so it shouldn't be hard for me to drop everything and walk away.

I feel like this is what's expected of me. Like everyone is standing around waiting and becoming impatient, wondering when I am going to make this big move and run. Of course, after writing *The Covering* with the happily ever after ending, all of that has to be destroyed and ruined. What makes me so special that I deserve the right to keep the happy ending?

One thing that I have learned is some people truly do want to see you happy. However, they also want to put a limit on that happiness. Don't start living your life better than those that are "rooting" for you and aren't genuine. Next thing you know, those that were for you become your worst enemies. You begin to realize what you thought you had in "friends" and "family" you really never had.

I wasn't anyone's choice for KB in the first place. Seems like it was more people who were against us getting married than there were for us, so why keep it together? I am pretty sure someone is saying they could have done a better job at being a wife than I did. I know there are women waiting for me to move on to show KB the great woman they can be to him and satisfy all his needs. Maybe, just maybe, there really is someone else out there who is just like Dion who will meet the approval standards to be KB's wife.

I'm done. Our marriage has stayed together this long, and that's an accomplishment, so I shouldn't feel bad about this at all. I feel so crowded and alone all at the same time. Alone because I can't think of anyone who can understand what I am going through right now who would want to be by my side to help me get through this. Yet I feel congested and crowded, almost to the point of actually being able to feel and smell the hard breathing on my neck of those that are impatiently wanting me to make a move.

No one else in my family has stayed in their marriage, so why am I trying to be the oddball out? My father divorced my mother, so I guess you could say I am following in his path. Not only did he divorce my mom, but he remarried immediately—basically before the divorce was even completed, so who would care if Mr. MarcTrain swept me off my feet now? My brother got married, and now he is divorced too—should have seen that coming, right? I can't forget my big sister, yep, married and divorced, so what am I waiting on? Clearly, these Nowlin offspring were not fit or made to remain married. Maybe that is why my baby sister hasn't married anyone—she is smarter than us all. I know that my family would be there for me. I was there for them, so why wouldn't they be? As long as I have my family, I will be okay.

What would KB's family say? I don't think at this point it really matters. I would be tarnishing that Hunt name. I would be bringing shame into the family. I would be tearing down that perception of unity. Or I would be showing I wasn't raised like a Hunt, so I don't act like a Hunt. I would be proving that KB moved too fast and married me out of grief. KB didn't know me, and marrying me was the wrong thing to do. Marrying me was probably the worst thing KB has ever done in his life.

What would the church say? Should I really care, but just thinking—what would they say? I wonder if there would be anyone that is shocked, or would everyone just say, "We knew it"? There are so many divorced people in the church right now; what would be wrong with joining in with the rest of them? From bishops to prophetess and prophets to missionaries, evangelists, pastors, and elders, all levels of leadership have been divorced and still operate. Hey, many of them seem to be elevated when they divorce, so I guess I should look at this thought as a "come up." Maybe I can use getting a divorce as a "ministry" to support other divorced people within the church. I can travel the world doing workshops and conferences on surviving a divorce in the church. If the church keeps pedophiles, adulterers, thieves, and liars around, surely they won't throw me away.

My "brother" on the job just got a divorce. Happily married to his wife for over twenty years, he began having an affair with a coworker who also happened to be married. Initially, I had no idea they were an item. I knew he was married because he had the picture of his wife and family on his desk. When we all went to lunch together, I just assumed she was going because she was a coworker and friend like me and nothing more. Talking about my book, The Covering, one day at lunch, I began to say how I had no respect for a woman that would entertain a married man. Imagine the silence that took place that day.

Once I found out there was more than just a work friendship going on, I refused to go to lunch as usual with them as if I was in agreement with what was going on. They were both married, for goodness' sake. There was no way in the world I was going to sit silently as if I was okay with their behaviors. I was saddened to hear that he left his wife and children and said that he wanted to have some time to himself. This woman married with children of her own said she wanted them to be together, and it looked like that was what he wanted too.

*Know this:* I will never have any form of respect for a woman who knowingly and willingly engaged in a relationship with a married man. Say it's a childhood scar if you want, but I call it just plain ole nasty!

Daily, I communicated with my "bro," telling him he was doing the wrong thing and that he needed to remain with his family. After a while of working on him and giving him scripture and praying with him, he decided to try God and attempt to put his family back together. I always wondered if it was because he realized it was cheaper to keep her, or he really did want his family back together again. He began going to church and wanted to fight for his family. His wife, by this time, was done with him and wanted nothing but to get away from him and get half of every dime he had. No matter what he did to try to keep his family together, his wife was more determined to keep them apart.

Well, his divorce was done. He had to pay out a lot of money to his wife and children and the lawyer, but it was over. But by the time the divorce was finalized, he had been back and forth with the woman he was having an affair with so much, on and off, even at one point telling her to stay away from him; it looked like he was going to end up with nothing and no one. This woman he was sleeping with never filed for her divorce. She said she wanted to be with him, but time passed, and she never made moves to back up what she was saying, never getting a divorce and staying in limbo with both men while becoming pregnant. It was scandalous, to say the least, wondering who the paternity test would proclaim as the father.

What could possibly be going through a woman's head that gets her in a predicament like this? What explanation do you have to justify this type of behavior? Maybe it is the television shows that nowadays glorify women who sleep with men that are married. It looks like the world is routing for this type of woman. Here we are setting the DVR and running home after church services to make sure we watch that show to see who's going to sleep with who and if the relationship remains intact.

Whether the leading man or the leading woman, the storyline someway somehow causes two individuals that should not be sleeping together to end up having steamy, arousing sexual encounters each episode that keeps us coming back every week to be glued into what could be considered soft porn on television. We even have the nerve to get an attitude and be seriously upset when the sex scene is cut short as the spouse displays guilt for their actions acknowledging they are still in love with the person they married more than the side piece. God forbid it looks like someone is going to do right and stay with their family instead of running off with the mistress.

The world we live in today. Yet women still wonder why each year there is a new derogatory nickname made for a woman, which describes what people think of a female based on her behaviors. From chicken heads to jump-offs over the years, and as soon as you are called out of your name, it's all about the individual that called you that name and never your behavior.

*Know this:* Every woman would love to be called beautiful things. Yes. Black women just call us queens, Nubian queens, but we must conduct ourselves accordingly to live up to the name. Be the queen, not the concubine.

My mind is on divorce. My family is familiar with divorce. My church has accepted divorce. My job is full of people who have been divorced. The world has made the answer to every troubled marriage divorce. So I am getting a divorce. But wait, if this is my final answer, there's something I need to understand—how did I get here...

# CHAPTER 1

# "Kenny's Wife"

*Know this:* Remember, it was said. You didn't marry the family or the church; you married your husband.

My name was now Lillian Nowlin-Hunt, correctly modified as "Kenny's wife."

Using Kenny's parents' timeshare to go on our honeymoon off to the Bahamas, we went by way of Ft. Lauderdale. I left Zion with his new grandparents and my BFF/sister Tina to take care of him while my husband and I went away to familiarize ourselves with the new territory God had given to us to have and hold for the rest of our lives. Oh, how sweet that sounds to say, my husband. I was married now.

We were so tired on the airplane we fell asleep the entire way to Florida. We were awakened by the Southwest Airlines staff who had made a wedding cake out of toilet paper with a paper bride and groom on top of it. Over the loudspeaker, the pilots and staff had the entire plane congratulating us. They also offered us a bottle of champagne that we turned down, but we were very appreciative and glowing with excitement as everyone acknowledged us as Mr. & Mrs.

KB and I made it to Ft. Lauderdale and headed straight to our room. There was a lingerie piece given to me at my bridal shower I was itching to put on only for KB to snatch it off. Yes, Mr. and Mrs. Kenneth Hunt wanted to continue celebrating our marriage ceremony. We had made a liar out of a lot of people and gave thanks to God for keeping us.

Contrary to all the rumors that were blasted all over about us being intimate prior to marriage, our first time was indeed on our wedding night. We couldn't help but think about our first time and the musical selections we made with one another, as we looked forward to getting to the hotel to originate more musical masterpieces. We made it to the room with no time to waste. I looked into his eyes, he looked into mine, and the orchestra began.

All of the physical activity taking place in our hotel room obviously made us hungry, so we took a break to get a bite to eat. Leaving the hotel room, we decided to go to a restaurant on the waterfront for dinner. KB ordered a lobster, and I ordered steak. We looked like a rich couple sitting at the table with a view of the water and the star-occupied beachfront homes across the way. Everywhere we went, we let everyone know we were just married and were on our honeymoon.

As we enjoyed the evening, I tried to be as dainty and ladylike as possible as my husband showed me off to the world. I was so hungry, but I made sure that I didn't swallow my steak whole. I took my time eating my salad and sipping my virgin strawberry daiquiri, only to look across the table at my husband, who was so into his food I think he forgot I was at the table with him.

He had eaten up his salad and was on to the lobster. I was never into lobster or crabs and things of that nature, so I had no interest in trying it now, which was a good thing because I don't think he was interested in sharing. He cracked that lobster and pulled out a large piece of meat. He dipped it in the little serving of melted butter and devoured it. It looked so cannibalistic to me and disgusting; I couldn't believe that he was enjoying it. He looked over the table at me and said, "See baby, I am going to introduce you to the finer things in life," as he pulled out more meat to dip in the butter.

I knew I had married a man who loved to eat and had a taste for upscale foods. As he continued to say he wanted to take me to places I'd never been before, see things I'd never seen, and eat foods I had never eaten, he was totally enjoying his meal. I was enjoying mine as well until he went in again to grab another piece of lobster. He tugged on it and had to pull a little harder to get the meat out, and then splash all over me were the juices from the lobster and the butter.

Stunned, I grabbed my napkin and began to wipe my face and arms off as I felt totally drenched. It was right then I knew that my life was going to be full of unexpected moments with this guy. All I could say was, "This is who I married," as we both enjoyed the rest of dinner with laughter.

When we got back to the hotel, he asked me if I wanted to go for a walk on the beach. My mind was nowhere near thinking about walking as I pulled him into the bathroom and began to take his clothes off. I started the shower, and the bathroom began to be filled with steam. Whether it was from the hot water or from us, who knows; the mirror was fogged up, but that didn't stop us from getting great views of one another or from seeing how flexible we could be.

No, we didn't need to walk on the beach and dip our feet in the ocean; we walked ourselves back into that hotel room and dipped our bodies back into a flood of love-making that was beyond what I could imagine.

KB looked at me as we laid our heads on the pillow and said he was looking forward to spending the rest of his life with me. This man made me feel like I was the best thing that had ever happened to him, and I was definitely being convinced that he was the best thing that had happened to me.

We needed to attempt to get some rest because we had to attend a sixty-minute presentation in the morning on time-shares. My new in-laws also told a preacher down in Ft. Lauderdale that we would be there, so they were looking forward to us attending church on that Sunday morning after the presentation. KB nor I had packed any church clothes, so we had to throw something together.

The presentation was the typical one trying to get us to purchase a timeshare. We put on the smile and made the "we are interested" face, but at the end of the day, we had our response already together. We had just gotten married, and we wanted to take our time getting into any additional commitments.

We left with the complimentary gift and had to make a trip to Walmart. KB didn't have a dress shirt or tie for church, so we needed to get him looking somewhat decent. I had on a black and white skirt with a sheer blouse to match with sandals and no stockings. It was not a church outfit, but it was "church" enough.

We knew in the Church of God in Christ you were supposed to have on pantyhose if you were going to church, but this would be one Sunday that rule was going to be broken by me. We made it to the church, and the service was just as live as if we were back in Baltimore. The pastor recognized us when we came in, and the church gave us a round of applause, congratulating us on getting married.

While in the service, we began to listen to the preacher speak on being filled with the Holy Ghost. In the months and days coming up to KB and my wedding, I really had begun to seek the Lord. I had been let down and hurt by so many, and there was a side of me that wanted to go mayhem on those that mistreated us.

Instead, I began to ask God to fill me with His Spirit. KB would tell me all the time that it takes the Holy Ghost to live right and to do right and stay right. I wanted it, and I needed it, so I listened as the preacher preached about receiving it. It is a gift given to all those who ask for it.

As saved and sanctified as I was, I truly was uncomfortable in the outfit that I had on because it was definitely a vacation outfit, not a Sunday morning one. So you know I was nothing but ashamed and embarrassed when the pastor called me up to the altar after he finished preaching. He began to talk to me, telling me how God had great things in store for my husband and me.

He said that God wanted to use us, and I needed to be filled to fulfill the call on my life. Here we are all the way in Ft. Lauderdale, Florida, in a church we had never been to before. None of the people in this church knew us personally, but the preacher knew what the desire of my heart was—to be filled with the Holy Ghost.

I knew my husband was filled with God's spirit, and I didn't want to be a hindrance or stumbling block to him. God had put us together, and I knew God was going to complete a work in me. It was important to me because I felt if I didn't get the spirit of God inside of me when I went back home, there were going to be some heads knocked off one by one for the way I had been treated because I agreed to marry KB.

There was some church folk who were due a good smackdown from me for trying to mess up one of the happiest moments of my life. This would do nothing but bring shame and disgrace to the union God had created between me and KB. I knew it was going to take more than me doing breathing techniques to stay calm, and I wanted God's spirit.

I wanted God to get the full glory out of my life and continue to use me how He saw fit. I wanted God to be pleased with my life and what He was creating me to be. I wanted my husband to never second-guess if he had made the right choice following God's instructions to make me his wife. I wanted my husband to never be ashamed of who God chose for him to be with for the rest of his life.

I wanted to be by my husband's side and allow God to use our lives as ministry to entice others to desire a relationship with God. I wanted to be able to love those who looked down on me. I wanted to be able to forgive those who spitefully used me and talked so badly about me. I knew I couldn't do it on my own, and I began to cry. With my eyes closed at the altar, I felt the women begin to surround me in prayer. The pastor laid his hand on my forehead, and I cried out to the Lord to fill me with His Spirit.

This was something that I wanted, this was something that I needed, but this was not the time I expected to receive it. I was on my honeymoon, not at a church convocation. I was in Florida, getting to know my way around the body of my husband, not at a revival. I was trying to have as many intimate moments with my husband as possible to try and get pregnant to see if I would be able to carry another child. So many things began to run through my head, and I could no longer even call on Jesus the way they were telling me to. I wanted it, but I was distracted...so I didn't get it.

The pastor gave us money to go out to eat after service, and we were excited to get back to honeymooning. We had to get something to eat because we knew we were going to be in need of some energy when we got back to our room. There was a little rainstorm that came through, but it didn't faze us at all. KB and I didn't care to see the outside but enjoyed the coziness of our room. As we lay in the bed together, KB told me he wanted God to fill me, and I told him that was what I wanted too. We talked about it being so strange that the pastor zeroed in on me with such urgency for me to receive the gift God had for me. We prayed and fell asleep in each other's arms.

I woke up to my husband sitting on the side of the bed eating pizza. He had gone out while I was sleep and got more to eat. I smiled as I looked at him and couldn't believe things could get any better than this. We packed our things and prepared to get up early in the morning to catch the boat over to the Bahamas to really begin our honeymoon.

*****

"Hello, baby," "Okay, baby" was how we were greeted getting off the ship and into taxi vans to take us to the resort. As we drove to our destination, we drove past beautiful resorts, excited to get to ours. The scenery was beautiful with the tall high rising hotels and water fountain displays. The palm trees surrounding the exquisite resort signs were made out of nicely manicured lawns.

The further we drove, the more anxious I became with great anticipation of staying in an exotic hotel resort that only my imagination could think of. Finally, we were there, and after checking in at the front desk, we were escorted to our room, and I then realized we would not be staying in a hotel with elevators and inside doors, but this would be a sure enough Bahamas experience.

Right in front of the door to our room, I saw something green crawl across the walkway. I screamed to the top of my lungs, jumping back with great fear. KB laughed, and we were told that there were little geckos all around and for me not to be afraid. Not to be afraid? Whatever! Since our room wasn't in a hotel high-rise structure, I was scared those creepy things were going to crawl into our room at any given time and scare me.

This was my first time in the Bahamas, and I was not used to seeing things like this and considering it normal. I made sure our bags stayed on the dresser, the desk, or the chairs and never touched the floor so that no unwanted guest could crawl into our bags unaware. I was on my honeymoon and should only have been thinking about my husband not being able to take his hands off of me and feeling all over me, but I knew that my mind was going to be on those gecko's being all over me instead so my eyes stayed open, and I was always on the watch for one.

KB wanted to get into the hot tub. We got into our swimsuits, and in the hot tub we went. I was so afraid because there were little geckos crawling around everywhere. As soon as we got into the hot tub together, KB knew just what to do to get my mind off those creepy crawlers as his hands crawled all over my body. We were the only ones in the hot tub, and we took full advantage of the moment.

As he held me in his arms, he gently kissed my lips. I felt his hands going up and down my back as his fingers gripped my skin. We were getting to know each other. I wanted to see how far he would go, and he wanted to see how far I would let him take me. There were no boundaries. We were husband and wife, and we saluted each other as such.

I knew KB wanted to have more children, but I forewarned him that there was a strong possibility that I would have complications or not be able to conceive at all. He didn't care, and all throughout our honeymoon, he made every effort to plant as many seeds as possible. I began to rub my stomach and call my belly KJ. That would be the name of the child I was sure I would be pregnant with by the end of this honeymoon. Kenny Jr., our first son together. Zion would be so excited to have a little brother, and KB would be excited to have a namesake.

We prayed together and fell asleep as happy as newlyweds could be. It was like a dream that I never wanted to be awakened from. This man took my breath away, and I couldn't believe that it was KB that was making me feel this way. Exhausted, we both fell asleep easily, but I planned to sleep lightly in the event I began to feel something crawling on me that wasn't my husband's hands.

Both of us were in a deep sleep, and suddenly I was awakened by a noise and felt a breeze-like feeling come over me. I was unsure of what I was hearing but knew that I had not heard the sound before. I knew there were no windows open because I made sure there was no way for the geckos to come in, so where the breeze came from, I didn't know. I couldn't find the words to explain what I was hearing because I couldn't understand what it was. It felt like someone was in the room with us. It felt like we weren't alone. I was scared but had a sense of peace all at the same time, thinking maybe I was just dreaming.

Half asleep, I tried to zero in on where the noise was coming from. I turned over and looked at my husband to find out that the sound was coming from him. Deep in his sleep, he began to speak in a language I didn't understand. I knew we were in the Bahamas, but he wasn't speaking in that dialect either. I was so stunned at the sound flowing from his mouth I couldn't try to wake him up. He went on and on and then began to say, "Yes Lord, yes Lord, thank You, Jesus, thank You, Jesus."

It was then I understood that my husband had been moved by the Holy Spirit and was speaking in tongues. KB was already filled with the Holy Ghost, something that I so strongly desired, and to witness the spirit of God upon him was beyond any words to describe. He was giving thanks to God, and I joined him.

Finally, he awakened himself and hugged me. I told him he was speaking in tongues. He turned over, opened the nightstand drawer, and pulled out the Holy Bible. He turned to Acts chapter 2 and read:

> And suddenly there came a sound from heaven as of a rushing mighty wind, and it filled all the house where they were sitting. And there appeared unto them cloven tongues like as of fire, and it sat upon each of them. And they were all filled with the Holy Ghost, and began to speak with other tongues, as the Spirit gave them utterance.

He knew my desire because it was his too. We wanted to be in a position where we had all power necessary to represent Christ and draw others to Him through living our life. We turned the light back off, and KB went right back to sleep. I laid there with my eyes open, wondering what just happened. How in the world are we on a honeymoon in one of the most exotic places, just the two of us with one thing on the mind—but yet the spirit of God came and met us right where we were.

This kept me awake, knowing that for God to do this, there was an urgency for me to seek receiving the gift. In the middle of our love-making week, God saw fit to bring to my attention that I needed to be filled. He brought it to the forefront of our marriage by allowing this abnormal situation to take place to show me that He wants to give it to me.

Falling back to sleep, I felt loved by my covering and by the One who put us together. I could only imagine greatness coming from this union and looked forward to every moment of it with him. We were in the beginning stage of our relationship, and the emotional connection needed to grow stronger. As I moved in closer to him, he embraced me and welcomed me with his warm arms wrapping them around my body and his warm lips heating my cool forehead.

The passion and the heat were there with only a touch. So quickly, we went from thinking about being in the presence of God to enjoying being in the presence of each other. What made the moment so much more exciting was that we had the right to have this passion. We had the permission to yearn after each other as we did. It was our duty to please one another with no condemnation or later regrets because we were Mr. and Mrs. Hunt—newlyweds that were together doing what newlyweds do. And then we could watch the sun come up.

******

*Know this:* A husband that is a real man will never let another man take care of his wife. She better know it, and any guy trying better know it too.

I had never been to the Bahamas and wasn't all that interested in being around all the water. Not for the typical "I don't want to get my hair wet" excuse, but because I simply couldn't swim. KB could swim, but all I would do was put my feet in the water. The hot tub was my choice of enjoyment. Getting into the resort swimming pool, KB swam around me like a shark. We couldn't get enough of each other, and it seemed as if we had the entire resort to ourselves. He would carry me over into the deep end and spin me around in circles as I held on to him for dear life.

While we were caressing one another while in the pool, I looked out the corner of my eye and couldn't believe what I was seeing. It was as if that moment was a scene out of a movie. My eyes opened wide as I continued to kiss KB, but he could tell something else had caught my attention. He turned me around only to find out that there was someone who had joined us.

I couldn't help but notice a lifeguard starting his shift as he climbed the tower ladder to take his watch, and by notice, I mean I took in every inch of his body. His feet were long and provided him a steady grip as he climbed up the ladder. With each step, I could see his athletic calves and the muscles bulging out of his arms and legs. Those little red lifeguard shorts. His skin was dark chocolate, and the drops of water dripping from his shoulders down to his six-pack abs sparkled as the sunlight shined on him. His body looked smooth and shiny, and when he smiled, a mouth full of luminous white teeth emerged from his full, dark lips. I must have stared long enough for the lifeguard to notice.

KB acted as if he was going to drop me in the deep end of the pool, so I screamed and pleaded for him not to let me go. He knew just how to snap me out of my stupor. I grabbed him tighter as he moved back over into the shallower end of the pool. KB began trying to teach me to float, but I was too scared.

I just didn't feel like swimming was something I could ever do. The lifeguard noticed us and began to smile at us again as KB insisted that I learn to swim. How sweet and romantic would that be for us to go home and be able to say for the rest of our lives that KB taught me how to swim while we were in the Bahamas on our honeymoon.

He kept trying, and I kept failing, and learning how to swim looked like it was going to be the last thing I would ever learn, definitely not during our honeymoon. After my continuous screams and battling the fear, KB gave up as I grabbed ahold to the side of the pool. He swam away as if he was tired of trying to teach me. Just as he came back towards me and I was getting ready to hold on to him again, the lifeguard smiled down at me. In his thick Bahamian accent, while smiling, showing all those pretty white teeth, he says to me, "I will teach you how to swim."

As the polite and friendly but happily newly married woman, knowing that my husband should feel one hundred percent secure, I opened my mouth only to hear my husband's voice come out and say, "Nah, that's all right, I got it!" I couldn't help but laugh as I told the lifeguard, "No, thank you," while KB held me close to him as if to say, "She is taken, so don't even try it."

The honeymoon left us a shade darker and even closer to each other. Never really having the chance to date or get to know one another and not having sex before marriage, we really needed to familiarize ourselves with each other. We definitely sealed the deal on consummating the marriage. Every place we went, we were certain to create a memory. But now it was time to go home and face the reality that marriage isn't just about love-making, erotic feelings, emotional highs, deep-rooted pleasures, and ultimate fantasy satisfaction.

I would never forget how in the midst of our honeymoon, God saw fit to make me very aware of the fact that He has a gift that He is trying to give to me, and all I needed to do was put myself in the posture to receive it.

Mommy said to write everything down because I was getting ready to experience life on another level, so writing a diary comes easy. But who is writing this diary? I know my name is Lillian Nowlin-Hunt, but who calls me that? Not to be mixed up with any other Mrs. Hunts, there sure are a lot of them around. Everywhere I go, I am introduced as "Kenny's wife." No one needs to know my name, where I come from, and who I want them to know I am because it has already been announced. My name is "Kenny's wife." Will people happily acknowledge me as such, or will I be invisible? Who wants to call me "Kenny's wife" anyway? What will Mr. MarcTrain call me? Will he ever talk to me again? Questions in my mind to jot down in a diary, questions that I am not sure I really want to know the answer to, yet I ask.

# CHAPTER 2

# Make This House a Home

Back home, reality began to sink in very quickly. I was no longer going to my apartment on Moravia Avenue but to a house—our home on Ready Avenue in Baltimore, Maryland. Ready Avenue... Was I "ready"?

Although God had given me peace about living in the same house my husband resided in with his late wife, my mind would often be filled with thoughts wondering how in the world I became strong enough to make this house a home for all of us. Your husband lived in this very same house with another woman he was married to. They lived here together, and this was their home. They were newlyweds here. They discussed and planned to raise a family here. They ate dinner here. They bathed here. They argued and cried here. They made love here. They were *in* love here...

But this is where I live now.

Allowing thoughts to penetrate my mind would only cause me to drift into unnecessary notions. Pointless concepts of beliefs would develop, unwarranted emotions would arise, and excessive fear would overtake me. God would not allow this, so these undesirable thoughts stayed at a minimum. Unhelpful deliberations were terminated, and damaging emotions annihilated.

*Know this:* Everyone is not built like you. You are unique, no matter how many try to replicate you. If they could be you, God would have chosen them instead of you to take on the tasks at hand. Stop wasting time saying, "I wonder what everyone else is thinking."

This house is the home where the Kenneth and Lillian Hunt family will reside. The Kenneth part of this family is already very familiar with this house, but the Lillian side must dig in and get comfortable. When you enter the house at the front door, you walk right into the living room. There was a small coat closet next to the front door, and I soon realized it was one of the only closets in the entire house. I didn't have a living room set at my apartment, so we kept the one KB had. We added the Black Panther glass coffee table of mine along with my thirty-two-inch television.

It was summertime when we moved in, so it was hot. The entire house had beautiful hardwood floors. In every room and even in the hallway and down the stairs, the hardwood floors made the house beautiful. We didn't have central air, but the air conditioners in the window did the job. KB had window air conditioners that kept the entire house cool as a winter breeze. Lying on the sofa with a nice comfy blanket was usual when we were home. Zion would be on the sofa right with us until he would fall asleep as we watched sports or a movie together. KB would order Stoko's pizza, and we would sit and enjoy our home together.

The living room and dining room were next to each other, separated by French glass doors. KB already had a dining room set with the china cabinet and buffet table to match. The dark cherry wood furniture was antique-looking and beautiful. It was all for show; we never really ate in there. I kept the dining room nice and clean, like a picture out of a magazine. In the china cabinet, there were dolls, dishes, and elephants that belonged to Dion until we removed them and gave them away to her family and her delta sigma theta sorority sisters that were close to her. The big kitchen was off from the dining room.

Although the kitchen was big and had one of my favorite colors (hunter green) in it, along with my black dining room table, I still didn't want to cook in there. The sink was an old cast iron single bowl white kitchen sink. It had brown rust water spots in it, and the sink countertop area had ridges in it to lead the water back into the sink when drying dishes.

The cabinets were outdated, and I could barely reach anything in the ones over the top of the stove because it was too high. The refrigerator, stove, sink, and microwave were all white. The floor was done with hunter green and gold stick tile. So being in the kitchen was quickly determined to be one of the places I hated to be.

The basement. This is the lowest portion of a house. Down in the basement, we stored all of the wedding gifts that we received. There was no space in this house to utilize everything, so storing it in the basement was our best option. This is the place where the washer and dryer were kept. KB had a huge box full of witnessing tracks down there. His omega paraphernalia was down there as well.

This was the place at 5639 Ready Avenue I did not want to go to frequently. It was dark and scary, and I didn't want to step foot into that basement alone. A lot of Dion's things were stored down there. KB wanted to throw things away, but he also wanted to make sure nothing of value was destroyed, so in the basement they sat. The backdoor of the basement had heavy duty locks on it and led to the backyard—another place I had no intentions of spending a large amount of time.

Our bedroom was painted a beautiful butterscotch color to match our bed set. The bed was so high off the ground I had to jump up into it. Our bed set came with a chest that we stored the television in. We loved watching television together late at night when we weren't doing other things. There was no closet in our room, so we had to make space to hang our dress clothing.

There was a second door in our room that led to the bedroom next to ours. We called that room the guest room that we put Zion's twin bed in. This room was small but had a huge window. I put white laced curtains in the window, which made the room even prettier. The large window with the lace curtains allowed the bright sun to shine into the room and make natural light. Under the window was a white radiator that would keep the room warm in the winter.

There was a bathroom upstairs. Although there was a bathroom in the basement with a shower, I never chose to use it. The upstairs bathroom had a tub and shower combo, and the shower curtain had to go around the entire tub because the tub stood off from the wall. KB did some upgrades in the bathroom before I moved in to give it a facelift.

A new floor, a new vanity, and toilet seat, along with a fresh coat of paint to make the gray and white bathroom be modernized. It was small, but I needed it to be comfortable. The bathroom is where I would sing. This is where I would sit and talk to God. This is where I would go and hide when I needed time to myself. So the environment had to be pleasing and pretty.

Zion's room was right next to the bathroom, which we thought was best with him being so small, and the room was almost just as big as our bedroom. KB had a mini-refrigerator in the room because that was the room he and his first wife slept in. We put my full bed in that room and made it nice and cozy for Zion.

This room had a small closet and a trap door to what was the attic. I never went up there, so I have no idea what it looks like. I stored all of my Coach, Dooney & Bourke, and Louis Vuitton purses that I purchased over the years there. Thanks to my big sister Linda I had plenty of designer bags, all colors and sizes.

Ready Avenue was a semi-detached row home, so we had a fenced-in yard with a driveway in the back of the house, which led to the alley. The back porch was small and was also another place I didn't want to be. It was covered with a screen, but because the screen had holes, it didn't protect you from the mosquitos.

There were too many stairs to climb to get up onto the back porch anyway, and the alley was as most Baltimore allies are—prone to have a rat running through it. Even with all the areas I didn't like about Ready Avenue, I had to accept them because this was the place we "the Hunts" called home.

Our baby boy Zion Noble was just as excited as can be. He was content having a mommy and a daddy in the home, shadowing KB as if he was his natural-born son. Zion was super happy about being the only child that everyone was going to spoil but also made it clear he wanted a little brother or sister to join the family too. The school year was over, and the head start had ended.

Zion was now five years old, and we needed to get him into the public school nearby. A good thing about living on Ready Avenue was that a school was just feet away from the house. Govans Elementary School is where Zion would begin his tenure in the Baltimore City public school system.

KB went right back into grinding and working hard, being a provider for his newfound family. My husband was no dummy with a bachelor's degree in criminal justice from the University of Maryland Eastern Shore (UMES). He was working at the church's restaurant "Heaven's Gate Eatery" as a manager. Clearly, working at a restaurant as a manager has nothing to do with a criminal justice degree, but this is what he chose.

When his father decided to open up a restaurant, he wanted to support and help his father in any way that he could. It was almost like going into business for yourself having your father as the owner, and you are a manager. I always thought it was a commendable thing for KB to do. He could have stayed in the school system and developed a way to utilize his criminal justice degree, but instead, he wanted to support his father and the church. That said a lot for the man God had given to me.

I sure didn't complain at all. Instead of me cooking, we would eat dinner at the restaurant, which saved me from being in the kitchen at home. We spent so much time at the eatery because it was right around the corner from my job and a block up from the church. Late nights and early mornings were routine for KB. Although he had set hours to be at work, his father looked to him, and he was there more than expected.

When KB wasn't at the eatery working, he was out serving civil summonses. Some nights he would have me in the car and Zion in the back seat as he drove around town with a map trying to locate individuals to serve them with court papers.

KB and Dion had a cat named Lexi that KB wanted to keep. Terrified of cats, I knew there was no way in the world that I would live under the same roof as one. KB explained to me that the cat would keep out mice, and it was necessary to keep her. I had to decide, which was I more afraid of, the cat or mice?

Living in Baltimore city and seeing a mouse wasn't all that surprising, but I didn't have them in my apartment and wasn't trying to have them in my new living quarters either. KB promised he would make sure that the cat stayed away from me and I would never see it. He locked the cat away and would let her out while I wasn't around so that her scent would remain to keep mice away.

We would go to bed together each night full of joy and happiness in our new life together. After tucking Zion in, I would leap up into our bed that was so high off the ground and snuggle up under my husband. Everything felt so comfortable, so right. I would try to go to sleep before him because he snored, but I guess looking at me sleep did something to him.

Many nights, I would be awakened by him turning me over and acting as if he was an explorer and my body was the new world he sought out to conquer. Just like an explorer would leave a mark, a flag, a symbol, or any type of sign to show that the land was occupied, so would KB. He would make it very clear that he was a long-term resident with no intentions of ever giving up or sharing the land that God had given him.

We constantly made explorative musical selections which made the both of us tired and exhausted, but we didn't care. We would pass out into a deep sleep, thankful to God for putting us together as we relish one another. To be in a sexual relationship ordained by God made it so exotic.

Knowing that we could enjoy one another and reach such a high left you speechless. He was mine, and I was his to have and to hold from this day forward as our vows stated. I was no virgin before we were married, and obviously, neither was KB, but we were thankful that God didn't allow us to fornicate and sleep with each other before the wedding.

No matter who, what, when, where, or how in our lives sex before marriage took place, knowing God approved what we had in this moment made it an exciting apogee worth waiting for. Being with KB predestined by God made me wish I had waited to have him only and not the others I had slept with. No one else compared.

I learned very quickly that no matter how tired I was, I had to make sure that before falling asleep, I was safe and secure under KB's arms. When I didn't, I learned that I would suffer the consequences.

Falling asleep one night, I was wildly enjoying our huge king-sized bed. I had drifted away from KB and was over on my own side of the bed sleeping. Life was good, and KB made sure

I was always "feeling" good, which wore me out and kept me desiring more of him and more of sleep. It would take nothing for me to fall into a deep sleep, trying to get every Zzz possible. I felt some movement in the bed, and it lifted me out of my deep sleep, but yet I was still in a resting mode. I felt more movement coming towards me, and although I was sleeping, I began to slowly come out of my dreams, knowing that my husband was once again desiring to go on an exploration.

I loved that he made me feel like he couldn't get enough of me. He made me feel wanted; he made me feel like I was too much and not enough all at the same time. I enjoyed anticipating his first touch to initiate the next exploratory musical. At this moment, I felt it coming, but I was struggling to wake myself up. I was tired; he had just worn me out earlier in the evening. I began to wonder if he would ever get tired too.

I began dreaming about our earlier moments of exploration. I was reliving each moment of desire, literally feeling every thrust of passion, craving every outburst of gratifying melodious resonance. Yes, I wanted more. Yes, I was eager to welcome him to my inner thighs. Yes, I wanted to feel his lips all over my body. Yes, I wanted to remain in this moment for as long as my body could take it. It started with him wanting me, but now my body wanted him. I began reaching for him, accepting him into my arms, wanting to dig my fingernails into him as I knew he was getting ready to create a new long-awaited verse in another original ballad.

I turned and opened my eyes to look him in the face and tell him I love being with him; I love the way he makes me feel; I love making love to him. As I opened my eyes, I was left shocked and totally surprised. I screamed at the top of my lungs and began to shake uncontrollably. My heart was beating so fast it felt as if it was going to burst right out of my chest.

KB jumped up, stunned at my behavior, trying to quickly understand what caused my response. He was just as surprised as he saw Lexi jumping off the bed and running out of the bedroom. All the while I was thinking it was my loving husband caressing me and moving in close to me, it was the darn cat!

Lexi was used to getting in the bed with Dion and Kenny when Dion was alive. She tried it and was quickly informed I was not having it! There will be no four-legged pets in my bed with me! That was the beginning of Lexi and I marking our territory.

*Know this:* I am terrified of cats. The feline family and I will forever have a beef all because when I was a little girl, a stray cat was thrown on me by a boy in the neighborhood, and that didn't end well. To be terrified doesn't mean to be weak. Lexi will learn the hard way.

All in all, we were a happy family. Blessed to be together, blessed to have a roof over our head. Only twenty-seven years old, it seemed like time was moving very fast for us. I was just living in an apartment with hardly any furniture, in love with a man that I thought was the world to me. KB was just married for four years to one of his college girlfriends, taking care of her throughout her sickness with lupus. Both members of Mount Hebron Memorial COGIC as brother and sister, and now we're husband and wife. His late wife had transitioned on, and who I thought was the love of my life didn't even fight for me; he stepped out of the picture for KB and me to begin this journey of life and love together—so we thought.

Together we were determined to please God and go in the direction He had planned for us. We wanted everything that we did to represent Christ and be, in one way or another, some type of ministry that God would get the glory out of. We didn't live a lavish life and didn't have anything to show off. What we did have in our possession, God had given to us. Everything we were responsible for, we wanted to be good stewards over it for God to be pleased with us. This included each other.

We both knew what we had was rare and unique. The love and the bond were created by God, not by a lustful thought, impulse, hormones, or childhood connection. It was our responsibility to keep what God had given us pure, clean, and without blemish. We had the duty of upholding the standard that was set for the two of us. Allowing any third parties in would be detrimental. We held the key to the future God had for us. Our decisions would map the way.

Would it be easy because God put us together, or would it be hard because hardly anyone else wanted this union to exist? Who could I trust as KB's new wife? How would I know what to do or to say and what not to do and not to say? So glad I had my best friend Bunch by my side. We'd been together through thick and thin, and nothing would change that. She could spot dangers for me miles away, so as long as she was by my side, I should be good to go.

But what was most important was this house was now a home. A real family lived here. There was the husband, the father, the head of the house, and the covering. There was the wife, the mother, the homemaker, and the fragrance. Then there was the child, the son, the future, and the life of the home.

# CHAPTER 3

# Bull's Eye

Going back to work as Mrs. Hunt didn't seem as if it was going to be much of a problem. I was going back to work under new leadership with a newly appointed director. This new director was put in place after the last director was terminated. The separation of employment for the last director Tina S. was so full of drama it went as far as involving police officers onsite for her protection and to keep peace.

Tina S. came highly recommended and seemed to know a lot about being a director; however, she was not the right fit for this head start program. She wasn't completely honest, and for some reason, she could not get along with the staff. She lacked self-confidence as well and had a lot of personal home issues going on that caused her inability to be as focused as she needed to be on the job. Having baby daddy issues, child emergencies, and relationship problems while trying to be a director just wasn't going to work.

But before Tina, I had the best leader anyone could ever ask for. My boss Isaac was African, dark-skinned, and short in stature. Isaac had resigned and left me with this young fireball who seemed to get into more trouble than she was able to handle. He was one of my best bosses ever. He treated me like a little sister. We had very few disputes, but when an altercation arose, we argued, said what needed to be said, and moved on. Isaac was very hands-on but never inappropriate with me.

He actually tried to marry me off to one of his African friends. I will never forget his friend entering the office, and the first thing he said to me was that he and I were going to have many babies. What? He was very controlling and told me to begin preparing a wedding. I responded to him as only I knew how—like a shorty straight from the East Side of the Roc in upstate New York with no chaser.

I told Isaac I couldn't and wouldn't ever marry any of his friends, and they would have to find another way to be able to remain in the states and become legal citizens. He respected me for my strong attitude and determination to never allow a man to dominate me in such a way but was disappointed that he couldn't marry me off. He was happy that God had sent my husband to me.

When I had surgery to remove the mass on my brain, it was Isaac who came to my apartment with a bouquet of red roses to cheer me up. He was the one I would talk to about anything relationship-centered like Mr. MarcTrain and how in love I was with him. He knew that I would never move back to Rochester because of Michael. He was that guy that was a good listener for me.

I trusted him, and he trusted me with personal and business affairs. He would always listen to my opinion, but as the African man he was, he made sure we all understood he was the decision-maker and what he said goes.

As Isaac's assistant, I knew everything that was going on within my job. I made it my business to inform my pastor that my job was getting ready to receive bids for a new food company to provide meals for the head start. If chosen, this would be a large income for the church's eatery.

I was so glad I was able to tell the pastor about this opportunity and did all I could to make sure they had everything the way that they needed to be able to submit a bid for service. I could not be involved in the bid process and was unable to witness the decision-making behind who would win the bid, so all we could do was pray that the eatery won if it was the Lord's will.

The eatery won the bid, and the pastor couldn't have been happier. This contract generated funds for the eatery that would not have been had I not introduced the idea. Isaac could have not allowed the eatery to submit a bid, but I had to convince him otherwise. He didn't have a lot of respect for Pastor and didn't really want to do business with him. I did all I could to try to get rid of that way of thinking with him, but it wasn't so simple because of the history behind his animosity.

Any food opportunity that would arise, I would call the eatery to get a deal just so that we could have good-tasting food at my job. All the workers loved the food, and the children loved the food too. At first, it wasn't easy to persuade Isaac to use the eatery, but after begging and tasting the food, he gave in. Isaac would always remind me of how angry he became with me over something I had absolutely nothing to do with that led back to him not wanting to do business with the church.

Isaac was angry because he fired a young girl that attended the same church as me and didn't know that by firing her, he was going to have to deal with our pastor. The girl was rightfully terminated, so Isaac was baffled when he received a phone call from the pastor, who, with a demanding tone, requested that his member get her job back. It took a lot of humility and keeping my mouth closed during this time because I was feeling it from both sides. The pastor was upset because he thought I could have done something to help this girl keep her job, and Isaac was upset because he felt I was loyal to the church and not to him.

I hated being placed in the middle of that situation. I couldn't explain to either side how I felt or help them to understand the entire situation. When Isaac pulled me into his office and said to me with his strong African accent, "Tell Pastor I don't tell him how to run his church. He don't tell me how to run my business," I knew that it had gone too far. I decided to not entertain anything about that situation anymore and backed away from asking Isaac to give her another chance at her job—she was wrong, a decision was made, and it was final!

Even with all of that chaos, Isaac still found it in his heart to allow the eatery to bid on a meal contract. I was glad I chose to back away when I did, which allowed Isaac to see that I was in agreement with his decision. Because I stood by him and supported his correct decision to fire this girl, when the time came for the eatery to do business with him, he felt comfortable knowing that I was not going to let the eatery take advantage of us just because we had the church connection.

Isaac and I became so close and spent a lot of time together. It was nothing for him to let me go into his office and just cry those days that I couldn't keep the pain from flowing out of my eyes as tears. Yes, in his office, I cried when Michael would threaten me that he was going to take Zion from me. In his office, I cried after I found out that Mr. MarcTrain was married, but I was too deep in love with him to end the relationship. It was in his office I cried when I found out that Mr. MarcTrain and his wife were having a baby and that there was so much more to Mr. MarcTrain I would later find out.

It was in his office that he told me he was leaving me and taking another job in DC, which caused me to have to go through the agony of these new directors. Oh, how I loved working with Isaac, but there I was under new leadership as a newlywed walking back into work happy and ecstatic about my future as Mrs. Hunt, but that wouldn't last long.

After getting rid of the fireball director, coming off my honeymoon, we acquired a "motherly" director. She even wanted everyone to call her Momma! She used her first few weeks with me as her assistant to gain information as to who was who and how everything ran. She pretended to be nice as I trained her and showed her the financials, the reports due, the basics of running the business. She was so happy when I came back from my honeymoon and immediately put me to work making unnecessary changes that she knew would cause an uproar with the staff.

We had just removed one director, and it looked like we were going to have to get rid of another. The stress was becoming a bit overwhelming. This new director that had everyone calling her Momma was so aggressive and rude. We had so many complaints about her overstepping her boundaries and coming down hard on the staff for no reason. I stood my ground and refused to support her poor leadership, and as her assistant, that clearly wasn't going to work well.

Every day I would come home to my new husband complaining about what this woman was doing. Talking to the staff like they were her children. Demanding that we call her Momma. Not approving people's schedules. Misrepresenting us in meetings. Doing reports incorrectly. Trying to get her friends in place behind closed doors. Arriving late and coming up missing during the day. The list goes on and on, and so did she.

I didn't want to be stressed. This was a great time in my life. I was newly married, in a new home, and finally could feel a sense of joy I had never felt before. I've been getting tired and began feeling sick. Because I was so frustrated with work, I would become frustrated with KB when I got home. We were supposed to be happy every day, I thought, but instead, I was wondering why my life seemed to be trying to take a sudden turn for the worse.

I didn't want to eat, and everything seemed to irritate me. I started noticing the habits of my husband that I didn't know about before we were married because we didn't live together prior to. I started wondering would things have been different if Mr. MarcTrain had fought for me and not so easily just handed me over to KB.

My hormones were clearly off. I hadn't been in a routine sexual relationship in so long, and my body was beginning to feel like KB was more than I could handle. It seemed as if everything was coming down on me all at once. My menstrual cycle wouldn't even come on, and I felt like I was getting ready to explode. It was only a few weeks since we had come home from our honeymoon, and I was expecting the bliss to last a little longer, but the truth of the matter is bliss must have some reality along with it.

KB and I had a disagreement, and we were being silent with each other, so I made an excuse to get away and went to the pharmacy. I couldn't help but wonder why my new marriage didn't seem to be going the way everyone else who got married worked. Everyone seemed so happy, so in love, years later they talk about how they are still on their honeymoon, and I didn't understand why that wasn't the same for us.

God was the one who put us together, so if anything, we should have been on cloud nine. I was hoping KB wasn't second-guessing God's decision to put us together. I knew our union was unique and quite unusual, but now I was wondering, *Will it remain worth it?*

*Know this:* Looking into a marriage from the outside can be very deceiving. Some people don't want you to know there are problems in their marriage and pretend to be "happy." Don't try to get to someone else's "happy" because it may not exist—create your own!

Nothing about my body felt right, and I couldn't help but wonder if there was more to these feelings and emotions that I was going through. Before leaving the pharmacy, I decided to pick up a pregnancy test. When I came home, KB was on the back porch keeping quiet and continued to give me the silent treatment. I went upstairs to the bathroom and decided to take the pregnancy test just to see if what my instincts were telling me was true. I didn't have to worry about KB busting into the bathroom because he was keeping his distance from me.

I knew I had been a handful to deal with. Everything on the job, along with the funny acting church folk gossiping about us, mixed with me trying to adapt to living with someone again and not being independent, had me all over the place with a bad attitude. I needed to tell him that when I knew I was right, he needed to understand that there was nothing he could say or do to change what I thought. I needed to tell him that even though I was right, I could be dead wrong in explaining how right I was. I needed to tell my husband I was sorry. I needed to tell him that I was learning and I was not perfect. I needed to tell him that as time went on, we would get to know each other better and try not to step on each other's toes. I needed to tell him, *"I'm pregnant!"*

Oh my gosh! How in the world did I know this? I couldn't wait to get out of that bathroom and run down the steps out the back door and tell him. But wait... Was this what I really wanted? I knew KB wanted a child because he didn't have any besides Zion. I knew my doctor told me years ago that I couldn't have any more children, so was I getting ready to tell him something and bring on false hope?

I knew I could get pregnant, but carrying a baby full term and actually giving birth was the problem. Maybe this was a good thing. Get pregnant immediately in the beginning of the marriage, lose the baby, and go through the pain and disappointment; then maybe we would agree to not try and have any more children. I never wanted kids in the first place, so hopefully, he would understand.

I came up behind him as he sat on the steps and just looked at him. This man that just a few months ago was my big brother is now the man I am having a baby with! I am carrying his child. Everyone is going to know that we actually had sex and conceived—that is the only way this could have happened.

I played back in my mind each time he laid me down, wondering which moment was the moment I became pregnant. I didn't know which musical selection it was; all I knew was that I enjoyed every single note, and now I was carrying his seed.

He turned and looked at me, and I handed him the pregnancy test stick. He asked me what it was, and I told him to look at it. He looked at it, and of course, he didn't know what it meant, so he asked me, "Are you pregnant?" I said to him, "Yes," and whatever issues we had that we called ourselves being upset with each other about were immediately forgotten. KB and I were successful in getting pregnant.

He got up from the steps and grabbed me and held me so tight, so excited and overjoyed at the news. He kissed me and looked at me and kissed me some more. He touched my stomach and smiled and then kissed me again as we moved from the back porch to the kitchen. Through the kitchen to the dining room, he hugged me, kissed me, and told me he loved me.

We made it to the living room and could go no further. He felt as excited as me. We ended whatever we were supposedly upset about and had only one thing on our mind. We celebrated by making a new symphony right there in the living room and then gave thanks to God and prayed that this baby would be born healthy.

We laid on the sofa together and called our parents to tell them the good news. KB was telling his father, and his dad replied, "You hit a bull's eye," as we all joyfully laughed, excited about what was happening. My mother was so surprised and excited too, but this was only the beginning. It didn't take much for the word to travel, and everyone knew I was pregnant.

Pregnant by your husband is something totally different from being pregnant by your long-term boyfriend or a live-in lover or your baby daddy! This man was the one who stood before God and made a vow, a promise, an oath and agreement until death do us part. This man became one with me to create a family to carry on the family name, create a legacy, and a new generation of blessed children. This man was the covering of our home, the priest of the home, the head, the protector, provider, and king. I had his seed growing inside of me. I had never experienced this before, and to be pregnant by my husband was a joy that is beyond explaining.

*Know this:* Don't think that your happiness will make those that are around you happy too. Some, saying they are rooting for your happiness, may actually be ones that are rooting for your demise.

Just as much happiness there was about having a baby, we knew there would be unhappy moments as well. Uncertain if I would be able to actually deliver a baby made the entire occasion bittersweet. I had already told my husband my situation, but now the world would know I couldn't have children if something was to happen with this pregnancy. The news about me being pregnant was out before I could actually get to the doctor's office to confirm a due date. The pressure was on, and the anxiety followed.

My BFF and big sis Bunch had Malachi at St. Agnes hospital and had a great doctor, so I wanted to use the same GYN group. We went to the doctor, and the doctor gave us our due date of March 8, 2004. The date seemed so far away, yet we were so excited. I explained my prior medical history to my new doctor, telling her I knew I was able to get pregnant, but carrying the baby and giving birth would be the challenge. KB was confident as we prayed and decided to trust what God says over man's opinion.

All we could think about was having another little boy in the house for Zion to be a big brother to. He accepted the news with a smile, overjoyed that he would finally have a sibling living with him. Kenny Jr. would be coming in March of 2004, and his big brother couldn't be happier.

*Know this:* If I have said it once, I will say it again. People want to see you do well but not better than them. When you've gone past their success, watch out for the backlash!

I was pregnant, and everyone was treating me like I had never been pregnant before. This was not my first pregnancy. Did everyone forget how Zion got here? Constantly being told what I could do and what I should not do was way too much for me. I just wanted to be happy that I was pregnant. Not sure how long this pregnancy was going to last, I just wanted to enjoy my husband being happy. He was never able to have a child with his deceased wife, so this was a big deal for him. He was the only son, and to keep his family name going through him, he must have a male child.

Every morning became harder and harder for me to get up and go to work. I was sick all the time, and my new boss made me even sicker! Just listening to her voice had become a nauseous trigger. I had gone to the head of the board of directors, and they seemed to be dragging their feet on the findings I had presented to them on behalf of the staff. Trying to keep the peace between her and the staff was more than I could handle, and something had to give.

I knew something was getting ready to happen, but I just didn't know what. I seemed to be losing grip on my life, and I needed to fall back and regroup. I put my head down at my desk and began to pray. I asked God to give me answers and show me what I needed to do to make things better. I didn't say a thought-out articulate prayer. I just said what was on my mind at the time. I asked God if I was doing something wrong to cause my life to feel like it was in chaos. I asked Him to give me a sign to show me where I messed up and how I could get back on track. I needed to know I was in God's will and that everything was going to work out for my good. I needed a signal, some type of indication, to get going in the right direction.

I lifted my head from prayer as the phone rang at my desk. I answered the phone, clearing my throat giving greetings to the caller. It was silent on the other end, so I said hello once again. Then I heard that voice. The voice that I hadn't heard in a while but couldn't easily forget its sound. The voice that, for the past few years, made my heart jump every time I would hear it over the phone. The voice that I would long to hear at the beginning of the day and the last voice I wanted to hear at night. The voice that told me goodbye once I accepted who God had chosen for my husband. It was Mr. MarcTrain.

I had no idea what I was supposed to say next. I was happy to hear his voice and, at the same time, scared. I wanted to know where he had been, what he did with the house, if he was upset with me, how he was handling me marrying someone else. I had so many questions but was too scared to ask any. He could tell I was speechless, so he asked me how I was doing. With everything going on around me seeming to fall apart, that was the last question I wanted anyone to ask me.

I quietly told him I was fine. He asked me if I was sure, and I paused. I wanted to tell him no. I wanted to tell him how the church folk started treating me once it became public that KB and I were getting married. I wanted to tell him how much I didn't like my new boss. I wanted to tell him I was pregnant, and I was praying that I could carry the baby full term and give my husband a male child. I knew he didn't want to hear any of these things, so I quietly said again that I was fine. He knew everything wasn't and said such, but I couldn't reply.

When he saw that I couldn't speak, he let me know that he didn't mean to bother me but that I needed to make sure that I paid my car note on time. He wanted to arrange picking up the payment since he no longer had access to my bank accounts. I told him that I would make sure to take care of it and would be in touch. He asked me again if I was okay. I said yes, and I had to go. I hung up the phone and sat at my desk, looking into space. I do not know what I was thinking; I do not know what I was contemplating. I know that hearing Mr. MarcTrain's voice made me have to confess to myself that I still cared about him. I began to hit my desk as if someone had heard my thoughts and was going to tell my husband. I don't like messy, so I needed to cancel every emotion that was going on inside of me.

My first plan was to not even share with KB what happened. I just didn't want him to know that Mr. MarcTrain called my job. I felt that if I told him, he would feel that there was something going on between us still and there wasn't. I didn't want him to have to wonder if he could trust me. I didn't want him to see the anguish in my face, which would lead to a flood of inquiries. I didn't want him to ask me what all we talked about. I didn't want him to ask me how I felt when I was talking to him. Most importantly, I didn't want him to ask me if I still had feelings for Mr. MarcTrain. I didn't want him to ask if I was over him or if I still loved him. I didn't want to tell KB because I didn't want to truthfully have to answer any of these questions.

The last thing I wanted to do was start a marriage based on keeping secrets and not sharing everything. When all the negative reactions to KB and I getting engaged and getting married started happening, KB and I were there for each other and said that we would always be there to communicate and support one another. I couldn't forget that and thought that it was okay not to tell KB about this phone call. I had seen in movies how an innocent phone call turns into something worse, like an affair. I had heard people keep things like this a secret, and then when it came out, there was a great misunderstanding.

I called KB and told him Mr. MarcTrain called. I told him because I wanted to be honest. I told him because I didn't want to fear him finding out any other kind of way. I told him because it was the right thing to do. I was thankful he didn't grill me like I thought he would. He didn't give me the third degree and try to make me take a lie detector test to be sure I was telling the truth. KB was a true man of God who loved me and trusted that God did not make a mistake when He put the two of us together. However, KB did not want me to keep my car. He wanted me to give it up and get a new car without any ties to Mr. Marc-Train. KB said that he just didn't feel right about it and thought it would be best if I gave the car up.

I was so upset. I couldn't believe that was what he came up with as a solution. I was pregnant, my job was tripping, the people at church were tripping, I had no family down here, and now my new husband wanted to be possessive and take my car away from me. I cried like a baby and totally disagreed with his decision. Being sick from this pregnancy didn't help either. KB and I wanted to do all we could to stay in the will of God, knowing that He was the one who put the two of us together. I didn't want to be without a car. I didn't want to let it go. KB decided he would handle any communications and transactions dealing with the car from then on and let me keep my car. I knew he didn't want to do it, but to make me be at peace, he did. To keep me happy, he did. To be that great husband, he did.

I wasn't sure how Mr. MarcTrain was going to take the news that he was going to be dealing with my husband when taking care of the business of my car. I wondered if this would be the opportunity he would take to express that he still loved me and wanted me back. Will the day KB calls him to talk about my car be the moment of truth, revealing all feelings and emotions? Maybe this wasn't a good thing. Maybe I didn't need to know how Mr. MarcTrain felt about me, and maybe, he definitely doesn't need to express how he feels to KB.

I knew KB was no chump, and Mr. MarcTrain didn't display one punk bone in his body. I would never want either of them to have to feel they needed to challenge each other's manhood. I should have agreed with KB and gave up my car. Part of me wanted to just let it go like Mr. MarcTrain seemed to have done with me—just let me go, with no fight or no push back. Honestly, another part of me wanted to keep things the way they were not just so I could have the car that rightfully belonged to me, but because I would be able to keep a distant eye on Mr. MarcTrain to make sure he doesn't hate me for not choosing to stay with him.

I didn't know why my mind took me to these places, but I was a married woman now. What Mr. MarcTrain thought or felt about me should have no longer mattered. God placed me with who He chose for me. I stood before God and witnesses and made the vow to be the wife to one man and one man only. No other man should matter, and no other man should be on my mind. What any other man thought of me shouldn't have mattered either. If they still loved me or not, if they cared about me or not, if they still had an attraction to me or not. It should not have mattered. It should not have been of my concern. It should not have consumed my thoughts. It should not, but...

One thing that I was learning was the more I looked to people to fill a void or an emptiness inside, the more disappointed I became. I now saw that everything I had been hearing and learning in church all my life about the Holy Spirit was true— He is the only consistent One. I was desiring Him more and more. I was more confident now that it was Him that I needed, and He was the answer, not Mr. MarcTrain, my son's father, or my own husband. I needed God's spirit to keep me.

CHAPTER 4

# The Gift

I had been asking God to fill me with His Spirit, especially since becoming married to KB. I wanted to be closer to God, and I wanted to get closer to my husband. I felt the frustration of my job and life, and I acknowledged I needed more of God's spirit to make it. This became a constant prayer for me, day in and day out, ever since our honeymoon. I just had to believe that God was really going to give His Spirit to me. He was a gift, after all, and I was ready to receive Him.

It has become a custom for folks that when you are having a rough time in life, you shut down. When things become overwhelming, we withdraw ourselves from everyone. We tend to create a pity party for one, but if anyone wants to join, there is a seat at the table as long as they are not being encouraging and keep the defeated atmosphere strong. When someone asks what is wrong, we act like we don't want to talk about it, but we really want the attention. We say you wouldn't understand, but the truth is we are trying to make life issues the end of life, and they're not.

We don't want to go to church, we don't want to pray, and we have become the only one in the entire world going through something that no one will understand, and there is no way out—we just have to stay depressed. Not so! I refused to allow these foolish thoughts to come into my mind as if I was the first and only person to ever go through what I was feeling. Others had survived it, and so would I. I was not easily broken, but I was getting tired. I needed more strength, and the only place I knew where I could get it from was the house of God.

I lifted my hands, I sang, I prayed, I cried, I moaned, I shouted, and repeated. I felt a little better; I let some things go; I released my assumptions and held on to what I knew. That's why I went. That's why attending service was so important to me. I didn't care that there may be some people in there that attributed to my pain, but God was greater. He was so great that right in front of them, He would bless me, strengthen me, and prepare a table for me.

I couldn't lose focus, or I would never receive the prize. So with a hurt heart, I went; I gave God my all and kept moving forward. Second services on Sunday evenings seemed to be the best services sometimes. The service was when the true soldiers came back, and the Lord showed up. It was even more exciting when your church visited another church on Sunday evening when you knew both churches together would be rocking. Uncle Willie's church was one of those churches. They didn't have the best singers or the best music all the time, but you better believe the spirit of God was there.

I enjoyed every minute of the service, even the altar call. This time I was determined to go up to the altar one way and return better than I was before. The preacher had preached, the atmosphere was set, and all that was needed was my strong desire to be filled. I called out to God. Uncle Willie and others were there laying hands on the people as we were all crowded at the altar. I felt the hand of the church mother on my back as she began to pray with me and for me at the altar. I began to remove all thoughts from my mind and tuned everyone and everything out. I began to cry and let God know how desperate I was to receive this gift. I began to ask God to fill me over and over again, just saying, "Fill me, Lord." I knew what I was facing. I knew what I was dealing with, and I needed God's spirit to dwell in me to make it through. I began to feel God's presence surround me. I felt like it was just He and I in a room alone. I opened my mouth, and I heard my voice speaking in an unknown tongue. Just as quickly as I heard myself, I then heard the church mother say, "Oh my, she is speaking in tongues." Then I heard someone else say, "Shhhh, be quiet." Well, by that time, whatever had just happened was over. Whatever tongue I was speaking in stopped. Whatever spirit that had come upon me to fill me left. I began to cry out to God, not understanding why He would allow this to happen.

I always would talk about the person who remains up at the altar after everyone else had gone to their seat. I would be saying to myself, "Can't they feel that everyone else has left?" "Why are they holding up the service?" "Someone needs to go sit them down." "If you didn't get it by now, you not getting it today." I would go on and on and would guarantee that would never be me. Well, after all those years of being in church and watching people get picked up off the altar or the floor, it was finally my turn. I had no control over it. I had no idea I was the last person there. Now I see, when it is something you really want, and you know you need it, it doesn't matter what else is going on in the room—you've got to get yours.

After that experience, I was thankful to know I was getting ready to go home and be around my mom and aunty, who I knew would encourage me. It was fun to go home and be with my family to see my big brother get married. I never thought he would because...well, he is a Brumfield, and hey, why would he. But my brother loves his wife—my sissy Shemeka, a.k.a. Meeke. They had been together for a while, and I was glad they decided to make it legal. Sissy fit right into the family as if she had always been there. I knew she probably wondered if we really liked her or not, but hanging around us, she got to see that not only did we like her, we loved her. Once my brother brought you into the family, you kind of never got to leave—stuck with us forever.

It was always good to see family and be around family. I was not a fan of living in Da Roc, but the one joy that remained there was family. Seeing my aunt Myrl was especially great. I loved to hear people say that we look just alike and sound alike too. I have always looked up to my aunty. She is my father's only sister. I had admired her life ever since I was a little girl. Her wedding was huge and beautiful; her hair was huge and beautiful; her smile was huge and beautiful. Everything about Aunty was a huge deal to me and most definitely beautiful. She was young and saved, and I never saw her doing anything ungodly. Even remembering when she was single and saved, and there were certain ones that attempted to make her their wife. Aunty made sure there was no hanky-panky, and then came Uncle Matt!

While I have many aunts, there is something special about Aunt Myrl. She took a special interest in my new husband, and I was so glad. I wanted her to know him and him to know her, so he could see why I loved my aunty as much as I did. One thing about KB is he loved to talk about the Lord, and so did my aunt. When we got together at my big brother's wedding, I guess you know that is all we talked about. KB began to tell her all that happened on our honeymoon. I was telling her how badly I wanted to be filled and what had taken place at Uncle Willie's church. She told me to hold on with patience. That God was going to fill me, and it was coming soon. She always knew what to say and how to say it. She really was like a second mom to me if there ever were to be such a thing. I always left her feeling more confident in Christ than before. I would say to myself, "I want to have that same impact on people when I grow up."

That was the great part about coming to Da Roc, but at the same time, there was still so much darkness about my past life here. My brother got married right in Corn Hill, a few feet away from where I spent my days at Michael's grandmother's house. You could actually see the house from the church. The memories (although not all bad) were something I did not want to think about.

The lies that were told, the mistreatment, the hurt, the embarrassment, the disappointment, along with the laughs, moments of joy, and the love were something I wanted nothing to do with ever again. But I looked down and saw Zion at my side and realized I had a ways to go before Michael was completely out of my life—if ever. That was the price you paid for the decisions you made. News of me getting married and seriously moving on with my life did not sit well with him, and being in the same city as him truly was not an ideal situation—especially not this close. I had to admit I still held bitterness because I knew that guy really didn't care or was sorry for what he took me through.

Mentally, every now and then, I had to fight myself to get out of thinking that the treatment and the words that came from him were true. Sometimes, I somehow fell into believing that he just may have been right about me, and I thought low of myself again, realizing that all that I had right now wouldn't last forever. So now I was ready to leave Da Roc and move on without having to face the hurts and pain of my past. Too much pressure trying to forgive and forget all at once, I realized some things would take time. I felt uncomfortable, and I could tell I was doing nothing but making myself sick. We gathered our things and went home, and I was so glad to see the sign that said "Welcome to Maryland" once again.

I had been worried about how this pregnancy was going to come to an end. KB and I had the discussion, and he knew that I had been told, basically, that I would not be able to bear any more children. Yet here I was, pregnant with little KJ. I knew it was early, and I did not want to get excited, so I braced myself for the worse so it wouldn't hit me so hard when it was time to face my reality. But now I began to ask the question, "Why?"

Why, when I was finally doing things right, it seemed to go wrong? Why, now that I was married, having a child with my husband, it looked like the baby part was not going to happen? Was I paying for all my past sins with this child? Why is it always when you have made the decision to go about things the proper way, you seem to get screwed worse?

I just wanted to give my husband one child. Was that too much to ask for? Deep in my word, I began to trust God like never before. Yeah, just like we all do. When we need God to do something for us, we become all attached to Him, wanting to chill with Him more than usual so that He can give us what we desire. I was praying more and giving Him more praise, hoping that He rewarded me by allowing my body to carry this child to term.

I hadn't been feeling the best, and this pregnancy seemed a lot different from when I was pregnant with Zion. I was praying this was a boy and that I was miraculously able to go full term and deliver a healthy baby boy, Kenny Jr, a.k.a. "KJ." I was always tired, and I felt like this was going to be the longest pregnancy ever. My emotions were all over the place—excited and totally not ready for all the discomfort that would take place.

I woke up to pink-looking stains in my panties. I called my doctor to let her know that I had been cramping, and now there was a pinkish fluid coming out of me. She told me to go to St. Agnes hospital right away. I was so scared on the way there, keeping quiet and not saying much of anything to KB as he drove. Zion was in the backseat, not knowing what was going on. He stayed happy and excited about the family that he always wanted finally coming together.

I began to pray under my breath, asking God to give me strength to know how to deal with the disappointment of not being able to complete a pregnancy. I asked Him to give me the words to say to my husband so that he would not be upset with me. I felt like a failure. All my life, I did not care if I had kids or not. I never really wanted any and wasn't the least bit upset when told that I couldn't have more.

But here I was—a newly married woman wanting to give her husband something he never had, and I was going to fail. This Oreo cookie, this broken, used-up crumb. No wonder no one else loved me enough, treated me good enough, and stayed with me—I had nothing to offer. I hated myself and regretted my youthful wish and desires to never have kids.

How could I have been so stupid and careless with my body? All of the sexual activity and wrongdoing were now coming back to haunt me. I could hear my ex-lovers laughing at me. Happy that I would never be happy now that I understood the detriment of my past behaviors. I wasn't a loose woman, far from it. I could use my hands once to count how many men I had been sexually active with.

I never hit double digits in sexual partners; that was never a goal of mine, and I'm glad promiscuity could never define me. I didn't sleep with every man I came in contact with, nor did I explore same-sex or any kinky behaviors of that kind. But I wasn't always careful. I wasn't always using good judgment. I wasn't with the right person doing the right thing.

I waited in the waiting room with my husband holding my hand. He had his game face on. I knew he didn't want me to see any sign of fear in him. He had never been in a situation like this, and he had to be strong for me. I hated myself for putting him in this predicament. I kept saying I was sorry under my breath. He did not deserve this. Maybe everyone who said I was not good enough for him was right.

He deserved a woman that was not used up already. A woman that was not broken. A woman that could give him as many children as he wanted. That was not me. I had to admit I was not the best choice for him. So did God finally make a mistake when He put us two together? That certainly was what it felt like right now. All these women out here ready and willing to give KB as many babies as he so desired, and here he was with me suffering through a miscarriage—a debt due for the past I lived.

We were finally called back, and as I laid across the hospital bed, I knew that this was not going to end on a good note. KB rubbed my hair back and kissed my forehead and told me that I was going to be fine. Why did he still love me after knowing I could not give him children? Why did he stay by my side? Why didn't he find a reason to run away like everyone else did in my life? The longer he stayed, the more I would hurt him through disappointment. I wished he would just leave.

This kind lady had me lift up my shirt and lower my skirt to put the jelly fluid on my stomach. She turned the machine on and began explaining that she was going to do an ultrasound to check on the baby. She rubbed across my stomach and quietly typed on the machine. She moved around again and typed some more. She began to press a little harder into my stomach with the probe, and the gel began to get all over me. After trying over and over and over again, her face began to look a bit concerned. I became frightened, already knowing that something was wrong. She explained that she could not see the baby, nor could she hear or find a heartbeat.

Hearing those words, I just lifted my eyes to the ceiling and gave up. I hated my life, and I could just imagine what my husband would think of me now that he knew for certain that I could not give birth to any of his children. But he wouldn't show his disappointment in me. He stood there like a trooper. Seeing him standing there, not being moved at all, hurt me even more. I tried my hardest to hold back, but a tear began to roll out of the corner of my eye down my cheek to my ear. He wiped it away and told me everything was going to be okay.

I then had to get up and remove my panties for them to do a transvaginal ultrasound. She put a condom on the probe and then put some gel on it and asked me to insert it so that they could get a closer look. I was already humiliated and felt it couldn't get any worse than this. With my husband and my son in the room, I was just wishing I could remove myself from the entire equation. As I inserted the probe, I felt like I could not breathe. I could hear someone saying, "Relax," but I felt like I was in the *Twilight Zone*. I was thinking I needed to divorce KB to give him an opportunity to be with someone that could give him a family, having children, and making him happy.

I had given up on myself and this fake trash we talk of a fairytale ending and happily ever after. How in the world did I fall for that and believe that it was something that could happen to me or something that I deserved? I drank the fairytale juice and fell for the shenanigans. Had me believing that I deserved a good man, a happy life, and be a good wife.

All wrong. I had to face the fact that I was not good enough and never would be. I had to face the fact that no matter how much I trusted God and served God, there were just some things I was never going to have or be a part of. The good life was for other people, not me. The happily ever after was for good girls, smart girls, rich girls—any girl but me.

I couldn't take it anymore. I wanted to jump up off the table and run out of the room. I was so embarrassed and ashamed. I looked over to KB to tell him I was sorry, and right as I opened my mouth, I heard the woman say, "There it is!" as we all looked over on the screen to see a black and white image. There was nothing in the shape of a baby. I didn't see a head, feet, or any hands and legs. I looked and looked but could not see any body parts.

Then she said, "Look right there," and we looked again. We saw the sack but no baby, and then...there was a flicker and another flicker. She explained to us, with joy, there was the baby's heartbeat! I could not believe what I was hearing and seeing. The tears began to roll down my face as I cried uncontrollably. The baby was alive and doing fine. KB looked down at me, kissed me again, and said, "I told you everything would be all right." Yeah...I was in for a journey with this guy.

*Know this:* Be careful what you say out of your mouth as a youth; as an adult, you will spend a lot of time eating those words.

Finally, I was in a state of happiness. All these years, I felt I never would care about having another child, but now I was so thankful to God for not going along with what I said and having His way in my life. He truly does know what is best for us, and even though we don't deserve it, He still blesses us. I knew for a fact this child was a miracle and a blessing, and I would praise God for such. Many times we are blessed with a second chance, and we blow it. We skip right over the fact that we should not be afforded this opportunity and go on matter-factly.

But I was pregnant. I was actually carrying another baby inside of me. That was a fact, and it was all because of God's grace. No one could make me believe differently.

# CHAPTER 5

# Physical Loss, Spiritual Gain

This pregnancy seems a bit different from when I was pregnant with Zion. Although there was a lot of morning sickness with Zion, this baby is an all-day sickness. I have lost so much weight not being able to eat. I am miserable all the time, and there seems to be no relief. No matter what I eat, drink, or smell, everything seems to trigger this nausea. I am crying all the time for nothing, and I don't get much sleep. Marriage seems to now have a different feel. I want my sleep while my husband, whom I love making sexual melodies with, wants to keep the symphony going. I am tired, sick, and have no desire to make love. What do you do in a time like this?

*Know this:* Every woman is different, so never compare yourself to others. It is okay to get insight, advice, and be aware of how others handle the same situation you are in, but by no means should you expect the same outcome. *We are different!*

My sex drive was on ten. Anytime KB wanted me, I wanted that much of him and more. Now I just want to be alone. And the two became one. No longer does my body belong to me; it now belongs to my husband. But if we are one and this body belongs to him, why isn't he nauseous? Why isn't he tired? Why isn't he an emotional wreck? How are we one, but we are not feeling the same things? How are we one, and he still wants to lay with me like crazy, and I just want my body back to myself? He cannot feel what I am feeling, and I am unable to articulate to him what an emotional roller coaster I am on right now. So when he wants me, I lay there. There is no participation on my part because this is not what I want right now, but it is something that he needs. We are one, and his needs have become more important. Why does he not even care that I am not as active anymore? Does he even know that I am not participating as much? How can you lose touch with your own body so quickly?

Truth is, we discuss we are one all the time, but in a new marriage, becoming one doesn't happen overnight. I want KB, and at the same time, I do not. How can you not want yourself if you are one? I have no idea how to tell him what I am feeling. I don't even know if it is appropriate to talk to anyone else about what I am feeling. So I keep it to myself.

Evidently, my body belongs to him and this baby now, and I have no say. I must endure and keep a smile on my face because, after all, I am newly married, and everything should be happy-go-lucky right now. This is still the honeymoon phase, so there shouldn't be any issues. This is not the time to question anything because I guarantee those that did not want us to be married in the first place are sitting by, waiting for a whiff of anything being wrong. So I cry and cry some more. What else is there to do? I cry, hoping that KB will attempt to find out what is wrong. Even though I don't know how to explain it, and

I don't know what to do, I still want him to seem like he cares enough to ask me what's wrong.

So here is where the mask is developed. So busy not wanting anyone to realize I don't know what to do next, I do nothing. I cry at night, and my husband doesn't see me. I stand firm in public, letting everyone think I can beat all odds with my eyes closed. It is getting harder and harder to wear this mask, and now there's a level of expectation I must keep up. The more I wear the mask, the more I see that the people I am wearing this mask for could care less about me. I want them to care, and at the same time, I don't care if they care or not. Remember I didn't marry the Hunt family, and I didn't marry the church; I married Kenneth Tyrone Hunt, so why now am I concerned about everyone else instead of being concerned about what he sees in me?

I need KB to see there has been a change in my sexual drive. I need KB to see that carrying this baby is a lot for me. I need him to know that I am scared of losing this baby. I want to tell him that I want to make melodies with him but just not right now. I want him to know that I need him to take into consideration what my body feels like, and I have no control over how I am feeling. Instead of saying anything to him, I won't eat, drink, or speak. I'm sinking into a dark hole and falling quickly into a place that seems to not have an exit.

*Know this:* Depression is a spirit and emotion that is real. Many times, when people begin to look at their life and not like what they see, that emotion begins to rise, and if you're not careful, that spirit will take over.

Between feeling like I am no longer able to sexually keep up with my husband and feeling like no one likes me at the church and my job isn't perfect either, my world is crumbling. I do not see any sign of relief physically or spiritually. I don't want to be a failure, especially at being a wife, but I don't know what to do.

Now that I am married and can have all the sex I want without sinning, I get pregnant and don't want anything. Am I being punished? I hear about other women getting pregnant, and their sex drive increases, so why has mine decreased?

One thing I am glad about is that KB loves God. I think about other marriages and see that it is at this point when the man feels he is not getting enough at home that he steps out on the marriage and gets satisfied in other ways with other women (or men...s.m.h....sad but true). I know KB fears and loves God, so being unfaithful to me is not on his mind, but I don't want him to be tempted either. I don't want women to see that I am not satisfying him and try to step in and take my place.

Funny how you think that because you are in the church, it would not happen to you. As I grow older and older in the church, watching those adults around me and listening to their conversations, I see the church is one of the most dangerous places for a woman to lose her husband. Church is where some predators prey on vulnerable and weak individuals. Not everyone in church is there to follow the teaching and morals of the church. Some are strategically set there to stop you from adhering.

I keep hearing and seeing the uptightness and unhappy faces around me, still displeased with the choices God made for my life, and I want to address them. I want to put a mirror up to people's faces and force them to see themselves and how foolish they look being nasty to me because God is having His way in our life. It was unreal to me that people actually stopped their children from playing with mine, didn't allow their children to talk to me; others would walk past me with disgust in their faces yet say they are a representation of Christ. How?

Sometimes, I wonder, *Do I really want to live through this for the rest of my life?* I love KB, and I am thankful God chose me for this assignment with him, but should I have to deal with this type of mistreatment forever? What happened to people being genuinely happy for a young couple loving God and living according to His Word? I try my best to ignore and brush things off. I do all I can to put the happy things in the forefront of my mind, but lately, happy things are becoming less and less.

They have no idea that we didn't plan for this love to take place. This is new for us too. No one is taking into consideration that this change is affecting us, and we must adapt. We need to get used to one another just like everyone should get used to us being with each other. We have to learn each other just like everyone else has to learn us as a couple together.

Day by day, I am getting sicker and weaker. I need to be able to handle myself at work because this woman who wants everyone to call her "Momma" has totally lost her mind. This is stressful and more than I feel I can handle. I do what I know to do, and that is going down to God in prayer. I find that even though there are some in the church that show very mean and rude ways towards KB and me, the church in the presence of God is where I am finding strength.

During this season of my life, I took solace in the little things that made me happy in a big way. One of them was having our dear friends Elder and Sister Farmer visit to celebrate Men and Women's Day at our church. Just thinking about it, my heart would leap with joy. After all, Elder Farmer is the preacher that confirmed what God told KB about marrying me. He and his wife coming to Baltimore from Memphis is always a highlight at the church, but even more so when God used Elder Farmer as confirmation that God ordained KB's union with me. So there I am, ready and prepared to encounter a move of God—just what I need.

In my white suit, with my little tummy poking out a bit, I embrace God's presence. It is something about this Sunday evening service that just isn't like the others. I feel a release, and I feel freedom; I truly feel the presence of God stronger than ever before. In the altar/well area at the front of the church, with my hands lifted high in worship, I begin to feel tightness of my skin as if something is growing rapidly inside of me. At first, I thought I was feeling this way because of my pregnancy. I was having a difficult time and thought I should take it easy; maybe this feeling wasn't bliss, maybe it was dizziness caused by stress or feeling overwhelmed. But something says, "Keep praising, keep worshiping, keep crying," and I do.

Then suddenly, just as it happened at Uncle Willie's church, I begin to speak in tongues. There is no one in the room but my Lord and me. As my skin gets tighter and tighter, I know He is filling me with His Spirit. I refuse to let the devil steal my gift this time. I won't let go. I won't let up. I am so overjoyed. He said He would give it to me, and He did. So excited, I refuse to let the service end without proclaiming to the congregation what God has just done in me. I want to say it out loud so that the devil can't whisper in my ear anything different. I want to say it out loud so that my outside can catch up to what I am feeling on the inside.

I want to say it out loud because God did it; He really did it, and I am overjoyed. It doesn't even matter to me if anyone is happy with me. I am happy because I look at me, I look at my past, I look at my shortcomings. I look at what others have to say about me. I look at what I see in the mirror and say, "Certainly, God won't give me this gift," but He did!

For so many, this is the reason they don't give the church a try. Everything and everyone reminds them daily of the condition they are in, and they feel defeated before even trying. The more you look at yourself, the more you will find wrong with yourself, the more you will believe what God has done for others and in others you are not qualified or worthy to be chosen for. "How could God love or choose someone like me?" we say, but God is saying, "How could I not?"

This happens because we don't see as God sees. God is the Creator of time; He is time and is in control of time. We are a moment in time. So while we see the moment, He sees our entirety knowing who we are before we ever get to His completion of us. It is good to acknowledge and recognize the moments. When you do, you get a chance to look and see how far you've come with every moment of your life. Realizing from one moment to the next, God was in control all the time.

While I was seeking His Spirit on the honeymoon, He already knew this moment was coming months later. While I was in the moment feeling like I didn't deserve it, He was on time, knowing just when to give me this precious gift. I am so glad He controls time and allows me to live in the moments. There was a moment in time where none of this spirituality and relationship with Him even mattered to me, and now it is everything. Just reflecting back on who I was and where I was just a few years ago and see what He has done with me in His time—God is amazing. And to think I'm still here, so that means He's not done with me yet.

Leaving out of the service that evening, one of the preachers at the church, Elder Washington, says to me the devil is going to come after me and try to tell me I don't have what I have professed. He tells me to be on guard and continue to pray. I believe him and know what he said to be true. I can't wait to go home and call my aunt Myrl and let her know what God has done. I am too pumped calling my mom and telling her that her daughter was filled with the Holy Ghost. That's me—Kenny's wife, saved, sanctified, and filled with the Holy Ghost.

I sleep so well. I feel so full. I am excited, humbled, and feel so strong. In my dreams, I see and hear God giving me instructions. When I wake up, I feel His Spirit pulling me to carry out His plans. What an amazing life I am living with Him living inside of me. Happy as can be, I approach life differently, listening to His instructions as I go. Like a little child feeling so free, not realizing what was ahead for me.

Even now, being filled with God's spirit, I still don't enjoy going to work anymore. I thought being filled would automatically resolve everything, but the reality is it is a process that I must be willing to endure. I used to love the fact that my job was at my child's school, so I could check in on him and see him from time to time during the day. I have met some of the greatest people here, but not anymore. I don't like my new director. I don't like how she treats the staff and how she forces them to call her "Momma." I don't like her controlling ways. I don't like how I am always in between her and the staff to calm every uprising that she starts with them.

I go to work with my mind on trying to be more of a mediator to calm the current situation down, only to see that the situations at work are getting worse. I am in communication with another director who is having trouble at her site also. Rhonda is so good to talk to and helped me keep things moving after Isaac left.

We had worked on some things together and hit it off well enough that she would look out for me, and I would look out for her as well with any reports and updates that needed our attention. She tells me she is going to have an opening at her site, and I need to consider coming to work for her. I heard that she was mean, but I never experienced such with her. I like where I work as far as location is concerned because it is right down the street from the church. I feel if I left, there would be a war that would destroy everything here. But a decision needs to be made.

I have to think about myself. I have to think about this pregnancy. I have to think about my marriage and the family God is developing with me. The daily stress on this job is not good, and something has to give. Every week it is something new. Every time I put one fire out, another irrupts. I tell Rhonda I am strongly considering her proposal, but I know I can't just run away, leaving things the way they are. I also know I don't want to lose this baby stressing over this director and her lack of ability to lead.

I don't enjoy going to work anymore because I can never tell when I answer the phone if it will be Mr. MarcTrain on the other end. I'm never prepared to hear his voice anymore. A part of me waits to see if he is going to call, but a bigger part of me doesn't enjoy the fact of knowing that any time the phone rings, it could be him. Calling to see if I am okay. Calling to see if I have taken care of my car payment. Calling just to hear my voice.

I can't enjoy it because I am married, and now that God has filled me, I feel God pushing out those feelings. I can't enjoy it because it is too late for this. His persistence should have been before I said, "I do," not after. I can't enjoy this because I feel like I am keeping secrets from my husband. Secrets. I don't enjoy keeping secrets because I can't...so I won't.

I know Rhonda is getting ready to fire her administrator, and I could walk right into that position, but I am pregnant. Rhonda is going to need someone there, not out having a baby, so I know I need to stay right where I am, no matter how bad it gets. I am already employed at this job, and they know I am pregnant. I have benefits and insurance to cover me and this pregnancy, so it is best I stay and tolerate what I know rather than quit not knowing what benefits I would be getting or when for certain.

*Know this:* God has a plan for all of us. That plan sometimes may seem very uncomfortable. It is wise for us to go with the plan regardless of how crazy or irrational it may seem when it is God's plan. When we don't, He will allow situations to take place to get us back on His track and not remain on our own.

I know the situation at my job is getting more and more intense between the staff and the director. This new director, "Momma," is setting envelopes on people's desks with a letter in it telling them they are terminated. I am getting yelled at from every side, not knowing that this is coming. Trying to keep the staff from beating her to death and explaining that we could go before the board to deal with her was terrible.

This is people's livelihood she is toying with. This is the way the staff survives, paying their bills and providing for their families. I am so upset with her behaviors and totally unhappy with the chaos she causes. She wants the staff she terminated to be off the premises immediately. She went into her office and hid, leaving me to deal with their anger as they pack their things in distress.

I was so caught up in trying to calm some of the staff down that I did not see the same type of envelope on my desk. Yes. Not only is she firing some of the staff, but she is firing me too. In a state of shock, I call the board chair. I'm not worried at all because I know that they will tell her she can't fire me.

I couldn't get an answer, and reading the letter, I know that I don't want an altercation with the police, so I too have to leave the premises. The eatery is right around the corner, so I drive over there to tell my husband what happened. The board chair finally calls me and says to me that they will get to the bottom of everything. He asks me if I have the keys to the building still and any of the company credit cards and administrative things. I tell him I do, and he says to me he wants to meet up to retrieve those things until they are able to work something out. This doesn't sound right to me, but I can't imagine the board chair or the board agreeing with doing me wrong, so I trust him.

When we meet, his demeanor is different from how he has always been. He is saying things like, "We will get back to you," and "We are looking into things," being real evasive. I am wondering why he isn't being direct and everything he says is very vague. It is almost like he has signed off on and agreed with the actions that have taken place. He says he didn't, but right then, I begin to wonder.

I decide I better call down to unemployment and apply because it is starting to look like I am not going to be walking right back into my job like I thought and that it may take a little longer for me to go back to work. I don't mind because I'm not feeling well anyway, but I know no matter what, after all the smoke clears, I need to still be employed.

Elder Washington warned me, and I could hear his warning so clear. In that moment, it was running through my head, "Where is that Holy Ghost now?" "Why didn't that Holy Ghost stop you from losing your job?" I was already saved, sanctified, and living for God, and, *Now with power from on high, life is supposed to be easier,* my naïve self was thinking.

You're just getting married, and now your husband has to take care of you and your bills because you don't have an income anymore. You're pregnant and have to go to prenatal appointments, but you are about to be without medical insurance. How are you going to take care of yourself now? This clearly can't be a part of that "gift" God has given you. Where's that gift now?

My heart is beating fast, tears begin to roll down my face, and I am in serious distress. All I can think about is what "people" are going to say about me. I lost my job on purpose so that KB and the well-to-do Hunt family and the church could take care of me, my son, and this baby on the way. What if they say this is a sign from God that He is not with us like we said He is? He allowed this to happen because this marriage was not His plan.

God couldn't possibly be a part of this mess. There is no way in the world He would allow poor ole' Bro Kenny to lose his wife to lupus and then put him with this girl he now has to support along with a brand-new baby on the way. I feel humiliated. I want to run and hide. But there stands KB to tell me that everything is going to be okay no matter what happens.

# DIARY 2

# Secrets

So it looks like marriages seem to have a strain on them because of secrets. Consider how your spouse would feel about a secret you are keeping from them if they found out the secret from someone else and not you. If the thought of this makes you feel troubled or uneasy, this is a clear indication that your secret no longer needs to be a secret.

Sometimes we think telling the truth will make matters worse, and that becomes our justification for keeping secrets. However, lying or simply not being forthcoming and remaining deceptive is worse. Not only do you have that secret, but now your spouse will always wonder, "Are there more secrets? Are there more lies?" You are living a lie and will get to the point where you no longer know who you are. Are you the lie you have been telling or the secret you have been keeping? Keeping secrets and privately holding things internally is a lot of work. It wears on your body, causes stress and anxiety of being exposed. The longer you hold the secret, the worse you begin to feel about it. Every time the secret is in danger of being exposed, you tend to make choices and decisions that are out of character only to save yourself from the direst of being uncovered.

Many times you fall into character trying to protect your secret, that you become many different people with different personalities. This causes your spouse to wonder if they know you at all. Having to walk on eggshells, not knowing what side of the bed you will wake up on. Depending on your mood and how the secret is affecting you on a certain day, your attitude towards others will fluctuate. This leaves your spouse wondering if they have made the right choice in marrying you. They wonder if you ever really loved them. They wonder if you are the person they fell in love with, or that was a cover-up as well.

Even worse, your spouse may blame themselves. Feeling that the reason things aren't going so well is because of who they are. They aren't good enough, they don't love you enough, and you are not satisfied with them. They begin to second-guess their attributes and how they look and how you value them. Their self-esteem begins to diminish, causing them to be in fear of losing you and never finding happiness with anyone else. They may begin keeping secrets, also in fear of losing you, which is the beginning of failed communication.

After a while, you will need others to cover for you as your secret gradually seeps out. You will cause others to agree to lie or deceive just enough to keep your secret under wraps. All while you say you love the one you're with. But how do you love them when they turn out to be the only one that doesn't know or the last one to know your secret? Trust and distrust become the topic of the marriage, not love, not forgiveness, not honor. God isn't even being mentioned, and the marriage becomes broken with difficulties in even trying to repair it.

Why is it that within a marriage, we tend to look outside the marriage for everything? Are your expectations not being met? Are you not satisfied? What void is not being filled that is causing you to think that something is missing or you are missing out on something? Or do you still have connections from previous relationships that you neglected to cut the cord, and somehow you are being pulled back into something you should have let go of?

Remember leaving an earring or some article of clothing or an item at a friend's house when we have an argument and break up. We go through the phase of not talking to each other, which turns to missing each other. Then use the lame excuse of needing to come over to find what was "lost" over there. This was only to keep ties to one another. Taking items that belonged to someone in order to meet up with them to give them back. This would only leave the opportunity open to start back up where you left off.

Well, when you get married, those ties need to be completely severed. Those ties honestly should be cut before you get married so that in the marriage, there are no third parties attached. Trying to hold on to something from a past relationship is a sure sign that you are not completely ready to move on. No need to marry someone that you are not ready to be committed to because you can't let go of your past relationship. Marriage is between one woman and one man. When you begin to add women or men to the equation, it is no longer a marriage; it is a mess!

The problem with keeping secrets is your secret may fall into the hands or ears of someone who doesn't particularly care for you and would love to tell all. I've noticed that with most marriages, there is someone that did not want you to get married in the first place, so they sit and watch and wait for the demise and downfall. They search for clues or anything to put an end to your marriage. In some cases of infidelity being the secret, it may be the other individual involved in the ordeal who feels they deserve to be treated better than being a well-kept secret. This label side chick or side piece at one time was okay for some until they realized they deserved better; they deserved more. At some point, they see that true happiness will never come from the sham of a mess they've entered in.

As close to the chest as you may have your secret, always remember your confidant has a confidant too. All it takes is for one person to get fed up or for someone to mistakenly say too much at the wrong time. Now you don't know who knows what and who will be loyal to keep your secret. You become paranoid, on guard at all times. You tend to start telling on yourself, getting your thoughts confused.

Then when everything is exposed and it all "hits the fan," the word "divorce" comes. We're not getting a divorce because of the details of the secret; we're getting a divorce because there ever was a secret. If you have married someone and you have become one, what is wrong with telling them everything? Are you really being yourself if you don't? If you choose to withhold information, aren't you pretending to be something or someone that you are not?

In marrying someone, you have come into a vow and agreement to always put them first. I have always been one to watch how someone treats their spouse. If you walk all over your spouse, I won't have much respect for them either. If you hold your spouse in high esteem, I see them living up to that and respect them on that level as well. Well, if you keep secrets from your spouse and leave them vulnerable to the dangers of that secret embarrassing them because of you, it shows just how much you respect them. Leaving them to wonder if anyone else would respect them if their own spouse doesn't.

Why do we keep secrets when we know the end of a secret can become the demise of a great thing? Is a secret really a secret if you are the only one who knows?

# CHAPTER 6

# The Voice

After a while, I'm starting to accept the fact that I am not going back to my job. I received a call from unemployment to tell me that the director stated it was my fault I was fired, so I was denied unemployment benefits. I appealed, and a date was set for us to go to a hearing. I know that what she has done is wrong, but we have to wait until the hearing to prove it. I've never been on unemployment before, and this is all new to me, and all I can do is pray that things work in my favor.

I am pregnant, and I know no one would want to hire me in this condition, and she blocked me from getting unemployment. I'm in a bad predicament, and I have no idea how I am going to get through this. I lie in my bed and rub my stomach, falling to sleep. In my dreams, the Lord showed me He was with me and that He was going to take care of me. But that was what happened in my dreams, and I need those dreams to be a reality.

Home with nothing to do, all I want is to sleep all my problems away. My husband would work all day from the eatery to serving summonses. I feel helpless and useless and wish I could offer some assistance. As I go from the bathroom to the bedroom, sick as I could be, I find no relief. Daily, my misery gets worse and worse. I cry when KB isn't around because I don't want him to see me that way. He is doing all he can do to take care of us, but we are still in a struggle to pay bills. Ashamed, I don't want to even discuss finances with him. I choose to ignore everything because I feel there is nothing that I can do about it anyway.

I know KB wants this baby as bad as me. This will be his first child, and we are looking forward to meeting KJ—Kenny Jr. I'm just tired of the doctor's appointments. I am finding myself in and out of the hospital constantly remaining dehydrated because it is hard for me to eat or drink and keep food down. KB tries to help me by purchasing me whatever I am craving at the moment, but as soon as it is placed before me, I no longer have the desire to eat, and the smell makes me want to throw up!

This does nothing but frustrates KB, but there is nothing that I can do about it. He threatens that he will take me to the hospital if I don't eat. He will make sure they put an IV in me to get me hydrated. I hide in my bedroom, feeling so low about myself, which doesn't help. Seemingly right when KB leaves to go to work, and I am feeling my worst, my phone rings.

All by myself in the house, my phone rings, and I answer, not caring who was on the other end, just hoping that it was good news in some way or another. My heart flutters when I hear the voice on the other end. I know who it is, and I know a buried piece of me misses him. It is Mr. MarcTrain. He asks me how I am doing, and I hesitate. He says hello again, and I tell him I am okay. He is calling because it is time for me to make my monthly car payment.

So many thoughts begin to run through my head, and I have to pause before I say anything else to him. With concern in his voice, he asks me what is going on. I answer, and he immediately knows there is something wrong. I can do nothing but cry. Mr. MarcTrain just sits on the phone and listens to me cry. He then begins to ask me questions, am I in danger, am I being mistreated, do I need him to come and get me. He just wants to know what is wrong so that he can help me. Why is it that he immediately asks the questions I want KB to ask? Why is his level of concern the exact concern that I want KB to have for me?

Feeling helpless and questioning my life, I tell him. I tell him that I am pregnant and that I am having a rough time with the pregnancy. I tell him how I cannot eat anything and how I have lost so much weight. I tell him how I thought I couldn't carry the baby. I tell him how I am constantly at the doctor's office trying to make sure that this baby and I survive this. I tell him that I was fired from my job and that the director blocked me from getting unemployment, and now I have no way of paying bills, and I feel like a big failure making one mistake after another.

He tells me to slow down and to calm down and start over, taking it slow. I stay on the phone with him telling him how miserable I am feeling and that I do not know what I am going to do. I want to know why he didn't fight for me. I want to know if he really loved me, why he gave up so easily and let me marry KB as if what we had meant nothing to him. I blame him for the condition my life was in. He tells me he loves me, and he is concerned about me and my health. He tells me that he is sorry. He tells me he wishes he would have done things differently.

I never took into consideration what he had to go through with my decision to follow God's plan. I didn't think about how it made him feel being cut off so abruptly after being together for so long. Right or wrong, I feel bad. He was nothing but a kind man to me, and I feel horrible about not even thinking of his feelings enough to have done things differently myself.

He wanted to go on, but I know that this is not what I need to hear. This is not going to make things better. This is not what my husband would want and definitely not what God would be pleased with. I tell Him that God makes no mistakes. I may be unhappy right now, but God is in control. I know that it is the enemy who is trying to make me feel like I have made the wrong decisions, and talking to him is doing nothing but allowing the devil an opportunity to fill my head with foolishness I do not need to entertain.

Everything in me is saying, *Hang that phone up. This is something you do not want to have to deal with later, so hang up now. This conversation can already be considered inappropriate so hang up now. Asking myself, Would I want my husband to converse with someone that tells him they love him, or would I want him to hang up now?* I know that my life is in God's hands and that this is a way to make me waver, but I refuse to fall victim to emotions of what could have been, especially when I am thankful for what really is.

I have to be honest with myself, Mr. MarcTrain, and especially my husband. When you care for someone, and you truly love them, that is not something that you turn on and off at your own will. I did not just have subtle feelings for Mr. Marc-Train; this was the man I was looking forward to marrying and being with for the rest of my life.

I could not have imagined being with any other man, but God saw different and had a different plan. While I accepted God's plan for my life, that didn't completely erase the emotions that were already there. It did not remove the past or anything that was said and done in the past.

I apologize to Mr. MarcTrain, telling him that I am fine; everything will be fine, and I will do what needs to be done to handle my car business with my husband. What we had is over, and although it may take some time for the feelings to be completely gone, my husband, the one who God chose for me, will be my focus. He tells me he is concerned about my health and that I don't need to stress over the car. I tell him not to be worried about anything and that it will be taken care of. I had to hang up. I had to let go. He had to let go too. But does KB need to know?

As quickly as I accept his attention, affection, and concern for me, I tell him I have to go and cannot speak to him. I am not mistreated. I am not in danger. I am not looking to cheat on my husband. I am, however, pregnant and full of crazy emotions that are all over the place. I am feeling unhappy about my body. I am always sick. I am in a hormone overload. I am looking for attention, but from the right person, and it is not Mr. MarcTrain. I am a married woman, and I love my husband, KB, *only*...right?

*Know this:* Everything that may seem like it feels good to you is not good for you. Don't accept every "good feeling"; emotions can be deceitful.

I run quickly to the bathroom to begin throwing up again. I hadn't eaten anything, nor had I drunk anything, so there was nothing coming up but a yellow acid-like substance. My mind begins to race. If I am not careful, I will find myself in a worse place doing things I know I would not want done to me and would frown upon if it was someone else. The emotions between Mr. MarcTrain and I are still strong and should not be. But like everything else with my body, I feel I have no control over anything, and I need God to help me if I am going to make it through this.

KB comes home with a bottle of Gatorade. He wants me to drink it, and I just can't. He yells at the top of his lungs, not understanding what is so hard about drinking something I would normally drink without a problem. Me, still not being able to put words in my mouth that I thought would help him understand, I do nothing but cry.

He tries to drag me down the stairs, threatening that I drink the Gatorade or go to the hospital. I don't want to do either, so I yell, I cry, I fight with all the strength I have. KB and I have never been at odds like this, and it feels like he doesn't love me. It feels like he could care less about me and just wants this baby. His father tried to explain to him that he needed to have patience with me as I cried to him, but we were new at this and had to navigate our way through.

All these emotions, knowing some of them are exaggerated because I am pregnant. Everything is way more sensitive than it should be. I find myself back in the hospital again. Part of me enjoys the attention that I am getting from those that seem to be concerned, but it continues to feel like something is missing. Every woman enjoys people catering to her because she is pregnant. She loves getting her way and making requests that she knows people will carry out on demand. But there is also a point where you just want to be left alone, and you'd rather have happy days instead of uncomfortable, unpredictable moments.

Every time Deacon Thomas would make spaghetti at the eatery, I would eat so much of it, then would become sick and throw it up until it became one of the main things I was able to keep down. Yes, I love that attention—who wouldn't? His spaghetti from the eatery is a main meal for me. I was so happy when it didn't make me sick. I could smell it and be fine. I can eat bowls of it and feel great! I love eating what I want when I want (which was obviously not much). I love everyone making sure I have a place to sit, asking with excitement how far along I am, and showing concern about this pregnancy.

Everyone is nice to pregnant women...right? I thought for sure that my being pregnant would maybe change some things for the better so that I could enjoy having a baby. It seems like for as many reasons we have to be happy right now, there are things that make us unhappy as well. All I want to do is enjoy this moment, but my mind keeps me focused on all the things I don't enjoy.

What I don't enjoy is my clothes not fitting me so quickly. The baby is growing so fast inside of me that I look further along than I am. I don't enjoy the stares that people are giving to me because of how big my belly is getting so fast. I don't enjoy rumors being spread saying that I was pregnant before we got married, and that is why we hurried to get married after Dion died, to cover up that we were in a sexual relationship while she was alive. It hurt to hear where the rumors started. Yeah, you guessed correctly, right in the church.

With my due date being March 8, 2004, I just wanted the days to go by quickly, but it seems to take longer and longer with each day. I don't enjoy that as my belly grows, frustration grows. I can't understand why people would start such a vicious rumor about my husband and me. So evidently, my baby is not due in March of next year; the baby is due in November of this year. The only way that could happen is if I had the baby early or that I became pregnant before KB and I got married.

Young and old spreading this rumor like telling it in different colorful ways would somehow make it true. I don't enjoy having to sit around and not defend myself. I know full well some of these married couples entertaining this rumor had sex before marriage. I see some of these older people have children older than their marriage, so there had to be sex before marriage for them too. Some of their children have given them grandchildren without having a spouse, but yet their mouth is on me and KB saying something that would never be true. Yes, I'm angry. Yes, I'm hurt. Yes, I'm ready to confront everyone that entertains this foolishness.

What hurts the worse is when you find out the very ones keeping the rumor alive are the ones who pretend to love you. They make believe that they are supportive of you. They want you to believe that they have no clue where the rumors came from when all along...it is them! To have to sit in church knowing what is being said about me behind my back. To have to hug and hold a conversation with these people and not let on that you know what they have been saying about you.

It is hard, but KB and I realize we have to go through this. Yeah, we know what is being said and who is saying it, and we choose to not confront them. We are choosing not to address their foolish, childish behavior. God spoke to me and told us to live. My husband explained that God was saying to me that we would outlive every lie being told on us. I had to hold on to that. I had to believe that in my heart. I had to accept the fact that I had no other choice.

I don't enjoy that I have no family here with me. I want my sisters and my mom to be around me and help me through this pregnancy. I have my BFF Bunch, but it seems like I put too much on her to always be there for me and everything that I am dealing with in life and never paying any attention to what she may be going through. I need backup, but no one is there. My family is in Da Roc, and that is where they will remain. So I don't enjoy being alone.

I feel like I am failing my husband as a wife, a friend, as a potential mother to his child, and all around as a person in general. I know he wants more sex from me than I can give him right now, and it is bothering him. I realize Dion as a wife satisfied him while she was alive, but there were some things they could not do because of her illness that he now with me should have free access to. Because my body feels the way it does with this pregnancy, he does not.

I am just not the same sexual person I was just a short time ago. I want to be, but I am not. Not to mention I am battling feelings for Mr. MarcTrain that did not just shut off because I married KB. I don't understand why I cannot accept the closure that was made. For some reason, I feel that there is more, and something at any given time is going to pop up to show that the closure I said was done really didn't happen.

I won't even talk to my husband about any of this because I don't know how he is going to respond, so how can we be friends? Friends are real with each other, and at this point, I am not being real at all with KB.

We just got married, and here we are with me unemployed and pregnant. Still trying to pay off some of the bills we had before the wedding, and I have cut some of the income by getting fired. We said we would be a team and here I am, not helping but making things worse for him. He married me, took my son and me in, and now he has to take care of us all on his own along with adding another child to the picture without any help from me. We are behind on bills. I have to catch up paying for my car through Mr. MarcTrain, and I have no money or income from anywhere.

My body seems to be rejecting this baby. Everyone knows that I am pregnant now, and they see this huge baby bump, but what if I don't make it through this? Everyone will know I cannot carry children. My husband will have to settle for Zion being his only child and never carrying on his family's last name. I want this baby, but I don't want to go through all of this, especially if the chance is still there that this baby won't live. I don't want anyone to know I may not give birth to this child because I will feel like less of a woman.

My heart is torn, my body is tired, and my mind is all over the place. So how could I possibly be a good mother to his child? I will not eat or drink, constantly in the hospital, and this baby seems like it will not have a chance with the way I am behaving. I want to eat. I want to feel better, but I cannot. I am failing. I am failing at everything. Happiness was handed to me on a platter, and I am letting it all slip through my fingers. If my husband knew what was going through my mind, I do not believe he would want to be with me. So I will keep everything to myself. I will fight through this in my mind. I will battle against any urges and struggle until the fat lady sings and exposes my secrets.

# CHAPTER 7

# The Policy

*Know this:* An open window or an open door is just as much an opportunity and a way for you to lose everything as it is an opportunity for you to gain.

Months after losing my job, I was still waiting for the unemployment hearing to take place and finally face this evil woman, "Momma," for denying my benefits. My belly had grown so big it looked like I was further along than I really was. Because of this, it was difficult to try and get another job. It is against the law to discriminate against a pregnant woman, but at the same time, no place of employment is willing to hire someone that will not be able to do the job they hired her for. This pregnancy was taking a beating on my body and leaving me with very little energy, yet I needed an income. I was between a rock and a hard place and determined to receive the benefits I rightfully deserved until I could come up with another plan for employment.

Every day, being idle and not having anything to do, I would seem to get more and more depressed. KB and Zion would be gone, and I would be home all by myself. Afraid of the cat, I would stay in my room unless I had to go to the bathroom. I didn't want to eat because every smell made me sick. It was so hot, so I wanted to stay in bed with the air conditioner blowing on me and my big belly to cool me off. Going from KB's side of the bed to mine, I would cry and sleep, sleep and cry.

Every now and then, I would pick up the Bible and read a few scriptures and would cry some more, which would lead to me feeling so sick, and to the bathroom, I would run. I kept trying to find scriptures in the Bible that would encourage me and make me feel better about my condition, but after throwing up nothing, I would just quickly fall asleep.

This was my routine, and I hated when I would come to the realization or be reminded that I had months of this to go. I chose to sleep as many months away as I could. After reading the Word of God and falling asleep, I began to dream. Dream after dream, I was so happy and wanted to stay in dream world forever. Everything always felt good and right in my dreams. In my dreams, all the problems went away, and there was nothing but great things taking place. In my dreams, there wasn't a worry or a care in the world, and all things began to line up. Yes, in my dreams.

Being awaken from my dream, I saw KB's face stressfully looking at me. He had been calling my name, but I was so engulfed in my sleep I didn't hear him. I was so disoriented it took me a minute to understand the words that were coming out of his mouth. All of a sudden, I became very warm. I felt sweat all over my chest and my forehead. KB was talking to me, but I couldn't hear him and was trying to read his lips. With his eyes as wide as they could be looking at me in my face, he said, "Baby, what are you doing?" I didn't know how to answer him or what to say, still not understanding what was going on. Then he said to me that the gas and electric company had come to the house for a payment and because I was sleeping so hard and didn't answer the door...they turned the power off.

It was then I realized the air conditioner was no longer on, and that explained why I was so hot. I never heard anyone knocking on the door. I didn't know the bill was due. Looking at KB's face, I saw one tear coming from his eye, rolling down his cheek. In that moment, I felt more useless than ever before. KB was a real man, and the last thing he was going to do was have his new family in conditions unacceptable to live in. He put his head into the blankets on the bed, and I reached down and touched his head, saying all that I knew to say at the moment, "Everything will be okay." I didn't know how, but that's all I had.

Newlyweds, new family, new living arrangements, new life, new beginnings, seeming as if the world was against us getting married, and then this happens. Because it was late in the day when he had come home, the lights would have to remain off until morning. No man wants to have the story that right after he was married, with a new family, his electricity shut off. It could leave the impression he was not ready to take care of a family, and he had moved on too fast, as many were saying. It could leave the impression that he did not know how to manage a family and bills. Or it could leave the impression that he had bit off more than he could chew. I saw it all in his face. I saw the despair. I saw the disappointment.

The car note was due, the electric bill due, phone bill too, and here I am pregnant at home contributing absolutely nothing. My heart hurt. I was scared KB was going to start second-guessing if I was the right one for him like the devil started putting in my head. I kept seeing all the faces of those that pretended to be happy for us, but we had already got word they weren't, so we went along with the façade. We let them believe that we fell for their evil antics. Those that were saying this speedy marriage is a mistake. Those that put up bets predicting that we wouldn't last a year. This was the perfect situation for them. The great laugh of the decade.

I could hear some ladies saying, "As good as Mr. MarcTrain was to you, you're a fool for leaving him talking about going with God's plan." I could hear other ladies saying if KB had married them, he wouldn't be in this mess right now. Voices from everywhere. Voices putting me down. Voices making me doubt. Voices taunting me to give up. I wasn't trying to hear these voices, but I had no idea what to do. So I put my game face on.

Evidently, KB didn't know what to do either, and before I could put my game face on, he lifted his head off the bed. Like the true man he is, he stood with strength and confidence. He took over the situation instead of allowing the situation to overtake him. He let me know we were going to be all right for sure, and without a doubt, we just had to trust God.

He said it with no fear. He said it with great sureness. We went to his parent's house without saying what was wrong and enjoyed the night with them as if everything was okay at home. The next day, the lights were back on, and we pretended like nothing ever happened. One thing I learned was that in this marriage, no matter what was going on, we had to have each other's back. We both needed to know that when it was one's turn to be down, the other had to be up. We had to keep a balance between one another and never doubt each other. Most importantly, we had to trust God, as KB said.

God had filled me with His Spirit. I wanted to tap into each and every benefit of it. First up was using the spirit of God to combat those negative spirits that were bringing bad thoughts into my head about this marriage. Thoughts that made me think that some of the nay-sayers may be right—this marriage won't last long. I needed something, someone to help me fight off the voices of negativity that tried to bring on doubt. I knew for a fact the way God placed my covering in my life validated his presence, but at times I still felt lost. I couldn't see what God was doing, so I needed Him to give me clear vision.

*Know this:* The scripture 2 Corinthians 5:7 says, "For we walk by faith, not by sight." It means just what it says.

Going into the state-building ready to fight for my unemployment benefits, KB said it again, "Trust God." While we awaited our turn to be called in the hallway, we saw "Momma" walk in. She had on African garb with gray dreadlocks in her head. A heavy-set woman, as she walked, her shoes bent to the outside. She walked with confidence, but we walked with God. She walked back and forth to intimidate, but for some reason, we were not moved or worried at all. We actually began to laugh at her, knowing that she was not a threat and she was getting ready to see who we belonged to.

She tried to speak with the arbitrator before the conference, and he rejected her. She tried to make it seem as if this was a waste of time, and she was ignored. She tried to make the people there think she had more power than she had, but they already knew and put her right in her place.

We walked into the conference room, and she sat at the head of the table as if she was the one orchestrating the meeting. The arbitrator sat across from KB and I. KB sat between me and the infamous "Momma" and made sure she knew that I couldn't be touched in any way, shape, or form. As we begin to tell our side of how things went down, "Momma" kept interrupting and saying it was a lie.

No matter what I said, she was denying everything. I was having terrible morning sickness and was not up for this, but all I could think about was KB saying, "Trust God." This woman thought it was going to be easy to come in and just deny my benefits by being misleading and aggressive, but she was wrong.

As she began telling her side of things, the arbitrator began to interrupt her, calling her out on every statement that wasn't adding up. She couldn't get her lies out correctly, and he was checking her on each one of them. He was able to see clearly that I had done nothing wrong, I was wrongfully terminated, and that my reason for separation of employment was valid for me to receive benefits. He ruled that I was entitled from the day she fired me. KB and I were overjoyed and so thankful. She left angry and bitter. As she walked away, I could see that God was not done dealing with her for how she treated me.

The arbitrator explained to me that I would receive all the benefits that I had called in for. Unfortunately, when I was denied, I stopped calling in to receive benefits, so I would only get the weeks of unemployment pay I called in for and any future ones I am entitled to. I didn't care about anything at that time, just happy God had proven Himself to us once again.

KB looked relieved, and God knows I was too. I would be receiving an income until I found another job, and that was nothing but a blessing. The only problem was that my medical insurance was still with my old job. God allowed for my medical benefits to continue, and there was nothing that crazy lady could do about it. I knew, at some point, they were going to get cut off, but I decided I would cross that bridge when I got to it. Rhonda had said that she had a job for me, but I hadn't heard from her, so I decided to just wait it out and see what opportunity would come my way after I had the baby.

God wasn't done teaching "Momma" a lesson, but He wasn't done with us either. I kept losing more and more weight and not eating or drinking, which would only lead to hospital visits. My doctor gave me every pep talk she could, and all I could do was tell her I was trying. I couldn't even take the prenatal pills. Nothing seemed to work, and all I could do was cry. I had never in my entire life cried so much and so hard. This seemed to be the worse pregnancy ever. I needed a relief. I needed something to make me happy, something to make me smile.

Accepting the fact that I was going to be home, I had to understand I had to do things differently if I was going to make it through this. I ventured out of my bedroom and began walking around the house doing little things here and there. I realized that the only way KB was going to rest easy was if he knew that I was going to be all right. I needed to see sunlight. I needed to stretch my legs. I needed to walk up and down the stairs as exercise. I needed to get out of the funk I was in and move on with the happy life God was trying to give me.

I went downstairs and walked around, straightening up the living room and dining room, picking up things behind Zion and KB. KB had so much mail coming to the house he would just put it all on the chest in the dining room. You could tell it was mail piled up for months. A lot of it was bills and mail addressed to his late wife. I knew it was hard for him to have to go through it and read it, so I took on the task to do it for him. KB wanted to throw away any old mail, so I would look at the date on the envelopes to see when it came through the post office and decided to throw it away or not.

I kept seeing different envelopes with a big deer on them with huge antlers in almost every pile of mail I would go through. After the third or fourth piece of mail, I decided to open it and read what it was about. As I began opening the envelope, I noticed that the deer I kept seeing was the logo for an insurance company, the Hartford Insurance Company. I knew KB said he didn't have any insurance, so I thought maybe they were trying to sell him some.

KB and I had many conversations about his late wife passing with him not having any life insurance in place. People from all over the country, family, and friends sent him sympathy cards with money to help with the funeral expenses. He still had a balance that had to be paid, but because of the kindness of so many, it was a lot less than what it could have been. He kept telling me how important it was for us to have those things in order to learn from that experience.

Many young people do the same thing. Thinking we have so much time ahead of us, so much life to live. We live every day not concerned about when we die. Naturally and spiritually, we skim over the subject ignoring the fact that one day we will die. Are we ready? Many families aren't prepared to bury their loved ones. We use every excuse in the book as to why we don't get life insurance. What we really do is set our families up for failure and unnecessary expenses. Young and healthy no longer mean you have years to go. Watching so many die so young has really made me become more aware of the importance of being prepared.

As I read the letter, I was in disbelieve of what I was reading. In my understanding, the letter was giving a deadline for a response to keep the life insurance policy for KB's late wife. Looking at the date of the letter, he only had a short period to keep the policy active. The letter had been mailed so long ago, and my first thought was it was probably too late for him to inquire. I started not to say anything to him, but I thought about it. Out of all the mail that was coming in that house piling up, God allowed me to notice the particular envelope that had a deer with huge antlers as the logo on it.

When KB came home, he was shocked I was out of my room and doing something different in the house. I was happy to see him smile. I handed him the letter and told him that he needed to look into that. I explained that as I was cleaning up the mail, I read the letter that said Dion had life insurance, and he only had a small window left to reply, keeping the policy active.

He again said to me he did not have any insurance, and he did not think it was anything. He began saying we needed to look into the company for us because he would not want me to go through what he went through if he were to die. I told him to read the letter, and then we could decide if it was something to it or not.

As he read it, he was still unsure. I did not want to seem pushy, but I told him it would not hurt to call them and inquire about it, and he agreed that he would. We could not help but sit there and imagine how this story would be told if there really was a policy. KB laughed, saying he was going to tell everyone how his new wife was going through the mail and found a life insurance policy for his deceased wife. Of all people to find such a thing, it would be me.

We chuckled as we imagined what people would say if they ever found out it was because of me. Obviously, in some people's minds, they were going to think that it was all a part of our "master plan" anyway. Becoming so big with the pregnancy so fast and church folk spreading rumors that I was already pregnant before we got married, it could not have been more humorous—if it wasn't rumors coming directly from the church house.

You expect the world to act evil, do evil, and speak evil but not the church. All the hugs I would receive, not for love, but to be able to confirm if I was pregnant or not. All the stares and side-eyes, along with the whispers stating that KB and I had planned all of this and had been together long before Dion's passing.

So here lay the plot. KB and I had a steamy sexual relationship while his wife lay in the hospital sick. We kept our love affair a secret, and no one knew that I was fulfilling all his needs that his wife could not in her condition. In the meantime, I came up pregnant, and we, by osmosis, knew that she was getting ready to die and got a life insurance policy. The policy would be for hundreds of thousands of dollars that KB and I would live off for the rest of our lives. All this while we were singing, preaching, praying, and dancing for the Lord every Sunday. What a scandal. It makes good for lifetime television.

At this point, I could care less. People were going to think what they were going to think regardless of what was true or not. Truth could be slapping some folks in the face, and they would still rather believe the lie. I knew the truth. I lived the truth. Truth was, KB had bills that needed to be paid, I was unemployed, and we had a baby on the way. It didn't matter to either one of us where the money was going to come from; we just knew that if there was money, no matter how much it was, we needed it. KB's parents were away, and we called them and told them about it. They were excited to know the outcome and laughed about how we found the mail too. The next day I made sure he gave them a call.

I stood in front of him as he talked on the phone. KB is a pacer. When he talks on the phone, he likes to walk back and forth. So there I was, belly and all, walking back and forth with him until I could not do it anymore. I sat and listened as he explained who he was and what his inquiry was. They asked for an account number from the letter, and KB gave them all the information they requested. All left for us to do was to wait and see. It would not change things if nothing came from this. I was not going to pack my bags and leave if there was no policy. We were not relying on there being one, but oh, what a great benefit it would be.

The insurance company got back with KB and explained to him that it looked like Dion really did have a life insurance policy after all through her last place of employment. She was working at a radio station when she became ill with lupus and went out on medical leave. Because she was never fired, and technically, she never quit, her life insurance stayed in place.

We were shocked, and at the same time, not surprised. We knew from the beginning, because of the way God put the two of us together, we needed to be prepared for the unthinkable to happen in our lives as God saw fit to show Himself in any way He pleases. This was just the beginning. No longer would my life be simple and ordinary, but with faith, God gave us vision to see clearly that our lives would be extraordinary with Him.

Anticipating the amount of money that the insurance policy was for, I was so happy for my husband. He said what he always said, "Trust God," and I learned really quickly to do just that. I knew there were bills that he needed to take care of, and without me working, whatever the policy amount is for, it would be a blessing to the house. We were shocked to find out the amount of money on the policy. Knowing that within a matter of days, the policy could have been canceled due to no response to the letters being sent, we knew this was nothing but a gift from God to encourage us.

KB's parents had come from out of town, and we were all in the car together making a night deposit from the eatery up at Mondawmin Mall's Bank of America. His mother and father asked how much the policy was for. KB got out and started running around the car. His father followed after and ran around the car with him, not even knowing how much it was.

We laughed and enjoyed the moment because it seemed so unreal. Here we were not too long ago with our lights shut off for a day, wife suddenly unemployed, and a baby on the way with not enough income to provide. God showed us He will provide. He made sure we knew it was Him by having the amount of the insurance policy be the same amount of money I would have made for a year if I hadn't been terminated. Who could do that? Nobody but God.

It took some time for the check to come, but when it did, we were overjoyed and thankful to be able to catch up on our bills and pay things off. I wished we could pay my car off so that I didn't have to keep facing Mr. MarcTrain each month. As long as there was communication there, the feelings didn't seem to go away.

My husband would tell me he loved me, and I would tell him I loved him back, but I knew I still had a love for Mr. MarcTrain too. How could I not? He didn't leave me; I left him to marry someone I had absolutely no feelings for. No matter what or how long it takes, these feelings will leave, and I will be at peace, but until then, I will keep my life busy, falling in love with the one God purposed for me.

I had to hang on to faith and believe that I had made the right decision. I had to keep the faith to see where God was taking us. The more faith, the clearer the vision. God had filled me with His Spirit, and I had to take advantage of that and not depend on myself. God allowed these things to take place so quickly in our marriage to show He was with us and all I had to do was stay focused. Staying focused on faith gave me clear vision. But if for a moment my eyes were somehow distracted, not only would my vision become blurry, but the defined line of marriage would too.

# CHAPTER 8

# One Head of Household

Zion had been excited about being a big brother but also anxious to see his big brother and family already established in Rochester. KB and my new in-laws didn't feel that it was wise to allow Zion to visit that family, but I saw things differently. All that Michael had done to me and taken me through, Zion was not aware of anything. All he knew was that he was to love his father, and that was all he would know from me.

As I have said before, I do not agree with telling children negative things about their parent. If the parent is truly a bad person, it has a way of coming out without you having to say a word. I feel it is important to never stop Zion from seeing his father.

KB and I had had discussions about changing Zion's last name, and I really didn't think I was convinced that was the right thing to do either. Zion had an identity, and we would be grooming him as his parents, but his last name should remain. Everyone got on me about this, especially because Michael refused to sign the birth certificate and acted as if he wasn't sure Zion was his. He embarrassed me and humiliated me at the hospital when Zion was born, acting as if there was a legitimate reason to question if this child belonged to him. Why would I give him the privilege of even having a connection after doing that? He didn't deserve to have this beautiful child carry his last name. He didn't deserve to be able to lay claim to a child he refused to take responsibility for.

Nonetheless, I thought about Zion. I thought about the questions he would have when he got older. I thought about the feeling of neglect or rejection he would feel not having something of Michael's. He didn't have any of Michael's time, love, affection, or resources. So the least I could do was give him his father's last name and allow him to keep it. Zion wanted his last name to be Hunt too. He loved KB and was happy he was going to have two fathers, one in Rochester and one in the home in Baltimore.

Zion may have been happy, but Michael certainly was not. While Zion was up in Rochester, Michael called to let me know he wanted to take Zion to Disney with the rest of his family. He wasn't asking; he was telling me. He wasn't trying to get my input; he was saying it matter-factly in a demanding way. I replied to him that I would talk to KB and get back to him about it. He told me that my husband had nothing to do with his son and he could do what he wanted and take him wherever he wanted.

Me being pregnant at the time, I didn't want to argue. In my mind, I wanted to know how he could find the money to supposedly take Zion to Disney but would never send money to help take care of Zion. I never sued for child support, never begged or asked for any money, so maybe he was saving it all up for the three years of Zion's life to take him to Disney. My mind was tired, and so was my body, so I decided this was one issue I would not give second thoughts about.

As Michael continued on to say that he was the only father Zion had and he would not allow another man to dictate to him what he could and could not do with his son, I just listened. For years there was no other man for Zion to call dad or stepdad, and he did nothing, so now that there was someone being a dad, he had a chip on his shoulder. I didn't know how to explain to Michael that KB was not trying to take his place or be a dictator. I didn't know how to tell him that he should appreciate KB and accept his role for what it is. I didn't know how to tell him anything because he was so angry, manipulative, and tried to intimidate. But now that I was married, and especially with me carrying this child, and I was already in a risky position, I chose to say nothing and remove myself from starting an argument.

After letting KB know what Michael's intentions were and what was said, KB felt Michael needed to better understand the dynamics of the environment. He feels that Michael may have misunderstood that being Zion's dad didn't give him authority or a say in the Hunt household. I could see that this was turning into a manhood thing quicker than I could react and before I knew it, here we were with the both of them on the phone, drawing their lines in the sand. Michael, trying to defend his position as a father, and KB, defining his position as the husband, head of the house, covering, father, leader, king, decision-maker, provider, and anything else in between.

KB wanted to make it clear that because he was the one taking care of this family, he was the one who made the final decisions. I was not sure I wanted Zion going to Florida with Michael alone, and neither was KB, but while he had my child with him in Rochester and we were in Baltimore, I felt we needed to table the conversation until my child was back home with me.

KB, feeling bothered and upset about the entire conversation, let Michael know that he wouldn't let Zion go if he didn't want to; we needed to think about it, and whatever decision he made, he would get back to him. KB ended the conversation telling Michael where and when to have Zion back in Baltimore, and that was that! Michael was angry, but there was nothing left to say. There was nothing left to do. The phone was hung up, and KB made it very clear to Michael that he would never rule or make any decisions for this household. Michael had lost this battle.

My mouth wide open, almost falling to the floor, I could do nothing but hold my belly and look at KB, asking him what he just did. He was so upset he would barely respond. I became upset, and we began to argue. Weak and totally caught off guard, I began yelling at KB, telling him he was wrong to end the conversation that way. I told him that man had my son in his possession right now, and if he decided to do something foolish such as not bring him back or run away with him, I was going to be more than a little angry. I could not understand why KB would make matters worse while Zion was still in Rochester.

It was not like Rochester was ten minutes away from Baltimore, and we could drive by real quick and pick my son up. It was not like Michael was already looking for a reason and a way to hurt me and make my life miserable, and we had now created an opportunity for him to do just that. KB didn't seem to care about my concerns, which made me even angrier. You couldn't just be the man of this house and not consider how I was feeling and how this situation was impacting me.

*Know this:* Blended families are a huge part of today's society. Many children are living in homes where one of the adults is not the biological parent. Communicating effectively without pride or arrogance is the beginning of having a successful parenting experience. Otherwise, be prepared for the storm.

I was so upset with KB. Concerned that Michael would try to get back at us by keeping Zion, there was not much talking after that. I began thinking about which family members and friends to reach out to for them to make a special ops recovery plan to get my son by any means necessary if things went south. All I knew was that my husband was going to see a horrible side of me if something happened to my child because of his decision to argue with Michael. I had experience dealing with Michael and knew how he played and manipulated and tried to get under your skin. KB, on the other hand, only had a few interactions with him, and they both wanted to determine who had the upper hand. Michael found out KB did. KB found out I do not play when it comes to my child.

I could hardly sleep through the night concerned about Zion. He was supposed to be brought back to the eatery while KB was working. I was home and wanted to be alert and near my phone so that I would not miss any calls. KB explained to me that a man had to make it clear to any outsiders that his home was not up for negotiation. He said to me that he could not and would not ever allow another man to dictate how his home operated. He wanted to make it clear that this home was off-limits for Michael in every way, and his intimidating tone had no effect and would not work here.

I understood what KB was saying, and I agreed. I just felt that it didn't need to take place while that man had my son in his possession. Anything could happen, but I had to trust God and believe that all of this would work out for my good and not for evil. Michael had the opportunity to be my husband, run the family, and be the head. He lost that opportunity years ago, and there was no reason for him to think he had a chance now. He made the situation the way it was, so now he just needed to accept the fact that the dynamics of my life and his son's life were no longer in his control.

Michael was supposed to call when they got to Baltimore so that we could meet at the eatery as planned. KB was preparing to go to the eatery, and I wanted to go along with him. Morning sickness and all-day nausea caused me to move slow and not as fast as he would like me to. My mind was stressed even after praying about this situation. I just wanted peace and did not want there to be a stupid argument between the fathers. I wanted my baby back with me. I wanted everyone to get along but understood it was easier said than done.

The house was so quiet you could hear the neighbors next door. There wasn't much conversation between KB and me, but I had plenty of conversation with the Lord. With silence in the house, my phone rang. I knew it was Michael when I saw the number. I answered in haste, excited to hear from my son. Michael, with this tone in his voice, said to me that he was pulling up. We weren't at the eatery; we were still at home. As I was getting ready to tell him this, he said to me he was outside. When KB and I both heard him say he was outside, I jumped.

The meeting arrangement was the eatery, not our home. KB did not want him coming to our home simply because, as he had made it very clear, the home and what goes on there were off-limits to Michael. Michael knew this, and showing up to our home unannounced and unexpected was his way of pushing back at KB. He told me to come open the door. Every step I took walking towards the door, I felt KB behind me. It felt like he was getting ready to push me out of the way to get to the door before me. All I could do was call on Jesus under my breath. I looked at KB and said one word, "Please."

I felt like I was getting ready to go into labor. It felt like my water was breaking. I knew it wasn't and that I just needed to go to the bathroom. I still had on my house robe with my belly big as ever, and I opened the door. I kept myself in the doorway as let the door open halfway. He had Zion in his arms, and Zion, of course, was sad to say goodbye. As I opened the screen door to get Zion into the house, I felt KB breathing behind me. I saw Michael looking past me at KB. I stayed right between the two of them with my belly and the door.

I had never seen KB like this, and I wasn't sure what was getting ready to happen next. I quickly took Zion's things from Michael and shut the door. The anger that was on KB's face broke my heart. Michael wanted to let KB know he knew how to make a statement too. The anguish that KB began to go through made me feel terrible. He was the protector of this home. He was the provider of this home. He was the king of this home, and it felt like the home was violated, and he wanted to do something about it.

The house remained in silence. Zion was sad; I was sick, and KB was mad. I sat there, unpacking Zion's things, asking him how his vacation was, and he quietly gave me short answers. So quickly, the devil had come into this house to disturb the peace, and it felt like there was nothing that I was able to do about it. All I could do was pray. I felt like, once again, here was the proof everyone needed that I was most certainly not the woman KB should have married. If he never married me, he would not be going through this "baby daddy" drama right now. He was an upright man, a God-fearing man, not a street man, not a hood man.

I didn't want to talk to KB about it because I didn't want to hear him say this was my fault. I already felt this way, but to hear those words come out of his mouth would tear me to pieces. I didn't understand why things had to fall out the way they did, but right then, Michael let me know that he did not intend to play fair. It seemed as if he wanted to show us that he was no punk and that he could pop up at any time and do whatever he wanted, and nothing was going to stop him—as if he had the upper hand. What he really showed us was that he acknowledged there was another man doing the job of a father that he should have been doing, and instead of correcting that and being a father, he chose to be a simpleton.

Michael showed us that he didn't have any intentions of raising Zion with us as a team in support of one another. He showed us that if it was not going to be his way, then it wasn't going to be a smooth way. He showed us he was a coward. He showed us he was not ready for this new way of parenting. He showed us that he was hurting and wanted us to take the blame for the hurt he was feeling and attempt to punish us—well, me.

Who would have ever thought that this controlling male-factor in her life would no longer intimidate this Oreo cookie?

The imaginary ropes of domination no longer had the effect or power that he was used to. But now, there had been casualties and others added to the equation that changed the dynamics. KB did not sign up for this. He did not deserve to be disrespected or insulted in any way. He chose to step up and be a man and father to a child that had none of his blood flowing through him. He did not have the pleasure of leaving the seed inside of me to make this child, yet he agreed to nourish, cultivate, and train the child.

As a man of God, KB had to take low, but that didn't stop him from being a man. That didn't stop him from expressing himself. It certainly didn't stop him from loving us. He took the bullet of humiliation for us. He took the sting of impudence from a coward for us. He took on the challenge to remain not only a man but a man of God through it all.

On this day, without a doubt, I saw that KB was down for me. He meant those vows when he said them at the altar on our wedding day. He showed me that nothing would prevent him from assuring this marriage be a success. He showed me God was with him and in him. He showed me I was covered and would remain that way with him no matter what.

Unbelievable ending to a day, yet we made it through. I had to stop second-guessing myself, wondering, *Am I really what God has for this man?* The problem was that it seemed like every day, I was presented with an obstacle that KB may not have had to deal with if he was not with me. So I wondered if this really was what it was supposed to be.

Thinking about Mr. MarcTrain, I wondered how he would have handled this same situation. When he and Michael met, there was no beef. Maybe it was Mr. MarcTrain's size and height that Michael wasn't trying to go up against, knowing from the first glance he would have been slaughtered. Mr. MarcTrain was already experienced with new-age parenting and parents in different homes. He had children that he did not have full custody of, so he knew what Michael was going through and possibly better understood. KB had never been in a situation like this, and neither had I.

It seemed as if every time something went on in my life, the bottom line tried to be that it would have been better if I had chosen Mr. MarcTrain. I didn't believe this myself, but the devil really was putting on a strong case to make me think about it. Funny thing is I didn't feel like I had a choice in the matter anyway. God placed me with KB, so obviously, this was bigger than me. Mr. MarcTrain didn't fight for me, so it was even more obvious that we weren't meant to be, right?

I just felt guilty, ashamed, and embarrassed that KB was going through this all because of me. I would not feel this way if it was Mr. MarcTrain dealing with this. I had to deal with his baby momma, who turned out to be his wife, so he would owe me to deal with this without making me feel bad. I had to accept his baggage, so he, of course, would have had to accept mine. KB didn't have this kind of baggage. He did not have children, so he did not have a baby momma. This life was not for him, and he did not deserve this. He was a good man, and he had lowered his standards taking me as a wife.

# CHAPTER 9

# Rumors

For some reason, KB and I were a target for rumors. I was so tired of them and not sure I fully understood why it continued to be rumors that lingered around us. A rumor is something talked about and widely disseminated with no discernible source. It is an opinion or story that most times are untrue. KB and I, before we got married, had to deal with rumors and lies and still had to deal now.

In my new home, with my new family, living my new life, I got a phone call from my close male friend. He was part of my wedding celebration and was excited for KB and me. But his phone call had disturbed me. His phone call made me question who he now was and who he wanted to be in my life. As I answered the phone, excited to hear from my friend, I heard him cynically asking me how married life was. I replied to him that married life was good. I told him I was having a baby, I was no longer working my old job, and how God had blessed KB and me in the midst of life situations happening. I told him how I was learning how to be a wife and appreciate what God had given to me. I told him how God had filled me with His Spirit, and I was super happy—even though things weren't perfect, things were truly good.

He then asked me to tell him the truth. I was wondering what truth I was not telling. What was I keeping from him that he already knew? He told me that he was getting the news and he had heard all about what had been going on with me and it was no need for me to try to keep it from him. I had no clue what he was talking about and sat wishing he would just tell me about me since he knew more about me than I knew about my own life! He asked again if I was all right. I told him, "Yes!"

My heart dropped to the floor as the next words flew out of his mouth. Sometimes when people are talking to you and what they are saying is so unexpected, you feel like you are going through what I called before the *Twilight Zone*. All I needed was for my vision to go to black and white and see stars, and that would have definitely been a *Twilight Zone* episode. Knowing that this man cared for me, and we were family like brother and sister, I listened. I didn't interrupt nor ask any questions. I let him tell me everything he heard and found to be true. He sounded so sincere as he shared how he got wind that I was being beat. That KB had been hitting and beating on me since the wedding day. He told me he got reports of me seen with a black eye. He was upset that I was staying quiet about it all and not trying to get help.

Knowing the abusive relationships of my past, this was a concern for him because now I was married. This was not just another bad boyfriend I could walk away from, but a husband who everyone knew came from a family deeply rooted in the church. Obviously, it was going to be hard for me to admit and let anyone know that the man praised as being a good man was a wife beater. Clearly, it was going to be difficult for me to let anyone know that I had once again become entangled with a man who was mistreating me. I was too ashamed to let anyone know that, in this man's grief of his late wife, he had been beating on me. I had been taking it not telling a soul because I didn't want to admit that everyone was right when they said we were moving too fast and should not get married until after he had grieved.

So I had married an abusive husband. Really? After all that I'd been delivered from, rescued out of, and fought to get rid of, I married a man that was abusing me. Sir. You have received bad information. You've been told wrong. You've been bamboozled. You didn't land on Plymouth Rock; Plymouth Rock landed on you! At no time did Kenneth Tyrone Hunt, affectionately known and called KB by me, had ever abusively put his hands on me. He had put his hands all over this body and made this body feel things it had never felt before in ways I never thought it could, but at no time was I abused. Why and where these rumors came from is my question.

If people only knew how much this man adored my body. How he would take his time loving on this body. How he makes me feel like he had never had another woman a day in his life. How he gave me all of him. From the honeymoon, when we made our first symphonic medley to this day, every contact that we had, had been nothing but pleasure for the both of us. So why would anyone waste time saying something different? Why would anyone want to paint a horrible picture of KB like that? All I could say was it was far from the truth. I was not in an abusive relationship. The way KB treated me every day showed me that the mess I accepted in my past was not for me, and I deserved better.

No, I didn't need anyone to come and check my husband for improperly putting his hands on me. No, I didn't need counseling because I was being abused. No, I didn't need a restraining order or an order of protection. No, I was not afraid or feared for my life. It was sad that someone would start rumors like this. It was totally uncalled for, but what could we do about it? They would have been better saying I was abusive, but why KB? We decided we were not going to entertain it or look further into it to find out where the rumor began. KB and I agreed we would just outlive the lie as we had all the others.

From one rumor to the next, we could not understand why we were the hottest topic. As I got bigger and bigger with this pregnancy, the rumors again came out that I was further along than I really was. This time the rumor was allegedly birthed from a group of older women in the church we call "the mothers." From whatever church and whatever ministry, the word on the street became that I would be having this baby soon, and I hadn't gotten to six months yet.

To make matters worse, the call from Mr. MarcTrain wanting to know if any of these rumors were true made me want to scream at the top of my lungs. With all that I was going through. The emotions I was going in and out of. Dealing with Michael and his behavior. Not having steady income. Living in a house that my husband was just making a future in with another woman. Being pregnant, afraid that any day I woke up would be the day I miscarried, and this baby would never make it out alive. I was at my wit's end. Mr. MarcTrain, with concern, called and wanted to know what was going on with me. He wanted to know if I was okay. He wanted to know if there was anything I needed to tell him. He wanted to know if I was happy.

Why would he ask me such things? Why would he privately show me that he still cared about me? Where was this before the wedding? Where was this when I told him what God told KB? I was married and pregnant, and now he felt that this life I was living should be with him. Well, I thought so too, but what happened? Why didn't it go that way? Why still talk to me like he cared so much about me? How would I tell KB about this so that he didn't hear it any other way? We had enough on our hands dealing with rumors that were so far from being true. Something like this only made matters worse.

I began to ask myself, *Is he doing this to ruin my marriage? Is he saying these things to make me second-guess my choice to go with what God gave to KB for our lives?* I heard it in his voice that he still loved me. I felt it through the phone that he still cared. I had so many questions and so many emotions I was going through that this just didn't seem fair.

"Wow" was all I could say. I had men in my life that wanted to be my knight in shining armor, but evidently, God allowed me to marry the only knight that mattered. My brother friend and Mr. MarcTrain both seemed sincere in their concern, but I knew there was nothing for them to be worried about in the area they thought.

*Know this:* Rumors, true or false, as they go from person to person, the words change, and the likelihood of them being completely true becomes less and less. So why keep repeating them?

Finally, coming into this new job at a new center, I could work from home for a while, which was a blessing. The crazy lady I worked for who fired me forgot to end my medical benefits, and what a blessing that was. I didn't have to worry about how my baby would be delivered and who would pay for it because everything was still covered. Evidently, the board made sure my insurances stayed intact because they knew what was done to me was wrong. Working from home trying to update documents for the center was a full-time job for me, and I was so thankful I could do it from home right now.

It was Zion's first year at a new school, and I was nervous. I wanted him to be happy, but this would be our first time not being with each other all day. It was fine when I worked for Isaac, and Zion was in a classroom right down the hall from my office. But now, I was not a part of his school. I couldn't just walk into the school and sit in his class without having to go to the office, get a pass, and sign in. The school was literally in our backyard, but it still didn't feel close enough. I loved my son so much, and I was having withdrawal symptoms and didn't want him to be alone. I needed my son to always know that I was with him, looking out for him and loving him as a mother should.

As summer turned to fall and fall turned to winter, my belly was ready to burst. The winters were so cold, and walking Zion to school had become more and more difficult. I kept going in and out of the hospital because of dehydration, and I was afraid if I was not careful, this baby's life would be in danger. Zion being the handful that he was, also wanted to be my protector. Holding on to my hand so tight as we walked to school together, he told me that he could do this on his own and I didn't have to walk him. I didn't know why he was so anxious to let me go. He quickly walked ahead of me and got to the school before I could cross the street most times. I loved the fact that he loved going to school. This was a new environment for him, and he had adapted well. With everything going on with Michael and Zion not having much communication with him, I was glad he had made new friends in school and was happy.

It wasn't until the teacher gave me and KB a call to inform us about Zion's side hustle that I fully understood why he didn't want or need my presence at the school like I used to be at the head start center. Zion's teacher told us that Zion had been selling pencils, erasers, and pencil sharpeners along with candy at the school, making himself some money. Zion told me that he wanted to make money to help Daddy take care of the new baby and me. We couldn't do anything but laugh. KB had been showing him the benefit of making your own money, and he took what he learned and what he had and made an honest hustle out of it. It was never a dull moment with Zion, and I was so glad he was excited about this baby.

With it being so chilly outside and icy, I had to take my time walking Zion to school. No matter how slow I walked and how careful I was, KB felt that I should not walk him anymore because he was afraid that I was going to fall. Because I was the mom that I was, I ignored him and walked Zion to school anyway, only to slip and fall just as KB said I would. Now I was feeling pain and discomfort and had to go back into the hospital. The Braxton Hicks contractions make it seem as if I was going into early labor. I was already at risk with this child, and now I had made matters worse. With all the rumors, people were just believing that it was time anyway.

My life was always under bright lights. Everything I did or say was being watched and scrutinized, and I was so tired of it. Why were there so many rumors about KB and me? The rumors didn't even make sense. Most people knew that these rumors weren't true, and others didn't believe them anyway. But there was a small group that continued to make the rumors grow and flourish. So these hospital stays weren't because I was having difficulties, but because the baby was really due.

KB got angry with me because he was tired of the in and out with the hospital. He was tired of the rumors. He was tired of wondering if this baby would be born alive or if all of this was for nothing. He was tired of struggling to make ends meet. He was tired, but we had just begun. I didn't know what to do to help him. I didn't know how to show more support to him. I wanted him to know and see that I appreciated him and I was thankful for everything that he did. But it seemed like I made more of a mess than I did cleaning things up.

I had fallen on ice, hospital ridden, and then back to bed rest again. My husband was upset because I was not by his side at any church functions, which led to more rumors and more tears. I wanted to be happy in this life, but rumors hurt, and the people who kept them going did not seem to care. Why was it so easy for people to spread rumors about each other? Why was it that before a gossiper spreads rumors, they did not think about how it would feel if the rumor spread was about them?

Almost everyone pays more attention to negative information than we do positive. When KB expressed that God told him I was his wife, that was positive and not so well received or cared about. When the rumors hovered over us that we had been having an affair long before Dion passed and I was pregnant before we got married, they were received and traveled much faster and more abrupt. More wanted to hear negative lies about us having an affair rather than trying to understand how God was using us and putting us together for something bigger than us. It seemed as if more people were fascinated by juicy lies than they were learning the truth.

All we could do was what God told us to do, outlive the lie, and the truth would be revealed. Interesting though, how rumors were horrible, evil, and hurtful, but they were considered harmless when they were not about you. Maybe if we all took into consideration how it felt, we would be less attracted to negative talk.

I knew how I could get on the phone with Bunch and talk for hours, going down a list of all the things I had seen, heard, and assumed about others. I realized some of the stuff we hear and assume may or may not be true, and some of the stuff we see, we don't see fully. It leaves us with opinions and theories about others that, most of the time, are far off and inaccurate. Yet, we are drawn to it. Why? I may not spread the rumor, but I will listen to it—why? People who listen to rumors and don't put them to an end are sometimes just as bad as the person(s) who are spreading the rumors.

Many times, people spread rumors about others that aren't true because it is something they are doing. For the attention to be taken off their wrongdoing, there will be a false accusation made just to cause a distraction. Spreading rumors about others helps people get away with the inappropriate things about their life they are trying to keep secret—but not for long. You can only cause diversions for a short period of time. You can only bring negative attention to someone else for a moment before the spotlight goes back to you. The rumors I heard about KB and me were so detailed but so false. How else could they come about unless it was something someone else was doing and chose to make the narrative be about KB and me instead of themselves? Some people do not realize the more you start rumors, the more people begin to look at you and recognize that you are really telling on yourself.

Others start rumors because they are jealous. They see wonderful things happening in your life, and it causes them to do an assessment of where they are in their life and become angry. Your life shows them just how much they have been lolly-gagging while you were making moves and getting settled and established. Just watching you bloom and do your thing the way God has blessed you to do it makes them upset. They seek out revenge by mischaracterizing you, destroying your reputation, and isolating you from others.

Remember people love to see you doing well until you start doing better than them. Well, as soon as it looks like you are doing better than someone else, they will come up with a rumor to bring you down. There is a need to feel superior. If you are getting all the attention, that means that they aren't getting any, and that makes some people miserable. The only thing left to do is smear your name to make people focus positively on them while looking down on you.

Some people are just outright bored. They live for drama and love to watch dramatic situations unfold before their eyes. With you being the main character of the rumor, their free entertainment has begun. Rumors come to make good things bad—and they intentionally come from bad people.

Then you have others that attempt to copy you. They see the shine in your life and try to replicate it or outdo you for no reason at all but because of jealousy. Mommy has been trying to tell me that a lot of the talk and the attitudes and behaviors are because people want what I have. I am trying to figure out exactly what that is. What about my life makes people feel that they want to tear me down to make themselves look good?

I have started noticing that although I didn't start rumors, I would listen, I would entertain, I would share, not realizing I was a part of someone else's awful plot to bring others down. Until you get tired of them, you will listen to rumors and wonder how true they are or believe them anyhow. You get to the point you are just glad the rumor isn't about you, so you don't care how it impacts others. But now that you have been sorely bruised by rumors, you want no parts in them at all. You don't want to hear them or be the topic of them, realizing rumors are full of hate.

The sad part is when you don't even realize how strong the hate is, and you are trying to be nice to people, not knowing that all along, they are the ones talking about you behind your back, spreading negative vibes about you, and portraying you as someone you are not. It hurts. You try to ignore it, but it hurts. You try to befriend to kill the animosity only to be talked about even more, and it hurts.

Rumor had it this baby was coming and coming quick. Only for the year to end with me still pregnant. That's the one thing about false rumors. When the truth finally comes around, there is no more disputing. Christmas and New Year's holidays had passed, and so had Valentine's day, and I was still pregnant. I was the first woman to be pregnant over eleven months. If I was sleeping with KB and got pregnant before Dion passed, I should have had this baby by now. To have been pregnant before KB and I got married would mean this baby should have been out of my belly.

I wondered what those rumor starters were saying now. What was their explanation of this baby's extremely late arrival? Why hadn't their lies and slander that they so adamantly declared as truth come to pass?

# CHAPTER 10

# The Perfect Family

This is my first time doing taxes as a married woman. It is different with someone else as the head of the household. But adding having property along with a dependent, our tax return has been a major help with the shortage of money. Sitting at home working, I can't help but try to make this middle room into a nursery for our soon-coming bundle. She is on the way; yes, it's a girl, and we need to be ready.

Living in a house that belonged to someone else before you is normal. Most people live in a house that has been occupied prior to them living there unless they have a house built from the ground up. But when you know who was living in your home before you, and the plans made for the house remain the same, just with you as the woman of the home, it feels kind of different. It was in this house KB and Dion were planning a future and a family, and now KB and I are living out that very plan in this same house.

I just don't want everything to look the same. I want it to feel like a baby room and look like a baby room. I am running out of time and need something done quickly. *800, 588, 23 hundred, EMPIRE* keeps ringing in my mind. Watching television, it seems as if every commercial is about this carpet in one day deal. I feel like the television is talking to me and telling me to call. I know KB needs every dime we have to keep the house bills in order, and we don't have a penny to spare, so getting carpet is out of the question.

So why I am on the phone setting an appointment for the company to come out and do measurements is beyond me right now. I make sure they come when KB is not home. They give me such a sweet deal if I do two rooms instead of one, so I decide to get carpet in Zion's room too. Just that quick, I am doing things behind my husband's back. This is not good. This is not right. I vowed not to keep any secrets. If it is this easy to keep something from him, this can turn into a bad habit. There is too much at stake here to hide things from him. I said I would tell him everything. I will—just not right now.

Thick blue carpet for Zion and a nice light sage look for the baby room. The baby walls were painted yellow with a beautiful white lace curtain for the big double window in the middle. And just like that, the baby room was about to be ready.

I ask KB to begin moving things for me in and out of the rooms to clear the rooms, and he can't understand what I am doing. I finally have to tell him that the carpet people are coming, and the rooms have to be emptied of all furniture so that they can lay the carpet. So fresh and new in this marriage, KB learned quickly when there is something I set my mind on, it will get done. Just that fast, I learned that my husband, while sweet and kind, is not a man that I can run over and do whatever I please without suffering the consequences. The head of the household is the head of the household in all things. Let's know our roles and conduct ourselves accordingly. Respect.

Preparing the baby room was my way of nesting. I am ready for this baby to come—even if she is late, according to all the rumors about my due date. I look back on the day we went to the hospital to learn if this baby was a boy or a girl. We had our hearts set on it being a boy, calling this baby KJ for Kenny Jr. The joy on my husband's face was priceless. After all he had gone through, I was so happy we had made it this far. He was getting ready to watch his first child being brought into this world. God is amazing. It was a girl, not a boy.

I wish my family was here. My mom, a sister, or someone. Being here all alone is getting to me, especially while I am pregnant. This baby is about to come, and I still feel unprepared for some reason. Bunch is here, but it seems like my new family likes to keep it clear that she is not family as they see it because we are not blood sisters. No matter where I am and what my last name has become, she will always be my ace, my sister, my best friend, my family. This is new for the both of us. With her getting married and having her family, and now I am married and having a baby, we are truly grown-ups. Life is supposed to be exciting, not dramatic. We can grow together, not apart.

It means something to have someone have your back no matter what you are going through. I have shared my entire life with Bunch, and I am so glad because there is no other best friend I could ever want to experience life with. She has been there through every rumor and hateful thing being spread about KB and me like it was hers personally. She is my sounding board. I can call her anytime and cry about how people are treating me, and just like a best friend, she is right there to agree with me and go in right along with me—a true big sister.

There is nothing like having a big sister that you can make proud. She shows me how proud she is of me every time I am the bigger person and allow God's spirit to lead me instead of me taking matters into my own hands. I know I really surprised her when I showed kindness to one of the main haters of my marriage. For someone to form their mouth to say how they want no part in my wedding as if they were boycotting it was hurtful and stupid. Only for that same hater months later to have to use the flowers from my wedding to assist with theirs. God has a way of bringing things back in your face.

Bunch knows how much I want to have family around me. She knows I need a support system in place. She knows that the people we have around us are suspect, so we want to only be around people we know are supportive without a doubt. That would mean family from home. I cannot say that no one in Bmore is in my corner. That wouldn't be true. But always trying to read through people's behaviors towards you to find out if they are sincere or not tends to become very played out.

In a normal family, the wife would become pregnant, and her parents would be overjoyed. Happy that their little girl has grown to be a woman and having children of her own. The mother would coddle her daughter and make sure she is doing everything she needs to do and show that she has been properly trained and raised for this moment. The husband would stand tall with his chest out because he has planted a seed, and it is being fruitful. His family is overjoyed because this means the family name will continue, especially if it is a boy.

All the family members get to brag about how the family is getting bigger with the new addition on the way. There is no competition; there is no jealously; there is no envy and strife. Where did this normal come from? And what happened that families aren't normal like this anymore?

It seems as if every time my husband's family would do something nice for me, spectators would have something to say. This is their first grandchild, and they have a right to be happy. Unfortunately, they have to hide some of their joy because anytime this baby or this marriage is mentioned, attitudes flare. It is easy to say, "Ignore it," but it is difficult when the chaos is only happening in the one place you thought you would be able to have peace—the church. Who knew being the pastor's daughter-in-law would have this type of drama?

Lucky for me, not only do I have to deal with a regular family, but as the pastor's daughter-in-law, I deal with church family as well. Not being an original daughter of this church, I am constantly reminded that my sister-in-law already has many sisters, although she was the only girl my mother-in-law gave birth to. I am also reminded that my husband has many sisters that mean something to him before his wife could ever mean anything.

Being members of the church and the pastor treating everyone like family, some seem to assume that me being the actual daughter-in-law and having a child has taken the attention away from them. Some feel that I have taken their spot as the one whom the family loves the most. I am subtly told how far relationships go back, so as others become pregnant, whatever my mother and father-in-law do for me, they expect the same treatment.

Me being me, I have no problem with family and extended family that goes far beyond blood. My mom has taken in and helped to raise many people that are not blood relatives, and we will fight if you say they are not my brothers or my sisters. So I get it, I respect it, I come from it.

However, what is not cool is treating me as if I came in third place in a competition, so I am a nobody that doesn't matter. It took me no time helping some to understand that I love the fact that my mother and father-in-law have acted as parents to so many. That speaks volumes on their part. But what these "children" need to understand about me is I have a mother and a father already.

Evidently, the plan was to secure a position in a family as a child and isolate me. What really happened was this behavior made me appreciate my mom even more. I am thankful my mother was a mother to me, and I had no need to look for motherly affection anywhere. My mom wasn't on drugs; my mom wasn't in the world; my mom never acted like she didn't have time to raise me and threw me off to the pastor's family to raise. My mom took me to church and never sent me. My mom never came up missing when I needed her. My mom taught me the way of holiness even when things got rough for her. So I don't need another mom. My mom is way more of a mom than any woman could ever attempt to be to me. I am fortunate, and I am blessed. I am thankful my mother-in-law gets an opportunity to be this kind of mom to so many.

No need to feel threatened by me. I'm not here to rain on anyone's shine. I'm just KB's wife, living this married life. I didn't ask for this; God sent me on this assignment. I didn't get married to finally have the family I never grew up with. As dysfunctional as some of the moments in my life were growing up, I can never take away from my mom and my dad that they raised me right.

*Know this:* The perfect family isn't perfect, as in nothing is wrong. The perfect family comes with perfecting love in the family and appreciating what is right while correcting what is not.

Being raised in the church, you were taught that a baby out of wedlock is wrong. Having children before you are married shows that you have been fornicating, and God is not pleased with that behavior. There is nothing to celebrate, so there is no baby shower that the church folk is going to attend. With Zion, I didn't understand why my mom wouldn't celebrate a new grandson coming into the family. I wanted her to be happy about it, but she needed me to understand where she was coming from. She was thankful for me, thankful for my life and the life of a child God was allowing me to give birth to. However, she, as a representative of Christ, could not and would not condone sin.

She was happy for me but sad for the way I went about things, knowing I could have done things the right way. It is one thing if you are not being taught right from wrong, but when you know better, you are expected to do better. When you don't, do not expect to be celebrated. Mommy had to back then step aside to show me that her displaying any type of approval of my behavior would send the wrong message.

Other young women would deem it all right to have children out of wedlock as if it were the norm. This was not the way

God created family, and if Mommy was representing Christ, I was misrepresenting. It wasn't that she loved me less. It wasn't that she would not be there for me and do whatever needed to be done to help me. She was right there for me, she helped me with everything, but she did not celebrate. Respect.

I understand why my mom didn't come to the baby shower I had for Zion. But now things have been put in the correct order, I am married and having a child. I am saved, in the church, and doing things the Bible way. This is to be celebrated to the fullest. This is a big deal for me. This is a moment I don't want to just pass by.

If we can show how we are displeased with sin, surely we can show how pleased we are by celebrating doing something right. My expectations are high with this being the first child birthed through this marriage. My family should be ecstatic, and KB's family should be even more excited with this being their first baby ever.

I wanted to plan my own baby shower, going big and hard this time around, but I didn't have to because I have Bunch. Inviting my girlfriends from the Roc that now live in DC, Georgette and Michelle, who I never get to see even with us living so close to each other, they must be there. This is an exciting time in my life. A moment in time I want to go slow and take it all in. Bunch wants to do whatever she can, however she can, because she knows how big this is for me. My finances aren't what I want them to be, so there is only so big that I can go.

Thank God for the eatery. Heaven's Gate, the church restaurant and KB's place of employment, was the perfect spot for the baby shower. Tasty food, good environment, and the inside hook up. It is only to my disappointment that my family is unable to come down for the baby shower. The weather is so terrible no one from the Roc is expected to come. No one from my husband's family, his aunts, or cousins showed up either. I still have joy and am excited about being a mom. If there was no one there to celebrate with me, I celebrate that I am doing things the right way. I am glad God allowed me to experience this moment.

My happiness truly comes from the best gift I receive, which of course, comes from Bunch. This beautiful yellow and green handmade blanket with a pillow to match. The blanket and the pillow are embroidered and say, "With love, from Uncle Chon and Aunt Tina Bunch."

Comparing pregnancies and labor is not always the best thing to do. As my water breaks with this baby, things are totally different from going into labor with Zion. With my heart beating miles per minute, I just want the baby to come out healthy and strong. I have come this far, and I am asking God to get me to the finish line. My mother can't be there with me, but I know she is praying for me. I have Bunch, and she, as normal, will not leave me.

More importantly, this time around, I have a husband. I am having a child with my husband, not my fiancé, not my boyfriend, not my ex, not my secret lover. I planned to have this baby natural, just like I had Zion. I am terrified of needles, and I do not want any if I don't have to have them. This little girl is being a bit stubborn, and the pain is out of this world. Nothing I do would bring me comfort. I can't understand why she won't come out. Zion and KB are anxious too, but we have to wait.

As the doctor and nurses begin to check, they notice her pressure going up every time I have a contraction. They take a closer look and see that the umbilical cord is wrapped around her neck, and they need to go in and take her right away. This natural birth turned into an emergency C-section delivery. It doesn't matter to me as long as she is healthy.

Welcome, Kennedi Joanne Hunt, my first baby girl. Today is March 8, 2004, the date the doctors said I would go into labor. They hit it right on the nail. Not a day later, not a day earlier. I went into labor on the exact due date. God has a sense of humor. He made sure all the rumors were shut down by making this baby come when the doctors said she would and not when all the rumors said. Now that's the way to shut a rumor down, and nobody but God was able to do it.

Five years ago, after having Zion, I became pregnant but didn't have any more children. I was told that because of my decisions, it was highly unlikely that I would ever be able to carry a child to term and most likely never have another baby. God changed that report, and I am a happy woman. All I wanted to do was give this man a child with his blood. Giving him something no one else has ever given him puts a smile on my face. KB deserves this after all he has had to go through. The Hunts, husband, wife, two children. One boy and one girl. The perfect family—right?

# DIARY 3

# Spirits

There are moments in life when feeling overwhelmed is an understatement. Feeling like no matter what you do, nothing comes out right. You put forth your best effort, but the outcome still feels like trash. Excellence seems far from you, and all you see for yourself is failure.

How do you get past this moment in your life? How do you recover from what you feel is your demise? What can you do to reset your life to start over and get a new chance to go about things differently? Is this even possible?

Sometimes escaping to a do-over world in your dreams seems like the best thing. To be able to get away from the reality that you are not in control of everything that goes on around you. Where is that happy place when you can just wake up, be happy all day long, then go to bed looking forward to waking up and doing happy all over again? Putting life on the repeat cycle of happiness.

I want to go to heaven. I want to get away from all life's disappointments. I want to be free from frustration and worry. I want to have a smile that is real and genuine, not a put-on for show. I want to cry my last tear and be done.

I want to stop thinking so much. I want to not care. I want to daydream all day and not be disrupted. I want to release, but I don't know what I want to release. I feel heavy, not just overweight, but carrying weight outside of my body mass. My legs are hard to lift. My arms feel like they are being pulled out of socket. My mouth feels paralyzed, and there is no hope for me to smile again.

Breathing feels like a chore now. Do I really have to? Opening my eyes to face another day is torture. Am I terrorizing myself? I am now my own enemy. I am the number one terrorist of me. Am I giving up? Is it time?

The mistakes made in life that are now your past seem to haunt you in a way that will overtake you. No matter what you do to better your life, someway, somehow, your past keeps coming up and making a fool out of you. How can you get past this? Is the reality that you never will get over your past and will have to live with your inadequacies? This cannot possibly be the way. If so, my life is doomed. There is no hope for me because my past is something I cannot wake to every day and survive.

This feels like I am killing myself from the inside out, and clearly, I am ready to die. I want the pain of failure to end. Does that mean I want to commit suicide? Do I want to kill myself, or am I just ready to die?

Spirits are real. Self-hate is real. Depression is real. Life is real. What causes us to have the wrong spirit, which will, in turn, cause us to make the wrong decisions, is something we overlook a lot. Many times, we look at people, places, things, and situations, but we forget to look at the spirit behind them.

We become angry and attempt to deal with and resolve things, but we are just addressing symptoms.

We find ourselves reacting instead of responding accordingly because we are faced with a spirit and do not have the right spirit within to properly reply. When things seem to be going wrong in your life, that heaviness comes upon you, and it is not easy to shake. Every waking moment is now full of doubt. You question everything about you, about your life, and about everything and everyone in your life.

The way you allow people to treat you causes you to believe you deserve to be treated that way, whether good or bad. Once people get into a habit of treating you a certain way, you begin to always expect that behavior. When you are treated poorly repeatedly, you begin to think of yourself poorly. That spirit of depression and heaviness is then joined with the spirit of self-hate. You now believe what is said about you. You now feel you deserve the bad treatment. You now feel that you are not deserving of anything good because you are not a good person. Self-hate is hard to get rid of when you have been fed this negativity by manipulative and condescending people.

Most times, it is people that you look to for validation. You look to them for acceptance. You look to them for approval. When you do not get it, you feel worthless. You feel like you are not a part. You feel like you are not worthy. You feel like if you were somehow suddenly taken off the scene, no one would notice.

Anyone who says they have never experienced depression, I now feel like they are not telling the whole truth. This spirit is so strong and so real that people who seem to have everything can't get away from becoming depressed. The fact that this negative spirit doesn't travel alone lets you know that this attack on your mind is not going to be a fair fight, and if you do not have the right one on your side, you are going to lose.

One minute you love life and see all your potential and what God has planned for you. The next minute you feel less than and never enough. So now that you are feeling low and want to give up, you accept every negative attack on your life as if you deserved it. Reminded of your past, you realize that you were in a Cinderella story; this is not where you really belong.

Allowing the negative spirits around you to dictate your future is a bad move. You will never be what God intended listening to those who have no clear vision for themselves and decide to keep you with them in a place of goallessness. Why are you listening to those spirits anyway? Why do you need their approval or validation?

Stop looking at the person and evaluate the spirit. People around you that continuously put people down always seem to put the blame on you, always victimizing but come out the victim are dangerous. So what is the point in keeping those types of people in your life?

# CHAPTER 11

# The Afterbirth

The way KB held Kennedi and loved her filled my heart with joy. She was still KJ, just not Kenny Jr. My daughter, so beautiful and smells so sweet. I loved her with all my heart. This moment made me forget about all I had to go through carrying her. There were so many hospital stays it felt like I was overdoing it. Every time you turned around, there was something wrong with me.

Who will ever forget me trying to walk to the bathroom during service by myself? Because I could not keep much down, I would not eat a lot, which made me weak. It was hard to walk because Kennedi was on my sciatic nerve, so I had to walk slowly. By the time I got to the back of the church, the pianist, Mother Carter, was standing there. It seemed to have been one of the longest walks ever. Next thing I knew, I heard her saying, "Uh oh, she's going down!"

And just like that, I woke up on the floor with all these faces looking down on me. I was trying to figure out what happened, how I got down here, and why everyone was in my face. I fainted. Trying to get to the bathroom, I fainted. Falling to the ground, scaring everyone, disrupting the service, I fainted. My father-in-law ran from the pulpit to the back like the protector he is to make sure I was okay. KB stayed on the drums—in shock, I guess. Explaining to everyone I just needed to go to the bathroom and that I was okay seemed to be pointless.

The ushers and Mother Carter got me into the bathroom to help me. When we got in there, them lifting my dress and trying to help me pull down my clothes caused the urge to go away. I could not sit on the toilet in front of so many people. I was embarrassed. I felt so ashamed. I could do nothing but cry. I was already being talked about and ridiculed throughout the pregnancy, and now all I had done was give the hecklers one more thing to talk about. I wanted to just run, hide, and never return to the church. I could not stop the tears from flowing.

But it was over now. My bundle of joy was here, and she was worth it all. Being cut was different from a natural birth, and I felt horrible. My head would not stop hurting, and I was so weak. I wanted to be happy, but I was in a lot of pain. The headache would not go away, so the doctor said they needed to do a blood patch to stop the spinal headache. Knowing that they were putting a needle in my back had me sweating profusely. As I held on to the nurse with my back bent sitting on the side of the bed, they stuck the needle in me. Immediately after feeling the injection of the needle, the headache went away. I was ready to go home and begin life as a new mom.

I love St. Agnes Hospital because of the atmosphere and the kind people. Everyone was so helpful, and it was an awesome experience, even with the complications. As it came time for me to be discharged, Cousin Omar came to see the baby and me. His mom, Shirley, my mother-in-law, and her sister, KB's aunt Joanne, were at the hospital when Kennedi was born.

Omar was the family cousin that was cooler than cool and loved to joke with me. I loved him and his wife and kids. They never acted funny towards me for marrying KB.

KB knew it was time for me to leave and said he was on his way. By the time Omar came, I had been waiting for hours. Omar offered to take me home, but I knew KB was coming and would not want him to miss the memory of taking his first child home from the hospital, so I waited. And waited. And waited.

My patience turned into frustration, as I was ready to get home, lay down and relax in the baby's room. When KB came, it had become nighttime. It was dark; I was hungry and not happy at all. He kept saying that he was sorry and that the eatery was very busy and he could not get away. Those words took my frustration up a few levels. If the car had broken down, and he was stranded trying to get to me, that would be one thing. I had been waiting to go home because he was working at the eatery, which is only five minutes from the hospital.

He began explaining how his dad needed him at the eatery because there were some coach buses filled with tourists from out of town who visited the National Great Blacks In Wax Museum and then came by the eatery for some soul food. I couldn't care less about the museum, tourists, or buses. This was KB's first experience with childbirth. This was his first time ever having a newborn baby—his reintroduction to fatherhood. Totally upset, I could not explain to him how none of that mattered and should not have been his top concern or priority.

This was supposed to be a happy moment, remember. The day we walked out of the hospital with the first newborn Hunt. Ready to drive home as a family and get settled in with caring for this new baby, enjoying the addition to the clan. I didn't want to fuss as upset as I was. I felt someone should have said to him he didn't need to stay. Manager or not, he needed to leave and take care of his family. Did anyone offer to work on his behalf so that he could be with his family? Did anyone think about it being his first time experiencing this? Not one person saw him and thought about the baby or me?

Omar happened by chance to come by the hospital long after I had waited for hours, not knowing that I should have been gone. Out of kindness and because he saw my frustration, he wanted to take me home, but no one else considered to come and get this new baby and me even though everyone was excited about welcoming this beautiful little girl into the world.

As I finally got into the back seat of the car with the baby, I was just happy to leave the hospital after waiting for hours. Being pregnant, going through labor, giving birth, having a spinal headache, trying to nurse the baby, staples in my belly, a needle in my back, and lack of sleep at the hospital will put anyone in a mood to want to find a moment of peace. As we pulled off from the hospital, although disappointed that KB had me waiting, I was glad he was there. We had a child together, and it felt great to leave the hospital with my husband.

Yes. My husband. Not my child's father, nor my fiancé. We were leaving the hospital as a legitimate family. Husband, wife, and child. A unit formed under God's direction and in His plan. I did not have to hear KB say he didn't know if he was going to sign the birth certificate or not. I was not embarrassed in front of the nurse because the father of my child did not want to own up to it this time. This moment was important to me. I had done things right. I had proven the negative onlookers wrong.

All this time, it was in my head that there was something wrong with me. There had to be something wrong with me for a man to lay with me and get me pregnant but refuse to claim the child. I always felt undeserving and not good enough. I believed the slurs spit out at me, telling me that I would never have this peaceful life because I was not worth it and didn't deserve it. I smiled as I saw in this present state the lies I was told were just that, all lies.

Driving down the road home, we went in the same direction as the eatery. As we came upon the eatery, we saw that there were still a lot of people there. KB decided to stop in and let everyone know he was taking me home. Before I could have a voice in the matter, he was already gone out of the car and in the restaurant. I was in disbelieve. Now I was mad—wanting to be happy, I was mad. As I sat in front of the eatery, my pressure began to rise. How this man did not get it was all I asked. Kennedi began to squirm in her car seat as I sat there upset. She began to make little sobbing noises, and I tried moving the car seat back and forth to comfort her.

After a while, her whimper turned into a solid cry. I had to take her out of the chair and hold her, trying to comfort her. We had been waiting for so long at the hospital it was time for her to eat again. There were no words to describe this feeling that I felt. There was no nice way to say how ticked off I was right now. As I took my coat off and lifted my shirt, pulling out my breast, this baby kept yelling at the top of her lungs. With people walking by, on the corner of North Avenue and Smallwood Street on the west side in Baltimore, Maryland, in front of Heaven's Gate Eatery, was where I first breastfed my newborn child after leaving the hospital.

Many days I could not understand why KB didn't see that I needed him to assist me. I needed him just to help me get into a routine. We were, after all, a family; we were one. We needed each other. After having a baby, there is a phase that we go through trying to get comfortable in the new dynamics. We are unable to articulate what we need and how we feel to the husband, which causes more problems.

I knew what it felt like to have a baby as a single woman. I knew what it felt like to have a child and wonder if the dad was going to come by or not to help. I didn't feel that I needed to tell KB to be a dad and a husband. He already knew what I had had to face having a child with someone who wasn't there. I expected him to be determined to be there no matter what. I didn't want to sound crazy saying to him I wanted this experience to be better than the last time I had a child. The dynamics were different, so I expected things to be different. Honestly, there should be no comparison because I was a wife and mother in a home, not a girlfriend/fiancé staying in a room in my mom's house.

Instead of trying to get him to understand what I was going through, I decided I wanted to leave. I felt if I went home to Rochester for a while, away from everything going on in Baltimore, I would be all right. I needed a break. I needed support. I needed my husband. He was working; he was helping his parents; he was on fire for the church; he was absent from me.

I didn't want to feel like the only time he saw me and paid attention to me was when we were having sex. It now turned me off. I didn't feel loved like I used to feel. I now felt like a piece of meat. In KB's mind, desiring me should have made me feel attractive like nothing had changed, and he still wanted me. In my mind, his desiring me made me feel like he didn't care about what I had just gone through having a baby. It felt like he was disconnected from me.

Communication between husband and wife is so important. I didn't need anyone else to tell KB what he should have been doing with me and for me; I needed to be the one to tell him. KB didn't need anyone to tell me how this experience was new and fresh for him and that he was scared and wanted to make all the right choices. He needed to be the one to tell me.

I could not help but feel like this baby and I were interrupting life, not adding to it. Anytime I needed KB for something, I always was made to feel like I was asking for too much. Telling him I wanted to go home to Rochester to be with my mom apparently triggered something. He finally called the job and told his dad he wasn't coming in and that he needed to stay home with me, Zion, and the baby. The assumption was that I needed "attention." It wasn't me personally, but the family needed tending to.

Every woman is made to feel like the emotions and anxieties that she has after having a baby are her going crazy, but I knew I was not going out of my mind. Listening to everyone say this is what a woman does after she has a baby and she will get through it doesn't help. Trying to make a woman believe that postpartum is the time when a woman loses her mind after a baby doesn't help either. After a baby comes, things change, and if we don't sit down and address these changes and get into a routine with a plan, the marriage will fall apart.

Not just the routine and the plan, but the expectations need to be addressed as well. There were many things I expected because I was not doing life in sin, fornicating and letting God down. I was living the life according to what we believed was the plan of God, so I expected God's plan to be happier than when I did it all wrong the first time.

I didn't know how to tell KB how I felt, so I said nothing. I cried, became quiet, and said nothing. My attraction to him and desire to be with him slowly diminished because I felt like he no longer understood me. I felt like I was not good enough for him. I had never been through this before as a wife, and I came in with expectations that maybe I should not have.

He thought being at work and making money for the family was his only job to make sure the family was fine, but there was so much more. Being led to believing that this was just a phase that I was going through made me even more upset—he was not even trying to understand me, just going off what other people were saying. If I couldn't talk to him, who could I talk to?

And just like that, my phone rang, and it was Mr. Marc-Train. Right on time, strangely perfect timing. How did he know I needed someone to talk to? How did he know I was going through an emotional time in my life where I felt no one understood and I needed an outlet? God, was this You sending this man to me as a sign? It seemed as if I could not get rid of the feelings I had for him; why? Mr. MarcTrain was calling to ask about the car payments, but as usual, he noticed that there was something more going on with me.

Just hearing his voice made me feel like the phone call was meant to be. He knew exactly what to say to me. So encouraging and so concerned. All he did was tell me what I wanted to hear, and I didn't have to tell him what that was. He was not trying to be my husband; he was being my friend. The friend he had always been to me. He loved me, and I loved him too, and that was what friends did—be there for each other, right?

Because this was what I needed right now, I couldn't find anything wrong with it. He made me feel valued again. He made me feel wanted. He made me feel appreciated. Was there really something wrong with friends being friends to each other? If he was a female, would it be any different? Please don't tell me I was wrong about this. Please don't tell me that I was engaging in something that would be deemed inappropriate. This was what my mind said, and this was what I was going to go with.

Know this: When you are walking the wrong way on the wrong side of the road, expect there to be a collision of some kind at some point.

Make no mistake, I was going to go with the plan God had for me, not make a new path. I appreciated Mr. MarcTrain understanding that he could not be my husband, nor would I allow him to pretend to be. But I appreciated the ear. I appreciated the support. I appreciated the love. After listening to me, he actually pushed me to communicate more with my husband. From a man's point of view, he explained to me what KB might be going through. After all, he had been married, and he had children.

I accepted what he said and took time by myself to see what exactly I could do to help KB and help myself get this family back on track. I didn't want to fail at this. I saw so many waiting for me to drop the ball, so I had to work hard to make sure I didn't. I accepted that there would be times things were not going to work the way that I wanted them to, but it was not the end of the world. I had to understand that being married didn't mean that there wouldn't be disappointments or moments of feeling low.

I listened to everyone telling me how to raise this baby. Everyone telling me who should be her babysitter. I listened to them tell me how to feed her. What to do, what not to do. How to do, how not to do. Everyone seemed to forget that although this was KB's first child, it was not mine. I had now five years of experience being a mom, yet I had people whose youngest child was in their twenties telling me what to do.

It had been over twenty years since being a new mom with so many new things that had been developed, but you could tell me what I needed to know. I had people with children younger than Zion telling me what to do. You'd only been parenting for a few years, and now you were an expert. If I didn't listen, I was rebellious, arrogant, and a know-it-all.

Truth is everyone raises children differently. None of us are the same. What we all have in common is that, for the most part, we all want to do what is best for our child. No, I would not be feeding my baby cereal in a bottle when she was only a few months old. I would continue to breastfeed no matter how difficult it was. Why? Because that was what worked for me; that was what I did with my first child. This was what I wanted to do with this child. She belonged to me to nourish her and take care of her. I just gave birth to her, so things would go the way I choose, not anyone else.

No, I would not allow anyone to hold my daughter that I did not feel comfortable with. Many had made it very clear how they felt about me, so why did you want to hold this baby anyway? No, I would not put a fake smile on my face to those who had given me grief this entire pregnancy and first year of marriage. Yes, I wanted you to see the beautiful, flawless-skinned, mocha-brown little girl that KB and I had, but touching her all the time—that would be a no, no.

Yes. I would dress my daughter the way I wanted to dress her and keep her styled the way I wanted to style her. She was my first baby girl. I had this right! I did not get the memo that because I was now related to the pastor, any and everything I did for my family—my husband and children—had to be approved by the "church folk." I didn't want my husband to ever be ashamed that he married me, so I decided to go along with and appease some of the recommendations.

Some, calling and telling me, "Don't listen to your in-laws; this is your baby. Do what you want to do—don't let them control you." Then others, calling and saying how they raised their kids, and I should have followed their way if I wanted to be successful. Not realizing how many people not only didn't care for me, but they didn't care for their own pastor either. The innuendos and code talking that I now endured were crazy. I felt I was being used to get to the pastor and the first family.

Technically, I was married into the family, so to some degree, I was not considered royalty until I was being used. People who had never held a conversation with me now wanted to ask many questions as if I was going to be their inside connection to an imaginary wall that was up around the pastor and his family. If I didn't carry the messages, I got mistreated. If I did carry the messages and the response from the pastor was public and abrupt, I got the side-eye for that too. I choose not to be a part of the church politics—but evidently, I didn't get the memo that once I married the pastor's son, I didn't have a voice in the matter.

Having a baby so quickly after being married was hard enough. Adding the stress of church relations didn't help. Church was supposed to be the place where I found peace. The place where I found refuge. The place where I could hide in God. Instead, it had become the place where I was on display. The place where I was ridiculed. The place where I was scrutinized far beyond what I ever imagined.

No, I would not allow my church family or my husband's family to tell me how to raise my child. I wanted to do this with my husband. I wanted to do this the way God intended for it to be done. I wanted us to have our family and have our memories and have our home, not living out someone else's dream.

# CHAPTER 12

# Betrayal and Hate... Me

Three years later, and it seems as if I have more people who hate me than I have that like me—not to mention I am pregnant again. I am not easily bullied or intimidated, and my pushback, quick, sharp replies, and hard outer core make me one that either you love to hate or hate to love. I have had to build a tougher exterior because I am being attacked from every side, it seems.

It has become too much, always listening to different ones tell me how I am not a true Hunt and that I am only part of this family, basically because of KB's stupidity. Yes, this coming from people who aren't blood, but nonetheless, they feel the need to let me know I am not blood either—even if I am the sole reason at the present time that this Hunt bloodline has gone to the next generation because of the baby I have given birth to.

Nicknaming my baby girl Moca, her beautiful skin so smooth and perfectly colored, I keep her hair done. I keep her dressed. I keep her looking like a little princess. It amazed me the time right after I had Moca what a church mother said to me that almost made me lose the little bit of respect I had for women in the church altogether.

I didn't even know this woman. I believe I had only seen her a few times around the church jurisdiction and at other churches, but I did not know her to have developed a relationship with her personally. That did not stop this woman from coming up to me after an evening service to share her thoughts about my parenting skills.

Already second-guessing everything, not realizing how close I am being watched, this life has become more than overwhelming. Moca was only a few months, two or three at the max, and this lady got right in my face and told me, "Your husband is a preacher, Bro. Hunt is a man of God. You need to have shoes on that baby!" Concerned that my sharp response would definitely send me packing moving back to Da Roc, I just looked at her with disgust.

My daughter did not know how to say shoes. Better yet, my daughter did not know how to walk. My daughter could not sit up at a dinner table, matter of fact, she just got finished sucking my breast, ma'am. Why did she need shoes right now? It was hot, and she was a baby sweating in the summer heat, and you wanted to tell me she needed shoes on. Of all the things you could say to me, you wanted to tell me to put shoes on her because my husband was Kenneth Hunt, son of the pastor! To H.E.L... with you and your demented thoughts, ma'am.

This woman I didn't know evidently knew my husband and his family and felt there was a standard that I was living beneath while carrying the Hunt name and child, and she needed to be the one to let me know. Little did she know she wasn't alone. Right along with her statement, I will never forget the other old church "mother" who told me that I needed to keep my daughter in the most layered, poufy dresses for every service. My response to her was simply stripping Moca in the back of the church one Sunday and allowing her to be in her onesie t-shirt to cool off instead of torturing her by making her keep on one of the most beautiful but hot dresses.

When are these people going to get that I do not care about what they think? When are they going to see that their comments and behavior do not make me listen to them but actually cause me to rebel against their foolery? So inappropriate, so thoughtless, so typical of how old church mothers are being characterized.

This is the perfect example of why young girls do not want to come to church now. They are talked to with no consideration or respect. They are judged and looked down upon. Here I am, a woman of God, living a godly life. Saved, sanctified, and filled with the Holy Spirit and happily married to an awesome guy but must deal with this type of behavior in the church. Imagine having a child out of wedlock. Single mothers truly are put in a position of scrutiny like none other. While I have my husband to yell at about my experience, who does a single mother talk to? I am doing it right and get this treatment; imagine the ladies who had babies the wrong way—what was said to them?

Thank God all of the old church mothers I come in contact with aren't like this and are genuinely sweet ladies. I am happy to be able to say all church mothers are not evil, mean, and rude. Some of them yes, most of them no. I would never give that reputation to all because of a few. Just because my reputation is being smeared doesn't mean that I should intentionally smear others.

Nonetheless, this is what I must deal with. I have no one to talk to because I am not sure who I can trust. I keep things to myself and realize I can't tell Bunch everything either. The more I tell her, the more difficult it is for her to look at some of these people mistreating me also. Their behaviors are unbecoming, and Bunch does not need to be exposed to all the things I am experiencing. I am glad she is there to be a shoulder to cry on and one who is ready to scrap for me if need be.

*Know this:* There are young women who want to glean from older women but are turned off by the way they are treated and talked to. The trust factor is gone.

My father-in-law has no problem utilizing whatever skills I have that will benefit the church. I am his daughter now, so there is no asking, just instructing. At least before, I thought I had a choice in the matter, but now that I look back—I didn't have a choice then either. *Ha!* But I was honored to serve then, and I am honored to serve now. I do it because I love God. I do it because I love my church. I do it because I was always a willing worker. I do it because it is in me to do—even if it causes more people to hate me.

Many things he asks me to do others have been doing and stopped or have slacked off. Instead of them getting back on track, they get upset with me for him deciding to use someone he knows is going to get the job done. When I am placed on an assignment, I choose to give it my all and do things in the spirit of excellence. While I am not perfect, I like things to be as close to perfection as possible. I want to enjoy whatever I do, and I want it to make a long-lasting impact. It is never to make the person(s) before me look bad, but for me to make something good be better. But of course, it is hard to look at it in that way.

I had to get even tougher and not feel intimidated by the stares. I cannot neglect to realize my eagerness to come off as strong is instead misinterpreted as arrogant to some. The pastor's daughter-in-law. If anyone ever thought to put themselves in my shoes just for one moment, how am I to respond to all the negativity? This is the church, a place where I felt was safe. A place where I felt there was peace and unity. I only feel targeted and like I am always being hunted from one Sunday to the next.

I hear that the pastor's children get it easy because they are the kids of the pastor, but it seems to me like I have it harder. I may have just had a child, but that didn't stop me from having to work. I didn't get extra sabbatical time or any special treatment. Many days it feels like my home and my family are being neglected because we are so busy trying to do all we can for the church. On my job, I am doing work for the church. At home, I am doing work for the church. At my in-law's home, I am doing work for the church. At the church, I am doing work for the church.

Only to hear that the sacrificial offerings that KB and I give are secretly being given back to us from my father-in-law. I cannot believe people really believe this. At no time do we ever get the money we gave in offering back. We never front or pretend to give, only to get the money back in the trustee office. It never happened, but of course, that is what is being said.

I try to tell KB that I am a target, and he says what others say, "Oh, it is just jealousy, don't play into it." I try to listen to that, but I cannot help but wonder who all is jealous and why. Some people are just outright evil more than they are jealous, and this is why I cannot have trust in anyone. I cannot talk to anyone about my marriage or my life because one would rather gossip over using the gospel to help me get through.

So I talk to no one. Me not talking to anyone causes me to seem more arrogant and the assumption that I think I am too good to speak. No one knows that the real reason is that the environment I am in has proven to be full of non-trustworthy people. It broke my heart the day KB and I were driving a young girl to church who needed a ride. She began talking about relationships and how phony some of the couples in churches are. KB and I were saying that our love for each other is real and we are glad we aren't one of those phony couples. Only for this young girl to reply to us we were phony too.

She began to tell how she knew that after Moca was born, we weren't having much sex. She openly said how my husband talked about me not giving it up to him and how he felt about it. I was so shocked I was speechless. How did she know that after childbirth, we went through anything sexual? Why and to whom would KB tell such things to? It didn't mean that our marriage was phony or weak—it actually showed how strong our marriage is, especially with me being pregnant with the next baby. It showed the transparency of marriage not always going the way we want it to go, but when you put God in the middle of it, things will work out in your favor in the end.

I was angry with my husband because I was embarrassed. Described as one that was not satisfying her husband, I was furious. Why couldn't KB say these things to me if he really felt that way? Why did some random young chick from the church think she knows our personal sex life? I didn't even want to look at KB. I didn't want to talk to him, nor did I want an explanation. There was no excuse for what just happened.

KB later explained to me that there was a brother who he knew was being unfaithful to his wife. The brother explained and used the excuse that his wife was not as sexual as he wanted her to be. KB, trying to encourage him, expressed that he had to go through deprivation of sex with Dion when she was sick, and he didn't cheat on her. He then told him, with my hormones changing after the baby, my drive wasn't as strong as it was in the beginning, but he remained faithful to me and did not cheat on me either. He never said that he wasn't getting any sex from me.

Instead of the brother taking this encouragement for what it was, a testimony that you can be faithful, he chose to spice it up, repeat, and make it juicy gossip to tell. I always thought only the women in the church spread rumors and negativity. I would always hear my father-in-law say, "Those skirts. Those skirts keep mess going." But this was a man. This was a brother. This was someone my husband trusted and was genuinely trying to help keep a marriage together. Only to find out the girl he told all of this to was one of the many this brother was cheating on his wife with.

So much for trust. So much for having someone to confide in or share your story to encourage. So much for thinking someone respects you for who you are and would never betray you and put you in a position of regret. I felt for KB because he always would tell me to give people a chance. He would say everyone isn't against me. He would say that I need to let people get close to me to get to know me better. Well, I guess he knows now that is out of the door. Never will I allow any new friends. "No new friends" is my motto, and no new friends it is!

*Know this:* If so-called men down here wallow in drama and conjure up rumors and strife, I want no parts in comradery with the women. No thanks!

The Young Women's Christian Council is the women's group at our church. This group provides direction, encouragement, and guidance on being a woman of God. Here is where we are taught how to be a good wife, how to wait on a husband, how to be a good mother, raise our children, and keep our homes clean, all while being faithful to God and the church and our family.

More and more, I have been hearing the dialog in the sermons directed at what it takes to be a good wife. I hear about what a woman should be doing in the home for her husband and children. There have been a few new marriages and young couples at the church, including KB and me, so I understand the teaching. It is important that things are done right in the homes so that the home doesn't fall apart.

I wanted to be a good wife and support my husband and our family. Daily, I would attend to our children and our home after I came home from work. The problem was it was difficult at times to figure out a schedule to make home-cooked meals. Zion and KB would be at the eatery every day after school, so they always had a delicious meal before they got home. I kept hearing the messages and listening to our YWCC leader say what we needed to be doing at home, and I asked KB what he felt.

I must be honest. Even with me making some changes to the house and putting some of my furniture in there, I still don't want to venture into certain areas as often as I should. The kitchen is one of those areas. It is to my relief, as KB said to me that it didn't make sense for me to try to cook meals every day, knowing that they have eaten already at the eatery. I smiled with ease, hearing him say he was pleased with me as his wife and that there wasn't more that I should be doing.

I told him what teaching goes on with the women, and he replied to me that not every home is going to be the same. He had me think about our leader and the fact that she does not go out to work but stays home. A lot of what she was telling us we needed to do, she was able to do because she did not have to leave the house. She was teaching us correctly, but it was based on one structure type of home that many do not live in any longer.

There was a time when women stayed home, and only the husband worked. The woman was able to do household chores and cooking and cleaning and meal prep to be ready when the husband walked through the door after a grueling day at work. I choose to work and help my husband take care of the home. Many women count it a privilege to stay home or have a husband who wants them to stay home.

I am the opposite. There is a significant difference between a stay-at-home wife/mother and a career woman. I am a career woman. I do not want to stay home. I enjoy going out to work and learning new things and being able to give support to my husband as he takes care of the home and family. I am glad my husband has no problem with me working. I am glad he respects my desires to have a career, gain experience and education, and not remain in the home only. KB said because this is the dynamics of our home, we cannot compare our routines and ways with anyone else.

So happy that we were on the same page, and we both stood by each other in saying while we understood what was being taught and why, we needed to take what was being taught and apply and adjust it accordingly to our home. This would have been great if KB did not just a few weeks later flip the script on me.

After a strong sermon from the pastor, KB decided to tell me that I needed to start having more cooked meals in the home. I was shocked at the way he approached me as if he was correcting and chiding me. We were just on the same page a few weeks ago, and now I was left to understand what happened to change things.

My reply was that I wasn't simply not cooking meals to be lazy. That wasn't it at all. *We* decided that I didn't have to cook all the time, multiple times a week. *We* decided that the guys eating down at the eatery would help because we didn't have to purchase many groceries to cook meals every day. *We* agreed that this would save us money and we would be fine.

Hurt and feeling confused and upset about the way he approached me with this, I just said, "Okay, fine." After he said what he wanted to say, I went to bed praying. I knew arguing with him was not going to help the situation. Many men, when they feel they need to do something or say something to feel in control of their home, will not listen to reasoning. There was no point in me trying to get him to understand. At this moment, his way of thinking was off.

I had to wonder if it was someone misinforming him, telling him he needed to be more aggressive with his demands for me in the house without fully understanding the dynamics of our home. Whoever told KB that he needed to demand his wife cook him more meals and convinced him to repeat those words to me clearly didn't belong in our marriage. They obviously didn't know what KB truly wanted, nor did they take into consideration how I would respond.

No. This was not going to be an argument. This was not going to be another thing I investigated to see who was trying to penetrate my marriage and cause me grief. Instead, I choose to pray. I went to God and asked Him what I should do. I asked God why this was happening. I wanted to make the right choices, and I didn't want to spend the rest of my life responding to what other people thought I should be to my husband. Besides, who was to say there was somebody saying things to him to cause him to act this way? What if he felt the way he felt because, well, that's the way he felt?

I left the conversation with KB alone and decided to do less talking and take some action. Without talking to KB, I came up with the plan to obey what he said. He wanted more home-cooked meals at home instead of the eatery, so that was what I would give him. I waited for payday to come around and went to the grocery store. For me to cook the meals he was eating at the eatery, I had to get many different types of meat, vegetables, and ingredients. Walking through the grocery store,

I went through every aisle. I didn't want to forget anything or leave any options out.

It felt good walking through the store picking up all the things I knew my husband and family enjoy eating. Getting snacks and all the things needed to fill my freezer, refrigerator, and cupboards made me feel different about what my husband said and how he said it. I made sure we had fruit, drinks, and lunch meat too, along with cereal and milk for the basics so there would be nothing they would need. Typical grocery run, but what made it different this time was that I planned to get food for every day of the week for every meal instead of getting a few things here and there.

I ended up being that lady at the grocery store that no one wanted to be behind in the line because my cart was so full. Everyone knew it was going to take a while for my things to be bagged up. As the cashier was ringing my things up, I began putting the bags in the cart neatly. Excited to see my refrigerator, freezer, and cupboards fuller than they have ever been.

Bag after bag, I strategically set them in the cart so that things like the bread and the eggs wouldn't get smashed. And finally, the cashier hit the total button, and all the discounts from the bonus card came off, and the total due came across the screen. Almost four hundred dollars' worth of groceries. I gladly pulled out my bank card and paid for the groceries to head home as the queen of my castle looking out for her king.

Cooking dinner waiting for KB to come home, I thought about third parties in marriages and how the Bible says, "and the two became one." Never should we allow any other entity to drive a wedge between us or add themselves to our marriage. This is us; we are the Hunts, Kenneth and Lillian with our children.

When KB walked through the door, the smell of dinner was in the air. Yes, it felt like home, looked like home, and he was getting ready to eat a home-cooked meal. His face, however, didn't look like he was as excited as me. His face didn't seem to get hypnotized by the aroma of the food. He stood there in the house and asked me if I had taken any money out of the account. Ever since we got married, we decided that everything would be together, including our money. I told him I didn't take anything, but I did go get groceries to provide dinner like he asked.

He asked me how much money I spent on groceries, and then he braced himself. I told him what I spent, and his hands went on his head. As he said, "No, no, no..." I asked what was wrong. He was so flustered and disturbed that I spent so much money, so I looked at him and said, "This is what you asked for!" He was the money guy that paid all the bills and portioned the money where the money needed to go every pay. I had no clue what bills he paid and when. I just knew that he took care of everything the best that he could.

Me spending almost $400 on groceries was not part of his plan for this payday, and now he was in a bind. He didn't have enough money to pay the bills that were due as he had planned, and now, he must figure out how he was going to fix this. As he asked me again why I spent so much money on groceries, I replied to him that he was the one that said to me he wanted more meals cooked at home. I cooked meals at home, but not all the time. He suddenly decided he wanted more after we discussed that there was no need for me to do more than what I was already doing for now. He changed, so I needed to go with his change. The only way to cook more was to have more to cook. The only way to have more to cook was to go to the grocery store and purchase more groceries.

Immediately, we learned what it means to communicate with each other. Immediately, KB learned I was serious when I said, "I can show you better than I could ever tell you." No, we didn't need $400 worth of groceries, but I purchased them to show him that our marriage and the dynamics of this marriage cannot be based on what other people outside of this marriage demand for us to be. We would be and do what God told us, but we would never be Doris and Henry or Irene and Douglas or any other marriage.

How our house is run may not be like someone else's, and that doesn't make them right and us wrong or vice versa—it makes us different. I love that KB wants me to pursue my dreams and goals as a career woman and not want me to stay home. He sees the benefit in me working and appreciates my willingness to work and assist in bringing in finances to the home. That also means he is forfeiting having dinner on the table when he gets off work some days because I get off work after he does. It means he may have to cook dinner or get dinner if he doesn't want to wait for me to get home to cook. On those nights we have church, he must deal with finding a meal on his own or eating leftovers because I have to go straight to the church from work.

It was an ugly lesson, but I think there was something we both needed to learn. God put me with KB to be his help, not a hindrance. Purchasing all those groceries, while it may have taught him a lesson, didn't help him take care of the bills we were facing. Being the head of the household is a tough enough job without your own teammate making it more difficult for you. He may have been wrong to change demands on me and lift his expectations higher, but I was no better, intentionally spending money he needed to cover other things on groceries. But we ate well.

So I'm not the perfect wife. I make mistakes. My marriage is not the perfect marriage, but that doesn't mean we are damaged. The betrayal and all the hate hurt me. I am disappointed in what I learn about the people and things around me. I am described as the person to hate, but truthfully, I see many people who hate themselves and direct their hate at someone they barely know.

No, I did not plan to marry the only son of the pastor, taking the one option away from many women who desired for him to be their husband or son-in-law. I didn't intentionally ruin the dreams of those young ladies who desired to become a Hunt for whatever reason. Don't betray or hate me for that. No, I was not born into this family, but I have born a child into it. Don't betray or hate me for that. No, I don't have a husband that is cheating on me right under my nose with women at the same church as me or anywhere for that matter. Don't betray or hate me for that. No, I am not a person that you can make be what you want me to be because I am committed to being who God has called me to be. Don't betray or hate me for that. No, I am not a woman that is going to stay home and not develop a career and excel outside of wifely duties and skills. Don't hate or betray me for that.

CHAPTER 13

# The Struggle

I am pregnant, but I am working. I am happy, and I am sick. I did not expect to be pregnant again so quickly, but I am thankful. I am excited at the fact the doctor told me years ago that I would not have any more children because of the decisions I made, but here I am on child number three. Praying that this is a boy, I am excited to grow a family with KB. We are in a financial struggle and not able to pay bills as we want, but here we are, having another baby.

That alone makes things difficult, and I see on KB's face the concern of being the head of the household and adding another mouth to feed. I want to show him that I am with him and I have his back no matter what. That we together will get through anything. Mr. MarcTrain and KB are trying to work out the agreement with my car, but KB just wants to give it up still. He feels that having Mr. MarcTrain anywhere in the picture is going against what the Lord is telling him to do. But we keep the car anyway. Not able to pay the car payment on time, but we keep the car.

The eatery has been going through transitions, and the business has slowed down. Busses have stopped coming through like they used to, and they must cut down on employees. It seems as if it is shortages everywhere, and there is no relief either. KB knows that with building a family, he must have employment that is stable, but he does not want to leave his dad. He doesn't want to disappoint him, so I encourage him to support his dad but also figure out what he is going to do to make up for the shortages.

It was nothing for my husband to work at the eatery and at night serve civil summonses. I was afraid for him working the civil summons, but I understood how it brought additional funds into the home, and we needed them. KB had been working summons for years and would always keep that as a side job for extra cash. However, just as everything else was seemingly being cut off for trumped-up reasons, the summonses job ended as well.

Looking at KB's face in the eatery after talking to his bosses that run the summons was hurtful. The way they talked to him and dismissed him, I felt there was more to the story than was being told. Since KB's start of employment, there were many others whom he referred to work there too that would do well working the summons. Sometimes there are shortages with the summons, and that would mean the workload would be light. Because this was KB's side job and not his main income like some others, I believe some of the ones KB helped to get a job assisted in him losing the job. Friends.

KB is not allowing this to stop him. Knowing this family is growing, he does what he knows best. He hustles. He went out to make money for this family. KB refused to go to his dad and borrow money, so we had to come up with funds on our own. KB, wanting to stay in shape and stay active, goes to the basketball court to play ball with his cousin Omar late nights. Me being pregnant, I worry about him when it gets late. I wanted him to be home with the family and me, but I know he needs his space and time to release as well.

KB came up with the idea to have fun working out and make money at the same time. He decided he would get cases of water and Gatorade and sell it to the fellas playing ball. When he was done with his games on the court, selling all he could there, KB would go downtown to where the clubs were. As the clubs were closing and people would be coming out hot and thirsty, he would sell water to them too.

Coming home late at night, I would lay in the bed waiting for KB to come through the door. We are in a struggle, but we are in the struggle together. He would come upstairs to the bedroom and turn on the light. Digging into his pockets, he would pull out crumbled-up dollars, wet dollars, and folded dollars. He would take his time unfolding and flattening them to count out how much money he made for the night.

I wanted to help him to make sure he understood that he did not have to feel ashamed or feel alone in this financial bind. KB made good money on the nights he went out selling drinks to whoever was thirsty. I would pray that God covered him, and God did.

I began discussing with KB that we needed to make some financial decisions. The eatery was closing, and he was going to need to find another job. KB felt that he missed the opportunity to go back and use his degree to start a career. Once he gave up working in the school system and in the criminal justice system to work for his dad at the eatery, he lost his experience time.

He has been working in the food industry and not using his degree, so now it is going to be hard to get back into that field. He did it for his dad. He did it because he believed in the eatery. He did it because he wanted to be a help. He did it, and no one forced him. That is what I love about KB. He is all for helping and supporting someone with a cause or a great idea. Now he needs to come up with one of his own to provide for this family.

Not to mention we are still feeling the effects of rejection by some who did not want us to be married in the first place. The more of a financial struggle we are in, it always brings into question: Was this marriage supposed to be? Even with us remaining together, getting through tough times, it seems as if this dark cloud still tries to hover over us.

Mr. MarcTrain found out that I was pregnant again and was again concerned. This time I wondered if his concern was really about me or about my finances. I am close to paying this car off, and that will be the end of our connection together. The connection should have been broken; nevertheless, it is what it is. At work, I had a conversation with his mom. She was very upset at the fact I married KB but was driving the car for which her son and I were responsible. I had to let her know that I was paying for the car, not her son. The payments were late, the payments were hard to come up with, but there were payments.

Things happened so fast when KB and I got married that there were many things that Mr. MarcTrain and I did not put closure on. It was both of our faults that we didn't handle things the way that we should have. His mom recognized this and was very vocal about it all.

The more the conversation went on, I realized that it was more than the car for all of us. Mr. MarcTrain's mom had never been mean to me. She was one of the sweetest women in the world as far as my contact had been with her. She showed love to my family and me and even told me what was wrong with her own son. Her opinion was somewhat objective, but at the end of the day, Mr. MarcTrain was her son.

In talking with her, she helped me to see that there were emotions and feelings, amongst other things, that needed closure. There was a need for finality. This moment made me have to confess that I still cared for Mr. MarcTrain more than I should. I could not be in love with my husband the way that I had a duty to until I released the link I had with Mr. MarcTrain.

As tears came to my eyes, I was wondering how in the world all of this was happening now. I wondered, *Is this just maternal hormones going all over the place, or is this something that I really need to address?* So when Mr. MarcTrain calls, I ask. I want to know what we need to do for things to be right. I want to know how we get in order. I love my husband, but being in love with him is something different. Fighting this while in a financial struggle, church drama, and being far away from family, I really need God to get my life together. It feels like if I take over, I am going to make the wrong decision and ruin everything.

I decide to fast and pray and not mention anything to KB for the time being. I need him to know that I do love him, and with everything else going on right now, he doesn't need something else to deal with. I pray that God keeps in me the love that a wife should have for her husband. I pray that whatever KB needs in a wife, I am able to fulfill. I pray that God breaks every connection to Mr. MarcTrain and anything else in my past that would hinder me from being in love with my husband the way I should.

I want God to give me a sign that He hears my prayers. I want God to show me that there is life in this marriage, and this marriage will live and not die. I need God to continue to show me that He is with me and in this marriage. God is love, and love is God, and as long as God is here, there is love. The more I focus on being in love with my husband, the more the love will grow. I will not allow the enemy to trip me up. I am getting ready to have a baby, and that is my focus and will be my only focus.

We are excited to find out we are having a boy, and there are no issues or concerns with him. There was a prophet to come by Mount Hebron one night to tell me that my baby was a boy and that he would be a preacher. He said that he would be preaching at a young age, and the anointing of God would be upon him. Well, he was right; this is a boy, and we are going to believe that indeed this baby boy will be used by God.

This pregnancy seems to be one that just flies by with no major problems. Yes, the sickness and the big belly, but nothing like Moca. We wonder why this baby seems to be more settled but can't figure out why until my water breaks and remembering what the prophet said. Mommy being here this time made me feel better even though I know I am getting on her nerves. We stayed home from church this Sunday morning and now must call KB to come take us to the hospital. I am happy about getting this over with, so nothing else matters to me. I don't even realize that my doctor is not the doctor on call, so I will be having this baby with complete strangers.

My mom wasn't there for the birth of Kennedi. When she finally held Kennedi, she really couldn't see her because she is a diabetic, and the disease temporarily took her vision. I know that time was hard for her, and it was hard for me too, so having her here this time around is a blessing—but I am a mess! It is a great thing that my mom is patient, kind, and loving. She loves me enough to be there for me no matter what. With all the scares we have had with her these past few years, I am thankful to have her by my side right now.

The contractions are strong and seem to be getting the best of me. I had an emergency C-section with Kennedi, so they are cautious with me trying to have this baby vaginally. Worried that the scared tissue from the last baby would cause internal bleeding, the doctors on call persuaded me to have another C-section and get the labor over with. I do what they tell me, and on January 22, 2006, my Kendrick Tyrone Hunt is here.

Wait. January 22. Why this date is so familiar is bizarre. It isn't until later in the evening, after coming out of labor and seeing my beautiful baby boy, that KB reminds me it was just three years ago on this same date Dion, his first wife, had passed. And just like that, this little boy's life had more meaning than we knew. Again, remembering the prophet speaking many things over his life, saying that he would be a preacher and that he would be unique, and his life was going to be a blessing. I am holding on to the prophetic word in anticipation for what is to come and already see it manifested.

Three years ago, this day was a day of grief because of death. A very special woman left here and left KB a widower. A whirlwind of events has taken place since then, putting us on this current path. The calmness and relief with this baby were as if God was putting his stamp of approval on the marriage and the family created. I asked God for a sign that there was life in this marriage, and He did. He turned a day remembered for death into a day now remembered for life.

Not for Dion to ever be forgotten. The secret tears that KB has to cry because he doesn't know how to express all of his grief in front of me show she will be remembered. KB loved her, and she was taken too soon, so forgetting her is not an option for anyone in this home.

Especially now that from this moment forward, we will be celebrating the birth of our first newborn son together on this day for the rest of his life. When he is older, he will know who Dion was as well. She will live on through this family.

*Know this:* This is not easy, but it is worth it. I may not see everything clearly now, but I just feel that it is worth it. I'm holding on to that.

The eatery closed, and KB was without stable employment. Not as happy as I originally was on my job when I first started, I want to look for new employment too. While I am the only one with stable income right now, I must be still for the time being. Trying to get on maternity leave and getting short-term disability insurance with my current director, who was once very sweet and nice to me, turned into more difficulty than I desired. Everything seems hard. Nothing at all comes easy for me right now, and I am trying to understand why.

I am doing what God instructed me to do. Why does it seem like everything is fighting against me doing what is right? If God wants us to do right, why doesn't he make it easy for us? Why does it have to be hardships? I wonder in my flesh, would life be better if I did things differently? I already know the answer to the question, yet I ask.

I have married the man God prepared for me. I work in the church and help as much as I can with everyone that I can. I even helped some get jobs—to my disappointment. From drug addicts to lazy, no call, no show, I have been embarrassed and humiliated on this job. Trying to assist people, young and old, retain employment has been a letdown.

I put my name on the line to get people jobs, only for them to not show up because they are sicker than sick but weren't sick on Sunday at church. If one wasn't sick, I had another just not show up because they needed to be at the hospital with their baby daddy's mom, who was sick. They weren't sick, their baby's daddy wasn't sick, but their baby daddy's mom was sick. They didn't need medical attention, but their baby daddy's mom did. She wasn't dying. She wasn't having surgery. This was just an excuse not to come to work. So if one wasn't lying about their illness or losing hours and money sitting up in the hospital room with their baby daddy's mom, it was the one coming in high as a kite with the Bmore crackhead lean. Eyes completely shut bent over the stove while cooking. I promised myself I would never use my name to help another person get a job in or out of the church.

These disappointments, along with me always doing work for the church at my job, caused a strain between my director and me, and I really didn't want to be there anymore. I am glad to go on maternity leave and take a break. However, a break in work hours meant a break in my finances as well, and that was the last thing KB and I needed right now.

KB went as far as purchasing vending machines to bring in supplement income. Whatever legal things he had to do, he did to make sure his family had provisions. But why does it have to be so hard? It seems like our finances are getting lower and lower, and just like that, Mr. MarcTrain seems to be living high on the hog. No worries in sight. Everything going well for him—just to plant in my mind once again that I made the wrong decision. I should have moved a little slower before getting in so deep with KB. This is what flesh says, but my spirit reminds me who put KB and me together.

KB's uncle Donald has his own cleaning company called Father and Daughter, and KB decided he wants to use Donald's company as an umbrella to work under. KB decided this was what he wanted to do and bring income into the home, so I support him. He and Donald plan cleaning jobs here and there, and KB was adamant about bringing an income into the home.

I want to show him that I am in his corner and begin doing whatever I can to show him I have his back. I see how hard it is for him to not have a nine-to-five job Monday through Friday, so I need for him to know that we are in this together and that it is not all on him. My prayers are going harder and harder for God to bless us with contracts and jobs to get this cleaning business moving. I need for God to send income to show me that He hears my cry and to show KB that we are not alone.

And just like that, KB has been contracted by a trustee from a sister church to do weekly cleaning of their sanctuary. The look on KB's face to win this and have income coming in was priceless. He even took Zion along as his work partner. Zion was happy to help, and it was another beautiful way KB bonded with him as a father. KB really wanted the job and wanted income coming in, so he took a low pay to get in the door and to show what he could do. Every dollar counts when you are in a struggle.

There is the struggle in our finances, struggle with acceptance in the church, struggle with Mr. MarcTrain, and then here comes Michael. Zion misses his father at times, of course, but is that my fault? Michael knows he can call Zion anytime, and he can do whatever he wants for him with our approval. I know he doesn't like this, but what else was he expecting? What type of woman would I be if I married and let my child's father dictate how my house would run? What type of man would my husband be if he allowed another man to control his home?

I don't want for the rest of my life to have to deal with the bitter father of my son. I want Michael to understand that I hold no hostility towards him for anything that he has said or done to me in my face or behind my back. I have enough relationship issues to deal with without him added to the mix. I want him to know that KB never wanted there to be animosity. KB sees that this boy needs a father, and he is going to be just that. He is not taking the place of Michael, but he is taking the responsibility.

These arguments over the phone are pointless and not necessary at all. I never ask for money; I never even call. I never bother Michael, yet he always seems to find a way to be negative with me. I have moved on without him. Healing from the wounds of my past with him, I say nothing negative about him to his son. He is able to participate in Zion's life, but he feels that he is going to dictate how that will be. The threats no longer work, the nasty, aggressive tones no longer work. The intimidation no longer works.

He should focus on participating in his child's life, not trying to make my life miserable. How is it that I free you from being responsible for a child you helped bring to this earth but come out the bad person? I hear so many stories about women who make life pure misery for the man with whom they had a child. Taking them back and forth to court trying to get their license suspended. Going before the judge to say the child support is not enough. Blasting them, telling everyone how they don't take care of their child. Calling the new woman and cursing her out, threatening her, and attacking her every time they see one another.

None of this is Lillian. None of this is even in my mind. I have no desire to know who is with Michael. I have no interest in fighting anyone. I don't want any money. I don't call his phone for attention. Then the only voice that seems to be a voice of reason is Michael's grandmother, Ms. Suelie. So, of course, she dies.

# CHAPTER 14

# The Love Triangle

The difficulty in the relationship between two human beings who, for some reason, separated is never about the child. Because two people could not fully understand or communicate their feelings across to the other accurately or effectively, they held onto bitterness, frustration, resentment, anger, hurt, and many hateful and negative emotions that eat away at a person from the inside out.

I feel like I need to try to understand where Michael is coming from, but because of my own disappointment with him and everything that he has done to me, I cannot do it objectively. I blame him just as much as he is blaming me. I don't understand how or why he blames me and can't imagine him saying he doesn't understand why I blame him, but maybe he does. Because we don't and won't communicate with each other, we will never get to the bottom of things like we should.

I didn't leave and kidnap my son to hurt Michael. He is my son; I can't kidnap him if I am the sole parent on the birth certificate. I didn't create a great plot to cause him pain and keep him crying like a baby for the rest of his life. I was not a bitter woman that was thinking of the cruelest way to get back at Michael for everything that I felt he did wrong to me during our relationship. I was done with him as he said he was with me. That part of my life is over. He no longer holds a position of importance to me, but he remains and always will be Zion's father. That I cannot change.

No, he never signed the birth certificate, but he is Zion's father. No, we would never be together again, but he is Zion's father. No, I don't feel bad about moving away from him, but he is Zion's father. Moving here to Baltimore, I needed to go on with my life. I was not going to allow a man to dictate the progress and positivity of my future. Michael no longer holds an imaginary chain around my neck. I know he thought over four years ago that I was going to run back to him, but I didn't, and I will never. Me being in a successful marriage and having a successful life this far disproved everything he tried to say negative about me.

After all I have gone through, I don't hold a grudge, but I am disappointed. Ms. Suelie passing away made everything seem like it would never be resolved. I feel an obligation to go to the funeral. I want Zion to see his family and say farewell to her. I don't hate Michael, but he sure shows how much he hates me. I do not ever want Zion to think that I am keeping him away from his family, so we decide to go to the funeral.

Driving to Da Roc, KB and I begin to talk about how God has blessed us. Here we are with three beautiful children making a wonderful family. We may not have all the money we need or all the success we see others possess, but we are a family. We are a happy family. We are a family that will stick together no matter what. I am so glad KB wants to be there with me and not have me go by myself. Zion is anxious, excited, and sad at the same time.

He really didn't know Ms. Suelie closely because he was not there in Da Roc to be around her, but he understood what she represented. She tried her best to make sense out of Michael and my relationship, but at the same time, she was more concerned about her grandson, which meant everything wasn't a fair assessment. She never mistreated me to my face, and she always made sure I ate good when I was with her. I have a lot of respect for her and what she stands for in the family.

We try to get to the church on time for the funeral, but we end up arriving after the family came in. The church, being a small chapel-like sanctuary, is crowded. My mother came with us, and when we come in and are being ushered to a seat, I begin to hear, "There's Lillian," "That's Lillian," "Oh wow, look, that must be Zion." I want to hurry up and sit down to get the attention off me. I end up sitting up close to the front and shed tears for Ms. Suelie as Zion goes over to his father to be with the rest of his family.

I realize I am sitting in front of Michael's oldest son's mother and wonder why she isn't sitting on the other side with the family. I do a silent hello, flashing back to all the times Michael made me out to be the side chick with her, using the excuse if she found out about us that he would never get to see his son. So many times I had run into her, and she never knew who I was. I was sure he was still dating her again, but because I don't keep track and really don't care, I shrug my shoulders and move on.

So glad I don't have to worry if the man I love loves someone else too. I don't have to worry about hiding myself so no other woman will come after me for being with the man she loves. I don't have to wonder if I will ever get past being a fiancé and actually go through with the marriage and live happily ever after. God gave me my love story, so I no longer have to wish or wait. Then Mr. MarcTrain comes to my mind, but I push him right back out. Now is not the time nor the place to give space to my mind to take me through any emotions regarding him.

The service is nice, and because some of Michael's family are my friends and people I have grown up with, I socialize to a minimum to make sure I don't seem cold or standoffish. We didn't plan to stay in the city long. We wanted to come for the funeral and immediately return home. Walking to the car speaking to the cousins and friends, I realize everyone isn't mad at me like I imagined from listening to Michael's reaction to me moving away. Some really act as if they are happy to see me, especially since it has been years since our last encounter.

I finally see Michael, and our eyes meet. He greets KB, and when he comes to me, we reach out to each other, and he hugs me. He hugs me tight. He hugs me with no barriers and doesn't let go. As I hug him back, my mind flashes to all the times we were together, and he emptied out all his emotions about his son's mom. I remember those moments we talked about his dad disappointing him and leaving him feeling abandoned. My mind goes to all the times tears were shed because he was disappointed with his mom and the way life would hit hard.

I squeeze as he squeezes. I feel in that moment the pain he is feeling, knowing what Ms. Suelie meant to him. Someone asked the question, "Can you forgive someone that has hurt you, someone who has done things to you considered unforgivable?" My answer, in that moment, is yes. I don't care about what has been done to me or said about me in that moment. My prayer was that Michael would live through the pain and grow.

I agreed to let Zion go back to the house with them so that he could spend a few moments before we get back on the road. KB, mom, and I decided to go to a family favorite, Friendly's, and eat there. KB is being so up close and personal with me. He made sure that I looked beautiful and told me so too. He made sure the car was cleaned and in good working order. He made sure that there was nothing that we needed or wanted. A real man. A real man making sure all who was watching knew that Lillian Nowlin-Hunt is well taken care of and is in need of *nothing* from Da Roc. I love him.

I am glad that I was able to be there and glad Zion was able to be with his family. I am glad I was able to hug Michael and be the bigger person showing that I do care. I am also glad to show that I have moved on and am not hard up for any relationship ties with Michael. I am glad everyone was able to see that Zion and I were being well taken care of by the fine man the Lord has blessed to be in our life. My after-a-third-child body is somewhat on point, and I am feeling good and looking good. I guess there was a part of me that wanted Michael to see what he messed up and missed out on. The way I care for my children, cling to my husband, and live for God was a woman he could have had, but not anymore—not this one at least. That chapter is closed. Just as Michael sees the happiness created, so does everyone else, including Mr. MarcTrain.

*Know this:* There will be moments when you think bigger of yourself than you should. Be prepared for the moment after, when you and your big pride can easily come to shame.

There is a difference between loving someone and being in love. I had to realize that. Getting married to KB immediately after Dion died never gave us time to fall in love, but we loved one another. I have been in enough relationships to know that I cannot make a man fall in love with me, so I don't even try. How could KB be in love with me when the woman he was in love with just died. They didn't break up; they didn't get a divorce; they didn't separate. The only reason they are not together today is she is not alive.

That feeling of being in love with someone does not automatically go away. I know I am not Dion, and I do not pretend to be. I wouldn't even try to be her or take on any habits of hers that made KB fall in love with her because he has to be in love with me being me, not me trying to be her. I am not upset, and I clearly understand how he feels. He wouldn't be an honest man if he didn't still have feelings for Dion. Their relationship was cut short. The ending not planned caught him off guard. Yes, the Bible says, "till death do us part," but that doesn't mean the feelings are immediately buried with the body.

KB cannot just blot out all memory of Dion. He can't just enjoy life with me and act as if she never existed. I loved Dion too, so pictures of her were not thrown away. Her belongings weren't given to goodwill, and all things concerning her weren't erased from the planet earth. KB needs to be able to speak freely on his emotions regarding her. He needs to be able to see things and hold on to whatever he wants that will help him to heal. Whenever he has a grief episode, he has to see that I freely give him that moment without hesitation. I not only give him that moment, but he chooses if he wants me to be a part of that moment or not.

I want to be the person he knows he can talk to about Dion and know that I will not be jealous. He already sees and knows that I cannot and will not compare myself to her. We already have enough people doing that. People who didn't have too many words for Dion while she was alive now are the ones who bring her name up more than KB does. Every time family or friends begin to talk about Dion or mention anything regarding her, I embrace the conversation. Individuals may do it to harm me, but what they fail to realize is that she was my friend/sister too. When her name is mentioned, it gives me a chance to smile at memories also, instead of making me insecure. I accept that Dion was who she was, and I am who I am, and there should be no comparison.

So now, KB has the task of loving me, falling in love with me, and making a family with me because God said so. Something like a prearranged marriage of the olden times. I am not the woman he dreamed of being with for the rest of his life. I am not the woman he fantasized about or with whom he prepared to create a family. I have given him children, a daughter and a son, but this was not his game plan. Not with me. Because God was the one who told him to marry me, I can't feel like a second choice, but I will obviously always know I was not his first.

The same way I know being in love with me wasn't the plan KB had for his life, being in love with KB certainly wasn't my plan either. Because I knew that God was orchestrating this union, I didn't fight it physically, but mentally, in my mind, I am still trying to understand how I can be in love with one man and married to another.

Did I just admit that? Did I really just say how I feel? I have had to admit to KB that I am not in love, but the love I have for him I have never had for any man ever—not even the man I feel that I am still in love with. This is confusing, and I want to find the underlying cause of it for the last time. I am tired of feeling the way that I feel and never saying it to anyone. I need help, I want help, but I don't know who to go to.

If I tell anyone, they will think I am cheating on my husband. If I say something, everyone will think I married KB for the wrong reasons. I don't want to be looked down on because of feelings I had no control over in a situation I did not create. What I feel with KB I have never in my life felt before. There is a freedom with KB I did not have with anyone before. Everything concerning KB is a new experience. The way he takes care of my body. The way he takes his time creating symphonies with me—they are all original ballads.

Spiritually, KB is concerned about my soul. KB proves his love for God by being obedient to God, marrying me when he had no previous desires for me. KB and I have battled in the trenches together to keep our family whole. He has proven he has my back, and I have proven that I have his also.

But then there is Mr. MarcTrain. He tells me he still loves me. His mom tells me he still loves me and is in love with me. I must admit I am still in love with him too. They both call me while I am at work; I find myself going into the conference room, shutting the door so no one will hear my conversation.

I just need to understand why I am still in love with this man after all God has put in place for me. Why do I hang on to the desire to hear his voice over the phone telling me he loves me and he wants me back?

Not telling KB about this confirms that it is wrong, yet I still won't tell. It feels good to know that Mr. MarcTrain cannot live without me and still wants me in his life. He makes his reason for calling me to be about the car payments, but we both know he just wants to hear my voice just as I want to hear his. More and more, I dive into false thoughts that maybe there is a chance he and I are still supposed to be together. He wants it, and a part of me that wanted it years ago still lingers.

How is it that I want KB to talk to me about the woman he loved so I can help him heal, but I cannot share what I feel in my heart? We both lost the persons we thought we would spend the rest of our life with. The difference is Dion has passed, and Mr. MarcTrain is still alive. I still have a chance to make that dream come true, or do I?

Being sensitive to the fact your husband is a widower. His wife didn't cheat, and they didn't get a divorce. The marriage wasn't horrible to help him be glad it was over. Their life of happily ever after had just begun, and there was no major trouble besides her illness. I moved to Maryland and fell madly in love with a man who was the best friend I could ever have. We didn't stop seeing each other because he cheated or told me he wanted to be with someone else. Even with all his history and baggage, our relationship ended because I said to him God told another man to marry me and make me his wife. Just like that, I ended what was my dream and desire since I moved to Baltimore. I was waiting for Mr. MarcTrain to put a ring on my finger, but KB did instead. How do you handle a man missing another woman? And you are missing another man.

Mr. MarcTrain calls me at work to tell me he has purchased a home in Baltimore. He wants me to leave my husband, take my children, and move with him. He promises to love my children and me unconditionally and take care of me for the rest of my life. This is all I ever wanted with the man I wanted it. I have been married for some years now and have children, so his love for me should have died away if it wasn't real, right?

Why is it that this man is telling me he still loves me after all these years and children later? Why is he so willing to take my children and me and provide for us as he has always promised? Why didn't he just secure the relationship before the wedding if he really wanted me? Did things not work out with someone else, and now he wants to pursue me again? Did he try to make his last relationship work, then realized she would never be me? "What is really going on?" is my question, and I need answers.

God allowing me to give birth to Kendrick on the day Dion died was a sign that I asked for. I wanted God to show me that this marriage was not dead, that it was not a mistake, and He did. Of all the days for our baby to be born, January 22nd was the day he came and changed our life. Since then, KB has been showing more and more love to me, making me feel like a queen, and us investing in our marriage together made my love grow stronger and stronger. I want KB to know he doesn't have to hide his feelings, especially because he is always so concerned about mine. Wow. After all he has gone through, all he has lost, all the changes that have taken place in his life, he is concerned about me and my feelings. Over everything, he is concerned about me, and that's when I fell in love.

I fell in love with a man that I never dated, was never attracted to, and was never interested in. He took me from a place of insecurity and uncertainty to a place of safety and assurance. With God orchestrating it all, we have come this far and now not just love but are in love. I'm in love with the way he makes me feel like a queen. I'm in love with the way he shows strength taking care of the family. I'm in love with the way he makes me laugh; he makes me smile. I'm in love with the way he makes me feel so important to him.

I'm most certainly in love with the way he satisfies me. He takes his time making love to every part of me. I'm in love with how he makes me feel like he can't get enough of me. He makes sure that pleasure isn't one-sided but that we both are pleased and more satisfied than I could imagine. Even in the tough times, I'm in love with the way he wants to assure me that everything will be all right and not to worry. I'm in love with the way he took on the responsibility of being a father to my son and raising him as his own. I'm in love with how he is not afraid to take on the challenge of father to Zion, knowing that Michael exists with a bitter taste in his mouth. He is everything to me, and finally, I can say I am in love with the man I am married to.

So why am I listening to Mr. MarcTrain plan the way to leave my husband? Why am I allowing him to continue to tell me that he cannot live without me and that he wants me? Why am I entertaining the thought of walking away from everything God has put together in my life? Mr. MarcTrain being so persistent, lets me know that he will not allow anything to happen to my children or me. He promises me that everything will be just fine and that, over time, KB will be all right once I leave.

So here I am at the address he sent to me. In my car, I hesitate but get out anyway and walk to the front door of the house. As I am approaching the house, the door opens, and there he is—Mr. MarcTrain is there to greet me as if he is welcoming me home.

CHAPTER 15

# Free Identity

KB and I realized that there were some things that we needed to change to make our marriage better. One thing was we
agreed we are not just a part of the Hunt family, but that we are
a Hunt family. There were family traditions and routines that
worked and were beneficial at one point, but with us having our
own children and more than one side of the family, we needed
to begin our own family memories. Since being married, I have
forfeit going home to Rochester to be with my mom, brother
and sisters, and the rest of the crew for some holidays when
times before I spent every one of them together.

Most times, it was because we could not afford to make the
trip and had nothing to do with anything else. Yet because we
live in the same city as KB's parents, there is no cost to spend
holidays with them. We see his parents on a regular basis, so
there is never a birthday present missed, gifts for Christmas, or
any other holiday forgotten. With my family, if we are not going up to see them, there really is no urgency to get a gift. More
time and energy is on those we see on the regular.

Holidays are and always will be a special time of the year that
I love, but with KB's mother having a birthday during the same
time, holidays were not about Kenneth and Lillian Hunt family,

but whatever everyone else wanted it to be as long as we were all together. I just wanted to have moments when it was just us. I want KB and I to be able to pick and choose if we are going to go somewhere or not for Thanksgiving and Christmas. I don't want to feel like if I say I want to stay home and cook or if I want my family to come to my home or if we are able to afford to go home, it should not be a problem. It didn't work out that way.

There is a congestedness that I feel with KB's family, and I don't know how to address it. Every family decision seems made through his parents, and I do not get a word in. I cannot live my life feeling as if I am a robot completing commands instead of actually living life with my husband and family. When I tried to express my concern years ago, it didn't work out for me, so I was left disappointed.

Like a whirlwind, KB's father sat us down one night and went up one side of me and down the other after accusing me of saying certain things that I did not say. I was unable to defend myself, and I was looking for my husband to have my back. I had to retune my ears after listening to the scolding I received based on an untruth. Instead of being able to talk, I was shut down. After saying that their children were raised to respect their mother, talking down to me as if I had no right to say anything, I felt like trash. Hurt and feeling attacked, I couldn't understand what happened. I kept telling KB I didn't say the things I was just accused of saying, and I couldn't understand why he didn't step in and stop his dad from jumping on me in that way.

I learned that day who I would never have a conversation with alone again. I had to learn who would never be someone that I would go to and talk or express myself. I was lied on and attacked for no reason and initially did not want to ever be around them again.

I think about my husband. This man that I just married, I am trying to be in love with. I cannot allow what his family does to stop me from trying with him. I don't want him to feel he made a bad choice in marrying me. I never want to embarrass him or make him ashamed in any way ever. I most certainly don't want him to think I disrespected anyone in his family. It was important to me that KB and his sister know that what was being said was not true. The only problem with that was telling the truth proving what was said was false would mean that I was calling someone a liar. So I humbled myself, cried, and took it. I hear people saying, "You are the daughter-in-law, not the queen, do not dare cross," so I stay in my place and say not another word.

I was angry at KB because I felt the same way his father defended his mother with something that was not true; he could have done the same for me while speaking the truth. It was hurtful talking to me as if I was improperly raised and not good enough for this family. When Christmas came around that year, I got the ugliest jean jacket as a gift from another family member, which was like an exclamation point on the matter. That day I learned the dramatics I was dealing with and knew to govern myself accordingly.

I have no control over my own life is how I feel. I have no say in the raising of my children, holidays, or any other matter. If I express this, it will only bother my husband, so I keep it to myself and choose to act as if everything is okay. To add insult to injury, every young girl at the church considers themselves a daughter, and I am constantly reminded that I am not a true daughter, but they are. I am retold that I just got here and that all others have been in my husband's life long before me. It is repeated that I am only a Hunt because of marriage and nothing more. I take it and say nothing, knowing I want to punch sense into some. I act as if I am good with it and move on in my own way. However, I wonder why I should have to take this.

I have been hit by family, church, and friends, and lingering in the background is an escape route to get away from all of this that I do not deserve to have to go through. Mr. MarcTrain hears and knows all about it and is that knight in shining armor telling me that life will be better with him. I would not have to worry about what the church or the family has to say about me if I remove myself from both.

It is so easy to go to where you know you will be loved instead of trying to understand why you are not accepted where you are. The feeling of rejection drives you insane. Why must I feel precluded with everything? It seems as if I am only seen as family when convenient. If there is a sermonic solo, an assignment to complete for the church, having the babies of the family to keep the family bloodline flowing, I may be included briefly.

I am in love with KB, though. I have fallen in love with him through all that I have had to go through with everything in our life. No, I don't think he defended me like I wanted him to in the past, but I know he loves me and is in love with me because he has stuck through everything with me this far.

*Know this:* There is a haunting question that never seems to go away. Can you truly be in love with two people at the same time?

I don't know how to tell KB how I feel about things that have happened in the family these past few years that we have been married, but I know I want to move past it all. There is no need to hold on to it. I never got the opportunity to love on my grandfather like I wanted to, so it is important to me that my children do. I need them to know their grandparents, even my own father. If that means me looking past things that don't sit well with me, that is what I will do. I love my family, and the God in me will help me through everything that I may not understand. Right?

There is no need for me to try to blame what is happening right now on the things that I have had to endure since getting married to KB. I can say that I am here at this house right now because I was hurt by the family that I newly joined. I can say that I thought the church was supposed to be a place of peace, not competition and strife. I can say that I am here because I feel like I have no one else that will understand what I am feeling or going through right now. But the real reason I am here right now is that I want to be here.

Once again, I feel like I am at a crossroads, and there is a decision that will need to be finalized once and for all. I needed to see Mr. MarcTrain face to face. I want to look him in his eyes. I want to see his smile that always melted my heart. I want to stand in front of him and know for a certainty what I feel is really what I feel. I want to know if he is stringing me along or he really has a plan for a future with me this time.

As I walk up to the door, Mr. MarcTrain smiles. His smile makes me smile. It is good to see him, to know that he is still doing well. Yes, we talked via telephone, but never face to face after my getting married. He looks the same, and as we embrace, his body feels the same. As it was in times past, him being such a big guy and me tiny, I get lost in his arms. He holds me tight, and I feel every emotion he has been holding. The hug lasts longer than usual, but that is to be expected.

As we stand and stare at each other, the silence has to be broken. I compliment him on his nice home, and of course, he lets me know it could be mine as well. And so it begins. We needed to unload. We needed to address all of the open wounds. Why I would so easily leave and marry someone I had absolutely no feelings for. Why I would give up everything we had planned to go into a marriage of uncertainty. Clearly, Mr. MarcTrain felt I had made the wrong decision and is giving me an opportunity to correct my bad choice.

Then there is silence again. My heart, beating so fast, unsure of how I should feel in the moment. I stay silent. Mr. MarcTrain again lets me know that my children and I will be fine with him. We would be a blended family, but of course, everyone would be loved the same. Everything he is promising is everything I ever wanted with him. Everything he is saying is all I ever wanted to hear from him. Mr. MarcTrain was the man I desired to be with for the rest of my life. Of all the men I have ever had a relationship with, Mr. MarcTrain surpassed them with his love, compassion, and care for me.

He was the one. There could or would never be another. To find love like this in your lifetime is rare. To find love like this is astonishing. To find love nowadays' period is quite amazing. Here we are. Two adults, affectionately caring for each other and seeming to fit like a hand and glove. Mr. MarcTrain had let me slip through his fingers once, but this time he had a good grip and was not willing to let me go easily.

Mr. MarcTrain so willingly volunteers to tell KB that I am leaving him and taking the children with me. He wants to stand by my side as I break the news to KB that I had made a mistake marrying him and that my heart and true love was Mr. Marc-Train. For some reason, I can only listen and not say anything. Over his voice, I hear another.

I came to this house today for some type of finality. I needed to have closure. I needed to make things permanent. I explain to Mr. MarcTrain that KB and I plan to take the children up to the Massanutten Resort for a family trip. Everything is set for the weekend to have some fun with the kids. With everything going on at church, the job, and a new baby at home, KB said we needed to get away. Mr. MarcTrain is unhappy with my response to him, but that is all I can say. The voice I am hearing is very clear and to the point. I came for closure, and that was exactly what I was about to get.

I tell Mr. MarcTrain that I will be in touch with him and that I need to leave. He doesn't want to let me go, and for some reason, my eyes don't want to stop looking at him, as if it was going to be my last time seeing him. He again wants to assure me that if I need him to be with me when I talk to KB that he is willing. My phone rings, and it is one of the women from the church. She needs my assistance with something and asks me,

"Can you hear me? Are you okay?" Right then, I know what I need to do by myself as I reply that I can hear loud and clear.

Driving down the road, I know this is exactly what I wanted, and now I feel anxious to be finally resolving this. KB and I had been up to our necks with bills and had decided to do a refinance on the house. KB had purchased the house for close to nothing, and equity in the home made it almost three times the purchase amount. With the monies, KB paid his car loan off, and we paid up other bills. With everything at my job surprisingly going bad between the director, who I was at one time really close with, and me, we didn't know how much longer I would be there. This refinanced money was going to help us stay above water in the event something went wrong.

Yeah. KB and I had a plan, but then I came to see Mr. Marc-Train. I don't know how I got here, but suddenly I'm home. My mind, so preoccupied, I didn't even know what route I took to get here. I come home, get the children's clothes together, and make sure that I am not leaving anything I need behind. I love my children and want the best for them. I want them to know that any and everything I do, I have them and their best interest in mind. I also realize that my life is not my own, and the voice I have been hearing was very specific. As I get the children in the car and all buckled in, I am ready to release. I had heard all I needed to hear, felt all I needed to feel, and was ready to liberate myself from it all.

KB gets in the driver's seat, and we are off to Virginia. All I can do is look at him and stare. The entire way to Virginia, my mind is on the voice I heard and the events that have taken place. Thinking about how things just went down and what I am supposed to do from here. Thinking about everything Mr. MarcTrain shared and the future he has planned. I sit quietly and begin to let it all sink in. I have never been one to make rash decisions unless absolutely necessary. This was necessary! Looking out the window at the beautiful scenery, I begin to think about my life and everything that has happened this far.

God has truly been good to me and allowed me to experience and go through many things when others would have given up. Many things that have happened in my life I am still trying to figure out how in the world I was chosen to be blessed like this. Every blessing God had ever allowed me to receive came across my mind—including meeting Mr. MarcTrain and marrying KB.

One of the most significant things that have happened in my life is that God's spirit truly has set residence in me. Because He dwells in me, there is a difference that cannot be ignored. God showed me He has a purpose for my life, and in order to live out that purpose, I must go through some things. I told God yes years ago, and He is going to take full advantage of that "yes" and use me how He sees fit. Had I not been sincere in saying yes, many things I have faced, including this situation right now, would not have played out well for me. I thought I was go-ing to Mr. MarcTrain's house for answers and closure, but God had an entirely different plan in mind. Hearing His voice speak to me let me know He really was real.

Telling KB that I have to tell him something is probably not a good idea, but I do. Of course, KB, being himself, wants to know immediately, but I don't want to talk in front of the chil-dren in the car. The drive to the resort seems long, as if we are never going to get there. But finally, we arrive. After getting the children situated, eating, having some fun, it is time for KB and I to be alone and talk.

KB needed to hear what I had to say without distraction. I begin to tell KB that I am still in love with Mr. MarcTrain. I have to tell him that the reason I shut down at times is I cannot understand why I am in love with one man and married to another. KB's face is in pure distraught. KB sits still to hear me say that Mr. MarcTrain is prepared to take care of the children and me and that I am his first choice and always would be. Leaving nothing unsaid, I tell him about Mr. MarcTrain calling and checking on me, being concerned about my health and me during pregnancies and my overall wellbeing. It is important that I leave nothing out. It is important I express everything that is on my mind.

KB is disappointed in me to find out I had gone to Mr. Marc-Train's home. Feeling betrayed, he wants to know everything that happened and how it happened. It is not my desire for him to feel betrayed, but I understand. The last thing I want to do is hurt KB, especially now. Anything could have happened to me, and anything could have happened with me. I am his wife, not his girlfriend, not a "baby momma." His reaction shows just how much he really does love me and is in love with me too. I tell KB the truth that I did not have sex with Mr. MarcTrain, although there was an opportunity. I went there for closure. I went there to end a chapter of my life. I went there truly to say goodbye to feelings that were clouding my mind.

People allow relationships to end but will have some type of string stay attached in the event they want to rekindle. I had to let KB know that I now understood while it was not the brightest idea going to Mr. MarcTrain's home, I really needed closure. I also needed KB to know that there was no secret romantic relationship going on. I must reassure him that I have not been married to him all this time while sneaking off to see another man. This was my opportunity and time to decide on how I was going to spend the rest of my life, and I was glad to be free to say exactly what I wanted.

What I want is for God to be pleased with me. I need Him to be pleased with my life. The life He has given to me, I do not take for granted. I realize that I do not have to be here, and all that I have and I am today does not have to exist but for the grace of God. So I tell KB everything because I am a true woman of God. I tell KB everything because I fear God. I tell KB everything because I am in love with him and him only. I tell KB everything because I do not want any secrets. I tell KB everything because I realize Satan is a deceiver and the father of lies.

Maybe choosing never to talk to Mr. MarcTrain again would have been good enough. I didn't have to tell KB. What would I do if KB no longer has trust in me? What would I do if things became worse? KB would have never known if I had not said anything. I could have gone on, and absolutely no one, not even Bunch, would know. The church, family, and friends would never get this ammunition to use against me. This is the last thing that I need. The only thing about that is God sees, and God knows. God was right there with me, standing in Mr. MarcTrain's home.

Telling KB everything that had taken place was the best release in the world. The need to see Mr. MarcTrain or even thinking there was something there for me to run back to came from me never expressing how I really felt. The Holy Spirit guided me into seeing how this was nothing but a trap. The Holy Spirit spoke clearly to me and gave me exactly what I needed. No man willfully accepts rejection as it seemed I had done to Mr. Marc-Train. While I felt that he had rejected me by not fighting for me, he felt I rejected him by actually marrying KB. Two children later, and Mr. MarcTrain still wants me, or does he want something else?

*Know this*: When a woman feels rejected, most times, she wants to get even, but sometimes, some women just want closure. When a man feels rejected, he wants revenge.

Looking into Mr. MarcTrain's eyes, I saw what I needed to see. More than love for me, there was a sense of displeasure for KB. How can you embrace this man's children and me when really you are upset that for the past few years, he has been living the life you planned for yourself? I asked God to show me, and He did more than that. He also let me feel what I needed to feel to be free.

# DIARY 4

# Emotions

Life is full of emotions. Emotions, a natural instinctive state of mind deriving from one's circumstances, mood, or relationships with others. Depending on what is going on in life, your emotions will change. Your emotions go with the mood, the path, and the direction of your life. Emotions express your feelings. Emotions display your real being. Emotions are your responses to internal and external issues and events that happen in your life. Joy, sadness, excitement, anger, surprise, disgust, fear, guilt, and then shame. Those are my emotions. Those are my feelings. While I know I must be careful when, where, and how I express these emotions, each one of them is real. Each one must be dealt with. Each one is a part of me. Each one has an impact on my life.

It is said over and over again that women are emotional beings. I just named a few of mine. Joy when things are going my way and happening to make my life better. Joy when things are running smoothly, and I can breathe easily. Joy when I look at my husband and children and see that I have a blessed life. But then the joy is short-lived and turns to sadness.

Sadness because everyone doesn't want me to have joy. Sadness because of the shortages and the struggles. Sadness when you feel like you are hated. Sadness turns into excitement when in the midst of hate, there is a breakthrough. Excitement to know that what you have been told you could never be, you begin to see a glimpse of a possibility to be more than that.

Excitement turns into anger as you realize you have been fed lies about yourself, and lies have been said about you because of your excitement. Anger as you see no matter what you do and who you are to people, there will always be someone hating you for no reason at all. Anger because you want to reply and defend yourself, but you can't. Anger because you just want to be happy. Anger because you cannot express or articulate your desires for a peaceful life. Anger then becomes surprise.

Surprised that the people you thought you could trust you can't, and the ones you thought you couldn't trust you can. Surprised that regardless of all the mistakes you have made in your life, you are still standing. Surprised at the way you were able to go through things that were meant to break you, but they made you stronger. It's no surprise that another emotion is disgust!

Disgusted at the way people treat you because of the family you have married into and the blessed union God specifically ordained for you. Disgusted at the fact that no matter how many flaws and emotions you have about what others have done towards you, you must be honest about your own imperfections. Disgusted at the poor choices you made that could ruin everything good you have going for you. Disgusted with the things I allowed to happen in my life and affect my marriage. Disgusted with my failures.

Fear. I'm afraid everyone will choose to never get to know the real me and accept the rumors about me. Fear that if they knew the real me, they would still hate me. Fear that I will never be loved or even liked. Fear that I can never be accepted or included as someone of value. Fear that everything I have been given will be taken away from me. Fear that the man that says he is following what God told him to do will have second thoughts and want to call it quits.

So then comes the guilt. Feeling guilty that I left Da Roc to live here in Baltimore. Guilty that I could not make peace with Zion's father no matter how I tried. Guilty that I have mixed KB into the drama that was never resolved. Guilty that I was in love but not sure if the feelings were for the right person. Guilty that everything that is happening to me is all my fault. Guilt over my past that keeps coming up to haunt me and possibly destroy my marriage.

So, of course, with guilt comes the shame. I am a failure. I tried to be a good mother doing all I could to give my son a better life. Here now, with more children, I am ashamed that they will never be able to say they have a great mom. Shame is all I feel as I must admit that I married someone I didn't know how to love. Shame that I can't speak up and say how I feel. I must confess I am not good enough to be this man's wife. Yet, I still live this life.

Emotions.

# CHAPTER 16

# God's Choice

Yes, I have love for Mr. MarcTrain; he has always been a true friend. He was there for me when it seemed no one else was. He always knows just what to say and how to say it and when to say it too. Nevertheless, he is not who God has for me. He is not what God wanted me to be entangled with. Saying that I am a woman of God and that God's spirit dwells inside of me is one thing, but what was I doing at an ex-lover's home? I am a married woman.

Many women and men, saved and unsaved, have found themselves in similar situations. Some make one choice, while some make another. I needed to understand why God had me here and what the purpose was. The scripture Hebrews 4:15 comes to mind, "For we have not an high priest which cannot be touched with the feeling of our infirmities; but was in all points tempted like as we are, yet without sin." Over and over again, you hear stories of infidelity, and you wonder why. Especially in the church when people are supposed to know better.

Many people say an affair just happened. They didn't mean it, but one thing led to another, and they had no control. I beg to differ. God allowed KB and me to go through this for many reasons, but most importantly, to discredit anyone who says that they had no choice in being unfaithful. If I was able to go over to Mr. MarcTrain's home, make love to him, and plan to leave my husband, then there would be a few things about me that would be true. One would be that I am truly in love with Mr. MarcTrain and not KB. Two would be that I have no respect for myself as a woman. Three would be the God I say dwells inside of me really does not—just to name a few.

But I did not degrade myself. I could have, but I didn't. I did not become unfaithful to my husband. I could have, but I didn't. I was tempted but would not commit adultery. I could have, but I didn't. I never want to have the story that another man knows what it is like to have been with Lillian Hunt. No man on this earth outside of KB can say they knew Lillian Hunt. Lillian Hunt is the wife of Kenneth Hunt, affectionately known as KB, short for Kenny Black. She has too much respect for herself and her husband to carry the title of wife and behave like a vixen.

When you really have the spirit of God, you will allow Him to guide you. You will listen to Him when He speaks, and you will get the understanding that you need. I was no longer in love with Mr. MarcTrain, and God needed me to see that clearly. I had a desire for the fantasy to live happily ever after, and the deceiver wanted me to believe that someway somehow, that happily ever after could only happen with Mr. MarcTrain. All of the ingredients were already there, the emotions, the history, the opportunity. All we needed to do was to put it all in the oven and let it cook. I chose to abort. I chose to listen to God. I chose to be the woman God called me to be, not the woman the deceiver wanted me to ruin my life as.

In Mr. MarcTrain's home, I stayed silent, and God showed me if I cheated on my husband, it would affect more than me. God would have forgiven me, and maybe KB would have too, but this one act would ruin my witness. If I had become romantic with Mr. MarcTrain, the divine union of KB and I would be voided. I would have been no better than my father or the woman he married.

While KB is clearly upset, he must understand God allowed it to go this far, knowing that I would not cross the line, even though the chance was there. I was tempted like many before and after me, yet without sin. God wanted to use me as an example that the Holy Spirit is real. God wanted to show His way is better than ours. He wants us to see and to know that His decisions for our life exceed what we think we want and need.

I had to let go of the dream of a happy ending with Mr. MarcTrain because God is giving a better ending with KB. I was feeling as if I would always be a second choice to KB instead of Mr. MarcTrain's first choice, and God wanted to change my perspective. First of all, God wanted me to see that everyone who brings up KB's first wife Dion is not bringing her name up to remember her, but more so to remind me that I am a "second" fiddle. The enemy used this to build the case as to why I should not stay around and go where I am without question number one.

I was never in competition with Dion—she is deceased. I accepted being second and was adjusting myself. It made me fall back into believing the negativity that I used to hear about myself spoken by the men in my past. Nobody would ever think I was good enough to make an honest woman out of me. This is why how Mr. MarcTrain felt for me was so important to me. With KB, being second wasn't really helping me feel like I was special to him. With tears in my eyes, God had to explain to me that I was not KB's second. KB loved Dion, and that would never be disputed.

His heart was with her, and now he is with me. My heart was with Mr. MarcTrain, and now I am with KB. No one has ever taunted KB with the existence of Mr. MarcTrain because he was automatically a better choice for me in the eyes of everyone who thought their opinion mattered. But he too had to fall in love with me, just like I had to fall in love with him. Tears flowing, I asked God how this is supposed to happen when he has been married before; there is no doubt I am his second. I wasn't married; he would be my first husband. He had no competition. God replied to me I didn't either. He clearly spoke to me. Dion was KB's first wife, yes, but that has nothing to do with me. I'm not a second choice; I'm God's choice.

God wanted us to see how easy it was to fall into a snare. He wanted us to understand that this could not and would not be tolerated if we were to be His servants. When I walked out of Mr. MarcTrain's door and got into my car, I felt like this would be the last day I would see him. The feeling of being in love was left there. The thought of what if was left there. Any open ties or connections were left there.

Crying to KB, I realize this is not easy to hear, but it has to happen. KB needed to know that this body, my body, is his body, and no other man has touched or will touch it as long as we both shall live. With every thrust, I am proud to be God's choice. With every moan, I accept being in love with one man—

the one God chose for me. Perfectly fitting, KB lets out his frustration through loving me, forgiving me for not talking to him or telling him how I felt before.

God was warning us never to go this way or attempt to be unfaithful. We must stay on the right path. God was also using us to prove that being unfaithful is a conscious decision many make, but then say they did not mean for it to happen. No one has ever made me feel like KB does, and I know for sure now no one ever will. God was showing us that we are all we both need because we are His choice!

*Know this:* Telling your husband you were at another man's house can turn out really, really bad. All the spiritual revelation was needed and is fine. But at the end of the day, husbands don't play that!

Enjoying the rest of our stay in the mountains with our children, we give thanks for God keeping our family together. I make the promise to KB that I will not willfully have any interaction with Mr. MarcTrain, and if there is any contact in any way, I will immediately let him know. We cry; we make love; we forgive, then KB lays the rules down, and I have no problem adhering to every single one of them. He looks at me and loves me, saying he knows he is in love with me, and this was meant to be because I didn't have to tell him. He respects that I want him to know everything.

I think of all of those movies that come out about married couples having secrets. When the secret comes out and chaos starts, I always look back at the point in the movie when they should have just told what happened. Not telling it all leaves the opportunity for something else to happen, something worse, and I was not willing to be a part of that, especially after the Holy Spirit warned me what I was feeling and thinking was a trap.

Preparing to leave the resort, KB and I were stunned about the events but happy we had come out of it whole. This was our first time at Massanutten together and as a family, and now we have this to remember it by. What kind of woman would I have been had I given my body to Mr. MarcTrain? How could KB ever want to look at me again? Thank God I have self-respect, self-control, and most importantly, the spirit of God. Thank God my husband has the spirit of God as well. I reflect back and realize things could have gone another way, but because KB loved and trusted God, there was peace.

On our way out, driving through the mountains, KB is driving slow. All of a sudden, coming down the right side of the mountain, we see a black bear. KB presses on breaks, and we just stare at it as it crosses the street right in front of us, looking at us but going on its way. It was as if that was God warning us both again, *"Do not get off the path* or be prepared to be mulled by a bear!"* Neither one of us had ever seen a black bear up close nor personal like that. It was scary, but at the same time, amazing. It was like God was saying, "Just in case you didn't hear Me the first time, I am always watching." We hear You, Lord!

I knew there was something on KB's mind, and I wanted him to share with me the same way I had shared and was honest with him. No man wants to have this story that their wife told them she went to another man's house. He doesn't want to look like he has been played. He knew I wouldn't lie and didn't lie when I told him nothing happened, but at the same time, a man is a man. KB's mindset was this man was trying to take away the wife that was God's choice for him. KB looked at Mr. MarcTrain now as a threat that needed to be addressed. As much as he is a man of God, KB is also a man of the streets. We need to go to Walmart before we get on the road, and KB gets me out of the car and tells me to call Mr. MarcTrain and tell him to never call me again.

As I dial his number, my heart is beating fast, but I am in a state of peace. All I have to do is remember that black bear to understand God's message to us was real, and there cannot and will not be any loose ends. Mr. MarcTrain answers the phone, happy to hear my voice. He says he was worried because he didn't know what happened to me; all he knew was that I was going to the mountains and would be telling my husband what was on my heart. He didn't know if I had told KB that I was leaving him, and then KB decided to kill me in the woods or what happened.

I say to him that I am in love with my husband and with my husband only and that he needs not to call me ever again. I tell him I will not call him again and that I am deleting his number. Any interaction dealing with my car would have to be between him and KB only without me anywhere in the picture. KB wanted to let him know we were a united front and that nothing was going to break up this marriage. I hang up fine with knowing that is possibly my last time ever hearing Mr. MarcTrain's voice again.

Going home, KB and I realized we needed to make some changes and adjustments to our life, starting with our home. Doing some small renovations, we put the house on the market.

It was time that we gave up the house and moved on, starting fresh with everything. We settled into knowing we were going to be a family for life, in love with each other making a family together. It was time we got a home that both of us could say was ours that had no previous history. I only had a few months left on the car payment, so we would be completely rid of Mr. MarcTrain as well.

Excited about moving, we are staging the home for house viewings. Hoping that during one of these open house events, we get a buyer, and at the same time, find our new house too. Our realtors have been working diligently to get us a new home, and we see that we really need it. KB asked me where Mr. MarcTrain lives. I have no problem telling him anything he wants to know, but I honestly cannot remember. It was like God had me in a trance leaving that house that day, so I would not remember. KB wanted to make sure wherever we moved, he wasn't close by. All I needed to do was remember that bear, and it didn't matter!

As it came close to the time to renew my tags on my car, KB began a dialog with Mr. MarcTrain to get the new tags. The conversations were no longer as gentle as they were before, obviously, so it was important that we just did whatever needed to be done to move on. By December, we were behind on the car payment, and Mr. MarcTrain stressed that he was not going to give the new tags until we paid up. Without the new tags, I would not be able to drive the car without being pulled over by police.

I understood that this was Mr. MarcTrain's way of being bitter with KB for again being chosen over him and wanted to put some misery in the happily ever after that we were living. After a few arguments here and there, KB finally said to me that he told Mr. MarcTrain to come and pick up the car. I didn't understand what he meant by that, so I needed him to repeat. He explained Mr. MarcTrain was not giving us a new tag, so he was not about to be held hostage and was tired of the entire situation. With just two payments left on the car, Mr. MarcTrain came and took my car away from me.

I was hurt and angry. I had paid for a car for it to be taken away. KB made sure I was not home to see anything go down, and just like that, the car was gone. I didn't want to be upset with KB because I didn't want him to think that I wanted to keep the car to stay connected to Mr. MarcTrain. That was my first brand new car, and it just hurt to see things end the way they did. I guess we all had to feel pain some kind of way, and this was mine.

Going to church that night, we rode in KB's car, and I was quiet. It was Bible study night, and I sat there with my head held down. Then I began listening to the Bible story being reviewed for the night. The story was about Joshua and the children of Israel. God had commanded that the Israelites destroyed Jericho, and all the gold, silver, and other riches found there were to be devoted to the Lord. If any disobeyed this command, then a curse was to rest upon all, and they were not to prosper. Achan decided he was going to hang on to some gold and some silver and hid it under his tent. When Joshua went up for another battle, they lost. He asked God to show him why they didn't win, and God told him there was sin in the camp.

I grabbed the Bible study book to read the lesson for myself. Hearing the reader read that there are some cursed artifacts that we are trying to hold on to within our homes that we need to get rid of caught my attention. KB and I looked at each other in awe. Once again, the Lord was speaking to confirm that releasing that car, no matter how many payments remained, was what God wanted us to do. We needed to remove any accursed from us so that we would be victorious.

I may be sad to lose the car, but I was gaining more confidence in knowing that God was with KB and me, and that was better than having a vehicle. KB kissed my forehead and promised me that he was going to buy me a better car and not to worry or think about that car again, so I tried not to.

Meanwhile, here I am, trying to sell and purchase a house, but I have no vehicle to get around in. My mother-in-law, not driving her old truck much, allows us to use it from time to time. I don't want to use the car and wish I had my own, but I have no choice in the matter right now. It is important to me that I don't look to my in-laws for anything, but at this point, I have to be humble. My job is getting harder and harder to deal with, and I am feeling like instead of things getting better, they are getting worse. I want to just quit after seeing so many things being done wrong on the job, but I know we need this money. Looking for another job secretively has become my hobby. Going in to work unhappy and leaving the same way.

Refinancing the house and putting the house up for sale, I feel like KB and I are on our way to a fresh start. It feels like the start that should have been put into play when we first got married, but nonetheless, here we are. The house is up for sale, and there is no turning back. Searching for a house is becoming discouraging, but our realtor Tonya Smalls keeps us laughing and uplifted through the process. The only problem I have with Tonya is that it seems as if she only wants to show us houses around where she lives that are convenient for her.

I have decided that I am going to go online and look for homes myself and send her the listings that I would like to see to move this process along. From one house to the other, there was always something missing. One house has a perfect renovated top-of-the-line kitchen with all new appliances right down to a tigerwood floor that is out of this world, but the basement is like a crawl space that even me, as short as I am, feel like I need to duck when walking down there.

We have gone to over eight houses, and they all seemed hopeful until we got there and saw something that was a deal-breaker. With every house, it may have been perfect on one part, but not so perfect because of small things that we just could not overlook. From location to price to number of bedrooms, nothing seemed to fit perfectly. KB decided that he was not going to go looking at any more houses and was ready to give up. I grabbed the children and said that I was not going to give up so easily and kept looking for the both of us. I am determined to make this move and give us the fresh start that we need. It seems like the harder we try, the more intense the resistance becomes. But I don't hear God saying, "Give up," so I don't.

Another house out in Rosedale, Maryland, seemed like the perfect fit too, with an outside deck in the big backyard that was huge enough to have parties on. My mother and father-in-law decided to come look at this house with me since KB was a bit discouraged. But when we went into the house, the oven was on, and the oven door was open. The rooms were perfectly large, but Tonya kept saying we didn't want to deal with a heating problem. The master bedroom had a bathroom also and enough room for me to have a chase or a sofa inside the room. I loved it, but I didn't have that "this is it" feeling that I needed.

I wanted to call it a night, but there was one more house that I wanted to see. Tonya being willing to go and my in-laws as well, we headed over to the last house. This house kept appearing and disappearing off the market, and we couldn't understand why. A four-bedroom home with a finished basement and a nice backyard sounded like what we were looking for, so we headed over with no delay since it was already late in the evening.

We arrived at the property with our real estate agent, and at first, it seemed very small, and I was wondering where four bedrooms would be in the house. Before getting out of the truck, I prayed, "God, please help us find what You have for us so that we can move on. This isn't something that we just want, but it is something that we need." As Tonya opened the door to the house and we all walked in, it happened. That feeling of "this is it." That feeling of "look no further." That feeling of "this is home."

Walking through the house, we all keep saying, "This is it, this is it!" When we walked to the open kitchen and looked out the back and saw a swing and slide set that sealed the deal. The basement looked like it was an apartment or another entire home altogether. The fireplace in the living room and the pellet stove fireplace in the basement had me overjoyed. Right down to the laundry room, everything was what I wanted. From the upstairs to the basement, there was a full bathroom on every floor.

The main floor bathroom with the clawfoot tub and chandelier had me with nothing left to say but "I'll take it." KB ended up meeting with a woman who had come by the house as a realtor that wanted to purchase Ready Avenue from us, so all that was left to do was make an offer on this home and get the ball rolling. The buyer of our house seems to want things to move swiftly, and we do too. When KB finally came to see the house, he prayed in every room. He talked to the Lord and blessed the house. I knew it was for us and knew without a doubt God was going to bless us with it.

Our realtor Tonya put an offer in for us, and the realtors of the home said that the owners of the house accepted our offer. Overjoyed, we began packing and getting ready to make this move. With it already being April, we wanted to be in our new home before our wedding anniversary. Getting closer and closer to the closing day, we get more and more excited. Crying and praising God, delighted that He found favor in us to be able to sell and buy so quickly.

Just as quick as the Lord is blessing, there always has to be something that is a distraction. As the school year comes to a close, I am tired of working this job, and I am ready to move on. I realize I am not alone, as many of my coworkers are thinking and feeling the same. I received the worse annual evaluation ever from my supervisor, and I realized that this place was not where I wanted to spend the rest of my career. It feels like because things are going well for me and my life is going in a good direction, it makes people around me mad.

All I want is for my family and me to be happy. I want us to have an amazing life with the adventures God will take us on together. I want my children to have a childhood home that they will remember growing up in. I want them to have that house they drive by when they become adults and say, "This is where it all started for me." Nothing like having a home to raise your children in. We are blessed and can take no credit for ourselves. It was God who prompted me to keep looking and not stop even though we had become discouraged. God knew this house was here for us, and all we had to do was trust in Him and not doubt.

*Know this:* Some people say it's not over until the fat lady sings. I have learned that in my own way too. Never believe that a deal is done until the deal is really done.

The realtor company that was selling our new home to us was eager to get the deal done immediately. We knew we had to close on our Ready Avenue home before we could close on our new home. We made requests for KB to be able to go into our new home and do the clean-out and treat the hardwood floors. Everything was done and ready for us to move in. Because both transactions were happening so closely, the woman purchasing Ready wanted us to move all of our things out so that she could move in. The realtors for our new home understood that we didn't want to put our things in storage and agreed to allow us to put our things in the basement of our new home until the deal was closed.

In between homes, we couldn't help but be excited. As the closing day approached, the woman who was to purchase our

Ready Avenue home began to act as if she didn't want to purchase the home anymore. We found out there was ground rent instead of the house being fee simple. This woman, being a realtor, was trying to make this be her excuse and reason to back out of the contract that we had agreed to. In doing this, we were unable to close on our new home and could not move in. We were also unable to live in Ready Avenue anymore because we had moved all of our belongings out, and they were stored in our potential new home basement.

KB and I wasted no time calling our lawyer, Susan Carol Bell Esquire, to resolve the situation for us. Susan knew exactly what to write and how to write it to make sure this woman couldn't back out of the agreement. The woman was upset, but we went to closing, saying goodbye to the past and moving on to our new home with a bright future.

Not having a vehicle of my own, KB rented me a Dodge Charger to drive around until we were all moved in at our new home. Staying the night at his parents' home and hanging out at his sister's house, we became more and more excited about moving into our new home. The closing day came, and we couldn't be more excited. Finally, KB and I would have something together. Finally, KB and I would have a place that we would make family history and memories. It had taken a while, but we were here. Then we got the news. The news that the house we put our belongings in, the house we planned to raise our children in, the house we felt was perfect for us, was actually in foreclosure, owned by the bank and not the owners with who we had a deal with. So now, we are homeless with no house to purchase.

# CHAPTER 17

# All Things Made New

Homeless.

*Know this:* There are times in your life when no matter far you have come, certain events that take place in your life have a way of making you feel like a letdown. When that time comes, look yourself right in the mirror and remind yourself *you are not a failure!*

This is the last condition I ever considered myself being in at this time in my life! How did we get here, and why? What's worse is there is nothing that we can do about it. We forced and made sure our home was sold but now have no place to move in to. This is so disappointing I can't even cry. Why cry? I was so excited about a perfect home for us that I am no longer going to live in.

It seems like everything always hits me to question my judgment and makes me feel like every decision I have made was a mistake or wrong. Why do I have to go to this state of thinking every time things don't go my way? Be it brief and short, I went there with my thinking. The attempt to fall back into old behaviors of self-assassination failed, and I am onward to praying with KB that God does something to get us out of this.

Susan Carol Bell, the best lawyer, period, is doing all she can along with Tonya Smalls, our realtor, but in the meantime, we must do what no one likes to do nowadays, wait. While we wait, we realize God is taking this time to humble us even more. I don't have a car because my husband gave it back to Mr. Marc-Train to rid him of our lives, now we have no place to stay, and I am on the verge of walking off a job that I used to love so much. Nothing is going my way, so it makes it hard to be the one witnessing to everyone and telling them to trust God while I am wondering where my trust and faith have disappeared to.

It is May, and all we want is to be in our new home before Memorial Day weekend. That is our anniversary and would be a great time to invite everyone over for a cookout. So many plans and ideas have quickly been shattered.

The bank explains to us that the realtor that was selling the house to us had been falsely advertising herself as a foreclosure realtor to her client. The bank is now saying that what we agreed to in the contract to purchase the home does not cover what the current owner owes to them, so the deal was not going to work. All I can think about at this point is how much of the DumbMax realty company I will be owning once this is over. DumbMax decided to terminate their realtor and put a new realtor in place to work with us to rectify the situation. Susan's strong hand and knowledge of the law is helping us to fight, but ultimately all KB and I can do is trust in the One that has the final say.

Praying to God for a way out of this is what KB and I decide to do. Down in spirit but up in faith. My sister-in-law welcomes us to stay in her home for a while until things are settled, and with no other choice, I agree. Her house doesn't have air conditioning, so on a hot May night, we are sweating, which adds insult to injury. We don't complain to her because she didn't have to let us stay there—plus, she is hot too. No need to make matters worse and everyone be miserable.

With the bedroom window open, we gasp for a wind, a breeze, a gentle blow, anything to come through to bring some form of relief, but we get nothing. KB and I, so frustrated and cannot sleep, turn to each other for encouragement. All we can do is look at each other and smile. It is too hot to do anything else. I turn to my side where he cannot see me and allow a tear to fall down my face. I know with his body turned away from me in the silence, he does the same thing.

*Know this:* Sometimes, when you have no one or nothing else to turn to, you just want to turn off. You want to throw the entire moment away. But when you come to know God, you know that Him, being the God that He is, will make a way out of no way for you. Just believe.

After tossing and turning and turning and tossing throughout the night, practically completely naked, we fall off to sleep from exhaustion. I have no real dream; by this time, I am sleeping not to dream but because I am simply tired. I am tired of feeling like the peanut gallery that is watching everything so closely in my life keeps getting the last laugh with me. I am tired of always feeling like no matter how much I trust God and ask God for things, it seems like my requests are put on hold for further review. I am tired of it looking like life comes so easy for everyone else, but with KB and I, there always must be an obstacle course for us to get to our finish line—only to find out it is not a finish line but a new start.

In the midst of it all, we have to recognize that the gallery is still full of people watching because God is still working. There remains standing room only because everyone is standing by to see how things will end. Because God is with us, He never comes short of His Word. The Bible says, "Yet have I not seen the righteous forsaken, nor his seed begging bread," so that means God has not forgotten us. It may be set up to feel like we have been left out to dry, but right then is when God shows up.

And just like that, on one of the hottest nights of the summer, a cool breeze begins to come through the window. It isn't just a cool breeze, but it is a cold breeze. Cold enough where KB and I have to finally get under the sheets and closer to each other to have a bit of warmth. In the middle of our sleep, we have to laugh and say God has a sense of humor and He hasn't forgotten us. He turned a very uncomfortable, hot, and muggy room into a naturally air-conditioned palace for us. The rest of the night is bliss because God showed up to let us know He is still there with us and will see us through.

Well, driving the rented Dodge Charger from place to place has been a blessing in many ways. While we really cannot afford to continue renting a car, we have no choice because the car not only operates as transportation but also as storage. The trunk is full of clothes, shoes, and other personal items we need; I go to work, church, and everywhere in between like a vagabond. Thank God the Charger is black with the darkest black tinted windows.

We are receiving compliment after compliment about this car, but no one seems to realize that we are just renting it, and the car duo operates as a storage unit too. It is a blessing because we are able to rent it right now. This eliminates me having to depend on KB for transportation. One can only think that if we didn't give my car back, we would not be in this position right now. Only if Mr. MarcTrain was more receptive to the fact that I was not going to be a woman that would cheat on her husband but wanted to keep the car that I paid for. Only if KB understood that no matter what Mr. MarcTrain wanted, I, being a woman of God who fears God, am not willing to have an affair but wishes I could have kept my car.

Keeping the things in the trunk is a valuable asset as well. If we end up at KB's parent's home some nights, we already have clothes and a change of clothes for the next day. If we are in town, near KB's sister, we can stay at her house and have what we need too.

I have never been so thankful for extremely dark tinted windows. While it seems as if everyone is watching, I am so glad it is hard for people to see past the tint. I can imagine some are so happy that I am going through a struggle with KB because they never wanted me to be with him in the first place. Hearing that we were purchasing a home had already created chatter, and now those that can't afford to rent an apartment are now trying to become homeowners too. Go figure.

Know this: This is what we mean when we say, "Do not envy people because of what you see," you never know what they are really going through behind the tinted windows.

Susan made it very clear to DumbMax and the realtors that they better do whatever it takes with the bank to get us into the home we signed a contract for. Not only have we signed a contract, but we have spent over $1500 on repairs, painting, and plumbing. Even though KB knows the people doing the work, we still had to pay. Now we have paid for plumbing and painting of a home that may not be sellable to us.

With Darlene, the buyer of our Ready Avenue home who is also a realtor, who tried to get out of her contract because of the mix up over the ground rent or simple fee, to the realtor Lying Latoya from DumbMax portraying herself as a foreclosure specialist on her website, this seems to be the worse home buying nightmare ever.

Here we are with three little children and no home to officially call our own. DumbMax tried to explain that they were not "foreclosure specialists," so we are trying to figure out why this realtor would advertise herself as one then. Each day my tolerance and patience decrease as my pain and suffering increase over this issue. Our realtor Tonya sending email after email with Susan to back her up is draining, but we have no other choice.

The bank was not willing to drop the cost for the house to move from foreclosure status. Lying Latoya, the lying realtor, was not willing to sacrifice her commission to pay the difference either. Going back and forth with each other, Tonya is very close to completely taking off Lying Latoya's head. Because of all these challenges, we reached out to DumbMax to file an official complaint and begin pursuing further legal actions against them. Once that happened, we were assigned a representative named Pam that we are to communicate with moving forward.

Effective immediately, we are no longer to speak with Lying Latoya, who was set to receive a commission in the amount of $7050 for the sale of the property. Here it is May 29th, and we have gone an entire month without a home, and we still have a ways to go. The contract on the new home is set to expire tomorrow, and if it does, we will have to look for a new home to purchase. This girl lied and misrepresented herself and then said that she was deserving of and not willing to forfeit her commission to save this deal.

At this point, it is not about money. It is not about Dumb-Max's reputation. It is not about foreclosure. It is not about a low sale cost. It is about a husband and a wife with three little children. It is about the discomfort in knowing you have no place to live even after you have fixed up one place and were the owner of another place for over nine years. It is about being treated as if we are not valued customers and left to figure out where the next place will be that we can lay our heads.

It feels like no one cares but us. I am looking at my children and how we have had to live for the past few weeks, and it is not fair. What else do we have to do to get the home we desired? This is the point when you start thinking that all the praying isn't enough, serving God isn't enough, believing that God is going to get us out this isn't enough, and we are defeated. My job is a wreck, my living situation is a wreck, and my emotions are all over the place.

We were distraught that our dream of buying our first home together was going up in flames, and to make matters worse, the title company is now trying to bill us fees for not going to closing when scheduled. Explaining that we are not the reason gets us nowhere. In the natural, one would wonder, Is this really meant to be? Because no one should have to go through so much just to purchase a new home. In the spiritual, one would understand that if the enemy is fighting us this hard, trying to stop us from getting this home, there is more to this home than we know.

Here it is, the end of the day, and finally, I get the email that we have been waiting all month for. The email from the title company telling us the paperwork is in, the bank will sell us the property, and that we can go to closing tomorrow. My heart is overjoyed, but I have to keep a tough presence and reply telling them that we are ecstatic to receive the news; however, we refuse to pay any additional fees. We would love to purchase the house; however, we will not be bullied into giving not one extra dime for anything.

In an emotional email, I reply:

> *"My husband and I are happy to hear that the property is ready for settlement tomorrow—this is truly great news. But...*
>
> *I would like to make something very clear to everyone: My husband and I are not willing to pay any additional fees! We have suffered enough throughout this. For the past four weeks, we have been displaced, spending money we did not have just to make sure our children were fed and as comfortable as they could be during this time. The keys were taken from the property, so we have not even been able to get*

to our belongings. We don't have money to pay for anything additional. The first and second settlement dates were not canceled by me! We are not responsible for the property not closing last week, nor are we the ones who set up the settlement date! We were told that the property must settle on the 22nd. Documentation that the payoff would be covered, to my understanding, was not cleared until the 23rd.

The bank is charging us an additional $300 for redrawing the paperwork! They waived the fees the first-time settlement did not go through, but the lenders are not willing to waive them again! Whoever set up settlement for Tuesday the 22nd and knew that the payoff was not corrected before then and did not make sure settlement happened needs to be prepared to pay the $300 tomorrow!

I am truly offended that with all parties knowing that we have been displaced for the past month (with three children!), no one will own up to their responsibility and pay the $300 or collectively come up with the money without me having to send an email. Do you all understand that we have paid for enough?

Please do not take this email message lightly—rest assured, without a doubt, I am angry! The negligence and lack of professionalism throughout this entire ordeal are more than I am willing to just brush off. I want to know today who will be paying the $300. No response to me means that no one is willing to pay the $300.

The next correspondence will be from my attorney Susan C. Bell."

Realizing sometimes you just have to let it out and be clear on your position for people to take you seriously. All I can think at this point is this house evidently will be a house that prays evil away, slays demons down, and rebukes in the name of Jesus, disrupting the plans of Satan. We have gone through so much to purchase this home, surely God will be operating in and out of it and will get the glory, and the devil is mad. Well, we want to keep him mad.

At the table signing the papers to our new home, we are tense but happy that it is almost over, but of course, the devil has to try one more time to defeat us. In the middle of everything being in a state of chaos, Lying Latoya kept the keys to the house. She was no longer a representative of DumbMax and could care less if we had the keys or not. Now we have to get a locksmith to change the locks on the doors. DumbMax doesn't want to pay for that either and tries to put it on us to figure out, but we have had enough and, at this juncture, are refusing to back down. This is nothing prayer can't fix. Just one conversation with our heavenly Father and Lying Latoya drops the keys off at the realtor's front desk.

Finally, we are able to move into our home. KB, the children, and I are so happy and excited. It may have been delayed but not denied. It was a fight, but we did not lose. It was rough but worth it all. Home. Yes, for the past four years, I lived in a house that was prepared for KB and Dion to create a family in. For four years, I made that house a home and tried my best to fill it with warmth, accepting that it was going to be my dwelling place.

I made it home but could never and would never remove Dion's mark. She started it, and I had to finish. I found out I was pregnant with our first child together in that home, had the biggest arguments, and made the most passionate love in that home. Now we have a place we call "home" together. We came into it together. We prayed in it together. We came up with renovations together. We may have moved the old furniture to our new home, but everything feels new, and that is how we live. New.

KB didn't waste no time doing what he promised me. Receiving the funds from the selling of Ready Ave, we paid bills off and down, but KB had something else he was determined to do. Taking me up to Auto Nation car dealership, KB and I drove off the lot with my silver platinum four-door BMW 5 Series. To see the peace on KB's face to have purchased me a car after all that I had to endure for the past six months can only be described as relief.

To think about a man being a real man coming into a situation and realizing another man has his hands in the provision of the woman he is supposed to be covering can disturb a real man's ego and pride. I never thought about how it made KB feel or look to have Mr. MarcTrain involved in my personal affairs after KB and I were married. It wasn't about KB being jealous or feeling insecure. It was the fact he knew as a man the door was remaining open for, at any time, drama to walk right in as it did. I never considered how unfair it was for KB to have to adjust. I never gave him a chance to cover me because I was busy trying to hold on to what I needed to let go of.

Proof that if you let go of what you think you need, God will restore what you need and more. I was in an Elantra, and now I am riding in a BMW with no strings attached. My husband purchased a car just for me. He made sure I had the "ultimate driving machine." I call her Miracle.

It all seemed like a dream. For the past half-year, I have been in a struggle. Not sure how long it was going to take me to get out of it. I felt like I was being punished. I was being chastised for failing God. I was in time-out for not going about things in the right way. I was put in prison or being held on probation because I had violated a law.

And suddenly, *free*. Free from the consequences of almost making the wrong decision. Free from being the laughingstock of those patiently standing by for my downfall. Free from the humiliation, discomfort, and uneasiness of not being able to be self-sufficient.

*Free.*

*Know this:* When things happen in your life, pay close attention to the detail. At the time, you may not understand exactly what is happening, but after a while, it will all come together. Something in my past prepared me for my future. Keep watching.

We have not heard from our realtor Tonya, and it has been a few months. I know the deal is done and complete, but we have grown to love her and her funny, no-nonsense ways. She finally emails us to let us know that DumbMax is offering us a home warranty, and we need to contact them to let them know if we want the warranty or not. Normally anything that goes on, Tonya would take care of it, especially when dealing with

DumbMax. But this time, she tells me to contact Pam and let her know our decision myself.

I am a bit taken back because I have nothing to say to Dumb-Max ever again. They put us through so much unnecessary drudgery, in the future, I would never want to purchase a home with them...ever. After going back and forth with them again, we find out that there was a home warranty policy that was promised to us that we didn't receive and all they want to do is give us the policy as they said they would. After making sure there is no additional cost to us, KB and I are willing to accept a check in the value amount of the warranty instead. DumbMax makes sure we are covered on all angles and now wants us to sign a clause so that we will not be able to sue them in the future for the negligence performed in this deal.

All I want is to start a Kenneth and Lillian Hunt Home of Memories for my family. I want to leave all the past in the past and keep my family growing strong and vibrant. I want to be able to say this is the house that KB and I raised our children in, and we purchased it together, we set the atmosphere together, we are proud parents together. That is not too much to ask for. That is not too much to dream for. A happy life with your family.

So after going through the worst closing on a house ever, Tonya, our realtor, quit her job. The funny thing is, I am so unhappy with my job right now, I want to quit too. Putting in résumés everywhere, other co-workers and I are trying not to spend another year in a place where we don't feel appreciated. And just like that, I get an interview with a Maryland organization and land the position as the director of human resources.

It feels good to know that an organization valued my skills and experience. Where I am now, it feels like I am taken for granted and looked at as if I couldn't or wouldn't be able to find employment anywhere else. To get this offer and the opportunity to make more money than I am making now is a sweet deal. I know my director is not going to be happy, but if she thinks about it, she should have seen it coming. I must go, and it is time. It doesn't make things better that other coworkers are quitting too and taking other job offers.

How much better can it get? A new house, a new car, and now a new job within one summer. Who could ask for anything more? With everything going so well and working in my favor, who is looking for anything to go wrong? Not me.

# CHAPTER 18

# My Color and My Calling

I'm the director of human resources—the one who does all the hiring and inform of the firing. I am one who believes that HR doesn't fire you; you fire yourself. As the director, I just inform you that you were successful.

This job is sweet. I love the fact that I have a huge corner office with big windows. Who would have thought that I would be this blessed? Immediately coming in, I gear up to learn my new environment and begin to hire more employees. Filling positions, planning HR workshops, and trying to get a feel of the land, all while introducing myself.

Getting acquainted with the staff, I see so much hostility. I put it on my agenda to do some workplace environment trainings to ease tension. The deeper I look, I realize that the line drawn to cause division is racial. Being the director of HR, I feel that I am exempt from that because it doesn't matter what color you are to HR; it is your job performance that matters. I treat everyone the same; however, that doesn't make a racist person not be racist towards me.

The executive director is a black man, a strong black man. Upon meeting him, he treated me like a daughter. So kind and helpful, he expresses he only wants to see me succeed. He, up in age, feels like a grandfather. Speaking to him, I understand more that there are issues between black and white employees. He, as an older black man himself, is clearly pro-black and will do whatever to see young black people succeed regardless of whatever they face. Me being a strong black woman but a saved woman of God, more importantly, I see an opportunity to spread God's love and empower others. I hire white and black employees—whoever is best qualified. I look beyond the skin and concentrate on the skill.

This job is like being on a roller coaster. Only here for a few weeks, and I have hired, warned of termination, and now dealing with the sudden death of an employee. A firm, straightforward, well-together black woman having a medical emergency being rushed to the hospital made things even more unbelievable. I am just getting here and don't know her all that well, but I decided to go to the hospital and check on her. I do know how to pray. I do know a God that is able to heal. I go as a woman of God and not just as the HR representative for the job. Having my daughter, Moca (Kennedi), with me is my way of making sure that I don't have to stay long but long enough to pray effectually and fervently.

As Moca and I enter the hospital room to visit my co-worker, there are already nurses and aids attending to her. I begin to pray, seeing how busy they look with her, and feel an uneasiness. I begin to plead the blood of Jesus and say, "Lord, have Your way." Alarms begin to go off, and more begin to rush the room. I quickly move out of the way and go into the hallway, where I begin to pray even harder. I know this is not good.

I don't know who to call or what to do besides calling on Jesus. I don't have her family's number. When the medical attendants asked, I told them we only worked together. They told me they needed to work on her, so I would not be able to go back in the room. I want to get Moca out of there, so I leave. Praying the entire time, I have a bad feeling about it. I call the executive director and tell him things didn't look good for her. This moment made me appreciate my mom even more.

Then I get the call. She passed. I have only been on this job for a short period, and I am now writing a resolution to read at a deceased employee's funeral. I hope that her death will cause others on the job to realize that life is too short to be evil to one another. Another coworker makes it so real, sitting in the church at her funeral service, listening to the resolution I wrote.

Comforting her daughter and making sure the life insurance policy is activated causes me to stay focused as HR. What a sad situation to know that this woman was dead and would no longer be here with us, but there are some who couldn't care any less. What kind of place is this I am working at? There is a separation between black and white and the old and young employees that needs to end. Hopefully, the upcoming event planned will help to do this.

KB and I enjoy going to Ocean City for the annual gathering for my new job. I have only been here for a few months and am already on an overnight trip with a gala to dress up for to eat delicious food. Excited about my future, I begin to dive in, trying to develop a more race-friendly workspace. The difficulty is with the higher-ups who choose to stay in their old ways and habits.

The executive director being a black man, and the president being an older white woman. The distention could not be any worse. I quickly had to make a choice not to be a pawn in this black and white chess game. Writing disciplinary memos for inappropriate behavior, I show that I am not a weak-minded or easily intimidated individual.

At the same time, the holidays are coming, and I would like the place to be more joyful. For the holidays, I decided to take it upon myself to get turkeys from the church to give to every employee. Everyone seems appreciative, and it feels like maybe there is hope after all. We make it through the holidays, and everyone is still employed, even the new employees I hired. No one else dies, and the young and the old are existing together until they are not.

Now that a formal complaint has been presented to me by an employee, I must address it. I cannot act as if someone didn't file a grievance, and I am HR. It is my duty and my job to investigate and take action. But for some reason, when I begin to do my job, the executive director gets fired.

Yes, the man who was mentoring me. The one who hired me. The one who was running things suddenly is fired. I am trying to understand how the director is terminated, and the HR department knew nothing about it. Me—I am the HR department. The board, lawyers, other staff, no one says anything to me. Now I am trying to understand why I am here if everyone else gets to do my job but me.

The president comes to see me and informs me that she fired the director and is now in charge. She is telling me to stand down on any investigations or complaints and that she would handle them. I advise against that, but she insists that she is the president and she will not share with me nor the corporate attorney what she plans to do.

Blatantly blocking me from investigating discrimination complaints would do nothing but cause this place harm, and I cannot understand why she would do this. I feel like my hands are tied, and there is nothing I can do about anything. I have decided to file a complaint down at the EEOC office and told the complainant to privately do the same.

At the staff meeting, the president is telling everyone not to come to me with any HR issues but to direct them to a white male employee that was not a part of HR at all. Their issues are not going to be addressed, just collected. She also is telling us that suddenly there is a budget issue, and some may be on furlough until the budget crisis is resolved. This is not good and clearly does not seem to be going to work out in my favor—or for anyone who has a complaint.

The managerial changes to my work and the complaint process were pointedly reinforced by my supervisor. I could only report to the corporate attorney that this place is absolutely crazy. Realizing with the attorney that there were other violations, he made me aware that I had to make them known to this place that seems to be going down in a heap of fire. After informing that there was a violation of a documented decree, and we were in non-compliance, I could feel that Madam President wanted to kill me because it looked like I was exposing her wrongdoing. I was only doing my job. And just like that, furloughs turned into sudden and immediate layoffs.

I am in a state of total shock right now and cannot believe what I am seeing and hearing. I can't even get to my office with my big windows and my big desk before hearing furloughs became firing. The black young man that was the complainant in the investigation I was told to stand down on is one that was fired. He, along with the former director's secretary, are both angry as I go into my office. Listening with disappointment and shame, I advise them to go down to EEOC, the Equal Employment Opportunity Commission, and file a formal complaint against this place. Telling them I will help them through this, I turn on my computer only to find out that my access to the database has been denied.

Another co-worker comes into my office, and now I am told I have been laid off as well. How is the director of human resources the one laid off along with the one who filed a complaint with HR? The response is "the budget." The decision made, without HR input, that the last three hired would be the first fired not put on furlough to end the budget crisis immediately. Yes, this decision was conveniently made after EEO complaints were filed.

As I pack my belongings, anger is the only soft word I can use to describe my emotions. I did my best to try and kill the ugly head of racism and discrimination in this place but to no avail. Adding insult to injury, as the director of HR, I was the one to hire the last employees, and they were white, but none of them were fired. If this was about a budget crisis and not race, why weren't there any white people fired that were the last hired?

I joined the other two fired employees, and we went straight to the EEOC office in downtown Baltimore to file complaints. Clearly, I was let go in retaliation for doing my job and being black. And now I must tell my husband once again I have nothing to contribute to supporting this family. I must once again be the let down in his life that could not keep employment.

No, it is not my fault, but it is on me. Yes, I am prepared to sue and demand punitive and compensatory damage retribution. Calling my attorney Susan with tears in my eyes, I cannot understand why my life goes from one thing to another, and I get no breaks. KB says, "Don't worry," but I can't help but worry. This was the most money I had ever made in life, and just like that, within less than a year, it was gone. My heart hurts.

I want to be successful in my career; I want to be a strong black woman that knows her stuff and is willing to help any and everyone, no matter what their color. But here I am, with an open EEO investigation, and I can't even fax my résumé to other places to find another job. Bunch takes my résumé and faxes it for me, and all I can do is feel pain and shame.

In this moment, God speaks. Instead of trying to understand why, I ask God what he wants me to do. Privately, I cry, feeling like a failure, and it is in my lowest moment, God is speaking, trying to get my attention. What can I do? Exactly what will get me out of what I am facing right now? The only response I get from God is He wants another yes!

So I am saying, "Yes, Lord" to His will and His way. Yes, Lord. As the Lord deals with me in my sleep and while awake. When no one is around and when there's a crowd. Everywhere I go, He is calling me. I take a second to reflect and realize what He is saying to me. I am trying to become the best wife, mother, career woman, but He wants me to be a better disciple, woman of God, missionary, and evangelist telling the world about Him.

Being called by God isn't something to brush off. I feel like God is going to continue to have me go through things I don't desire to go through unless I answer the call. Being called by God, I have a fear. I don't want to let God down. I want to be all in. I want God to get full glory out of my life. This is real. I am being called. Not answering, He continues to chase and call and beckon for me. I ignore and now realize I am not just ignoring but being disobedient. I don't feel worthy. I don't feel like I will be accepted. I don't think the anointing on my life will be received happily. I want to turn the opportunity away, but I owe God. So I say *yes*.

I think about all the funny-acting church folk who already have an issue with me being the pastor's daughter-in-law, and now God is elevating me spiritually? I am not good enough to be in the family; how could I possibly be good enough for God to use me? This would do nothing but cause people to hate me more and to be unnecessarily jealous. If I get called to speak, who will say amen? Who will stand in agreement with the word that the Lord gives me to say? I can hear people saying, "Now, the pastor is only making her something because that is his son's wife—his daughter-in-law. It's a family thing, not a calling." Little do they know I don't think my father-in-law even values me as his own.

God causes me to look at all that I have been involved with this far. Before marrying KB, where was my dedication? My "yes" to God came before I moved to Baltimore. Running from it, I made poor decisions, but I still said yes. The discipline, the obedience, the gift of singing and worship, the ministry of serving are in me. What I am was not given to me by man. I didn't start serving because I married into this family; I kept serving after marrying into this family. I didn't inherit gifts and anointing by my last name changing to Hunt; I added more gifts and anointing to the Hunt name. Now with no fear, I must walk in the calling that has been set on my life.

I tell KB, and he is ecstatic, telling me he knows God has a plan and a calling for the both of us, and I must get in position to carry out these plans. He prays for me, and as we pray together, I cry tears of joy that my husband is supportive. I cry because I feel God's presence. I cry because I know I am making a serious move, and I don't want to let God down. Before I chicken out, I go to my father-in-law, my pastor, and let him know I want to speak to him in his office.

I tell him what the Lord is saying to me, but then I add my own part. I tell my pastor I'm not trying to be a preacher, missionary, or anything behind the mic; I am merely doing this out of obedience because I don't want to keep getting in trouble with God by running from him. My pastor accepts what I say and prays for me. That is it. That is all. Nothing more. I feel I made the wrong decision saying something, but the Lord wasted no time letting me know it is all good; it is all God.

Drained and tired after a long day of service driving home, I engaged in a conversation with someone I was dropping off, and the dialog was personal and convicting. The Lord spoke to me and gave me what to say in response to guide this soul down the right path. As I was speaking, I was wondering where the words were coming from and had to acknowledge it was God speaking through me once again. I was not smart enough to come up with the things said on my own. The words were right on point and right on time. As they got out of the car, the Lord encouragingly spoke to me, saying, "Man didn't give you the anointing, don't wait for man to accept your calling—be humble, be subject, be obedient, be respectful, say only what I give you to say, wait on Me, and I will lead you and guide you and open doors and opportunities for you as long as you are willing because I chose you for a reason." I said, "Yes, Lord."

*Know this*: There are many that can say the Lord called them, but few have been chosen. To be called and chosen is more than what is seen with the naked eye—only the spiritual will understand.

KB has just started his cleaning company, I Just Want It Cleaned, following and branching off from his uncle Donald's cleaning business Father and Daughter Cleaning Services. Here my husband is making a business, and I am a complete failure. KB has already been cleaning a church, the Good Shepherd COGIC, for the past two years, and now he has an apartment complex as a client. He is trying to build up, and with me not having a job, I feel I do nothing but tear down.

Now home with my two-year-old son Kendrick, I can't do much but wait as the EEO investigation is underway. KB decided we, as a family, needed to get away. We plan a trip to Myrtle Beach and pack our bags. With nothing left to do, I clean my house from top to bottom as if I am going to have to move out since I am no longer working, but KB reminds me our faith and trust was never in my job but in God. He will provide.

The drive to Myrtle Beach was just what we needed, but I couldn't help but wonder what I was going to do next. Just lost my job, and we are on vacation like we are rich. When Zion jumped in the hot tub with KB and me, the splash wet my hair up, and immediately, I wanted to zap out. I'm frustrated. As we drive around, we see nothing but half-naked black women riding on motorcycles.

So we are here in Myrtle Beach on Black Biker's Week of all weekends. The loud engines and music, along with the fast driving, were enough for me. It didn't get any better when we went into Cracker Barrel, and my baby boy Kendrick could do nothing but stare at a woman who had on nothing but a two-piece bikini with a fishnet coverup. He prayed for the women... as he stared at them.

Welp, we needed this trip, and the family time was essential. We don't know what is going to happen after this, but we are thankful in the moment that if we don't have anything else, we have family. Everything was going well until Kendrick decided to see what it was like to jump off a big bed in the resort. Flying off the bed, he hit his head on the sharp edge of the dresser splitting it open with blood everywhere. It was Sunday, our last day on vacation, and now we needed to go to the hospital. KB, in total father frustration mood, having such a spiritual need for us to be in church, decided the place Kendrick would get treated and healed is at church. KB found a Walgreens purchased some gauze, tape, and band-aids. There would be no emergency room visitations on this trip.

We didn't know if not getting Kendrick professional medical treatment right away would affect the gash on his head, but we trusted God more, and we are glad we did. What a service we had with Pastor Lee at Mason Temple COGIC in Conway. It was just what we needed to encourage us to hang in there because help was on the way. Nothing but confirmation after confirmation that God was leading us to bigger, greater, and better. So we head back home to face the reality I no longer have a job, so I begin working even harder to help KB build up his business.

Doing all I can to find more clients for KB's business, I just don't understand why I must go through this. I take this time to help with the church selling dinners on Fridays. Gathering orders and sending out emails, I try to get as many orders as possible to bring in as much money for the ministry I possibly can. Looking into and checking on this case every day, I am consumed with clearing my name and retribution.

"Helping the church has been a blessing for me," I try to tell myself. This has become a way to engage with other adults while in my house all day, every day. Looking for new employment, selling dinners, finding new clients for KB, and going to every church service there is has been my way of feeling like I am contributing in life. This weighs so heavy on me. This makes me feel really low. This feels like depression that I am fighting, and I need some relief. Each week dinners are sold, I try to connect with someone just to be able to have something to talk about and someone to talk with. Small talk or church talk, whatever, it doesn't matter to me.

First Lady Nakia Daniels is a regular customer. A talkative little lady that is always excited to eat. Talking to her over the phone, I wonder if she is fat or skinny the way she loves food so much. She and her coworkers praise the food, and she is great at getting orders each time. Her being nice to me means so much to me right now while feeling my worst. She doesn't even know how much her holding conversations with me, talking about how good the food is, means. Yes, this is depressing. This is my life.

All summer long, I have been waiting to hear how this EEO suit will end, but I got no answers. On unemployment, I am ready to give up because the finances in the house seem lower and lower. I have no idea how we are going to make it. We have been borrowing from my in-laws with hopes once this case is resolved, it will be a six-figure payout for all the pain and suffering. All the while, I am to just trust God that He will see me through this. How? How is God going to see me through? When? When is God going to make this all be over? Enough already.

Through it all, we remain faithful to our church. As we prepare to go to the Sunday morning service, the phone rings. It is my brother telling me that Mommy has been put on life support. I do not understand what he is talking about because I am trying to figure out when she got sick, when she went to the hospital, why I don't know anything. Not only am I a terrible wife, now a terrible daughter.

My father-in-law, understanding my pain, pays for me a ticket to go to Rochester, so instead of going to church, KB drops me off at the airport. Just that fast, thanks to my father-in-law, I am home with my mommy. With the tube down her throat, she tries to talk. She tries to say how happy she is to see me. I am glad I am here. Glad I am able to just stay in the hospital, never leaving her side.

I don't know what I would do without my mommy. She means so much to me. After all she has gone through in her life, this doesn't seem fair. *But God!* Already frustrated with my own life, I have zero tolerance for anyone taking this time to make any type of scene. Mommy was upset to see my dad there. She felt he had no place since he walked away years ago; he lost that place and opportunity to be there. Concern would be his only reason for being there, but Mommy was not interested in his concern when she pulled through and realized he was there.

I understand why she feels that way, and I don't fault her. This is not about him; it is about her. Telling him that he was not welcome in her room had to be done, but no one cared if he was out in the waiting room. I am not for the family drama right now, especially with all I have going on back in my own house, but I certainly do not want my mommy to feel uncomfortable given her condition.

I know Dad cannot understand this and will take it, however, like a victim, but at the end of the day, it is all about Mommy. Hearing Daddy say, "*If* I have done anything to hurt you, please forgive me" to my mommy made things even worse for me. There is no *if*. You know what you did. You know you were wrong. You know you cannot skip over that—have your cake and eat it too. Moving right along.

We are looking for a miracle, and we get one. Mommy is fine and able to go home. My KB drove all the way up to come and get me, and I am going home too. I reflect on this visit and the way my uncle Clay prayed in that hospital over my mommy, and I am reminded right then, prayer still works. Redeem-Bethel Church was right there for my mommy, being so concerned and thoughtful. This church is the best church, and I appreciate Pastor Prior and all the congregants for being so kind to Mommy.

Coming home, I am still stressed because I have no job; I have no future plans; I have no idea what I am going to do. Mommy calls and says she wants to speak to KB and me. We both get on the phone to hear her tell us she is leaving Redeem-Bethel Church to go back to her childhood church, where my aunt and my grandma still attend.

Shocked, I am speechless. She says the Lord told her to leave, and she was stalling and taking her time, but when He put her in the hospital and told her to leave now, she decided to follow His instructions, giving up her title as a district missionary and humbly following the will of God. This is huge, but God is bigger. We do nothing but agree with whatever decision she made.

I just need to know, while God is speaking, can He say something on my behalf to get me out of this state I am in? In front of everyone, I've got to put on that all is well. I cannot break down and cry. I must always be strong. I think back when at the hospital, one evening, as I was walking down the hallway, there was a family so distraught and in tears. They weren't the same color as me, but they felt pain and were in a moment of sadness and desperation, just like me.

I was there for Mommy, but God had me go over to them and have prayer. It didn't matter their color or where they came from. It didn't even matter what they believed in at that moment. They were so thankful and so appreciative, like I was an angel, and I wondered where my angel was. Black women always got to be strong, always got to be tough, always have to have it all together, no matter what. Until they don't.

I have been racially discriminated against, lost a job again, almost lost my mother, my only solid day one, and back to feeling hopeless. How do I stay the strong black woman? How do I keep everything together? How is it that I am there for everyone, even people of the same race that discriminated against me, but I can find no one to be there for me? How do I keep living knowing I am hanging on by a thread?

# CHAPTER 19

# Surprised Delivery

I could not get out of my bed without my back hurting. In so much pain, I just lay there. Turned to my side, I just cried, not understanding what was going on with my body. Being unemployed, I had no medical insurance, so I could not just call my doctor and go into the office to see what was wrong with me. Assuming I had a bladder infection, I had to find a way to be seen. The agonizing back pain was unbearable, and with all the other bills we already had, I could not cause us to go further into debt.

Doing a search for free clinics in Baltimore, I reached out to a lady from the Maryland Department of Health. I explained to her the layoff situation, loss of insurance, and that I thought I might have a bladder infection. She was very helpful and gave me a number to a free clinic. I called the number, and the woman at the clinic informed me that they only see ten people each day, and I had to be there by 8 a.m. if I wanted to get a spot.

KB took me along with Kendrick. I was told I would not have to pay for anything and that a doctor would see me and run diagnostic tests. I made it just in time, looking around the waiting room at the teenagers and other people there waiting to be seen. My number was called. I went back to a woman's desk, where she began asking me personal questions regarding my sex life. Questions like when and with whom was the last person I had intercourse with, if we used protection, how many partners I had, how many partners my partner had, and so on...

This was very embarrassing for me because I was a Christian woman with very spiritually strict morals. KB was a minister, and to be asked these questions was just outright invasive. She explained to me that this was an STD clinic, so they had to ask these questions and also test me for syphilis and chlamydia, as well as do an HIV test if I consented. In total shock, I told her I had spoken to a woman on the phone explaining my symptoms and why I needed to come to a free clinic because I had been laid off and had no insurance to see my regular doctor. I went further, telling her outside of the back pain, I was fine and did not need any additional testing.

The woman told me that the doctor would see me and test to see if I had a bladder infection, but before I was able to be seen by the doctor, I had to take the STD tests. I went from one person to another trying to get out of taking additional tests but could not because that was the way the clinic operated.

Going back out to sit with KB until they called my number again, I wanted to scream. Sitting down next to him, I saw that he had brought in his Bible for reading pleasure as he waited for me. I was mortified as tears of total shame began to fall down my face. He asked what was wrong, and I told him this was no ordinary free clinic and that these people were here because they had come to be treated for STDs. With his Bible in his hand and my son sitting next to him, he could not believe what I was saying.

Just being in there and for someone to come in and see us sitting there—a married Christian couple, the minister and his wife. The thoughts people would think about us, *Which one of them cheated? The so-called church people catching STDs,* and so many other things. We already had enough rumors going around about us; we didn't need to add to that.

I wanted to leave immediately, but the pain was so bad in my back there was nothing left for me to do but sit there helpless and wait to be seen by the doctor. My number was called again, and they took my blood. I had to sit with another woman, and she grilled me about not wanting to take an HIV test. I explained that my husband and I were in a monogamous relationship, and that was not why I was there. Of course, they took it as just another made-up story because if it were true, why in the world would I be seen at an STD clinic? And even further—was he really my husband or was he someone else's, and that was why we came there?

Finally, I was seen by the doctor. He checked me and said that I was having muscle spasms in my back and gave me a prescription for pain. I rushed out of there as fast as I could in so much pain. I could not disguise how disgraced I felt as I walked back into the waiting room to see that my husband had decided to just wait for me in the car instead of keeping my two-year-old son around the different people that were there.

A week later, still in pain, KB refused to let me go another day suffering. He rushed me to the GBMC emergency room, and it was there that I was diagnosed as having an inflamed disc in my back. After the ER physician prescribed me inflammatory medicine, I went home feeling somewhat better. On our drive home, there was such a sting in my heart to know that after all the humiliation I had gone through at the STD clinic, the doctor at the clinic had misdiagnosed me. I had gone through all of that and had not been properly treated or given the right medication to resolve the issue. All of this took place as a result of being unemployed with no medical insurance, which made me more upset with my former employer!

It is going on a year later, and this case has not been resolved yet. But God is dealing with me to use this time to get closer to Him, so I do. I find myself reading His Word more, crying out more to Him in prayer and seeking help and an increase in faith to make it through this moment that seems to be tougher than any other moment ever. The church is in need, and there are sacrifices that need to be made.

KB and I don't have any money, but we do know how to cook. Starting Kenny Black's Outback, on one Sunday, we make $1000 to give to the church selling ribs, macaroni tuna salad, and baked beans. In the dead of winter, yes, KB is pulling this grill down North Avenue to the church, causing the smell to permeate throughout the entire neighborhood, and people are coming from everywhere to get some BBQ in the middle of winter.

Know this: The saying "Where there is a will, there is a way" is true, especially when you desire to do for God. He will turn nothing into something quick for the way to be made.

Sometimes God wants us to get our minds off what we are going through to help others. I would have loved for that money to be for us, but putting God first is what we need to do, and I trust He will take care of us. I begin to have dreams and visions that I don't understand. They seem so real, so I pray to God for understanding. Not realizing God is birthing a gift in me, I am not sure how to handle it.

So many dreams and visions that I decided to share some. I talked to a young woman about a dream I had of her hurting and in so much pain and disappointment because of her dealings with a man that was not her husband. This man happened to be a preacher. He pretended they were just roommates as they went to the same church together, but they were in a relationship, and he was sleeping with her, and God allowed me to see right through it. I couldn't understand why at first. I had never seen this girl but saw her clearly in my dream. I didn't know they were in a relationship, but God revealed it. This scared me. I just wanted to mind my own business.

I realize the more I tap into God, the more He develops me into who He wants me to be. If I can't find a job, can't get my old job back, and on unemployment, I might as well be working and employed by God. The pastor says there's a need for a Sunday school teacher for the young people and looks at me all the way in the back of the church. I am shaking my head no, and he immediately asks me what was I saying. He reminded me that I had gone to him and explained what the Lord said just a few months ago—that I was being called into ministry. Humbled, I accept the call to serve as a Sunday school teacher.

Remembering my favorite Sunday school teacher, I immediately ask God to give me favor with the children to keep them interested and excited about me being their teacher as much as I was excited about Sister Hopkins. I start seeing the great impact that she had on my life, and a lot of the biblical stories I know are because of her. I get excited knowing that I will be ministering to young people and sowing a seed of spiritual growth and knowledge about God that they will never forget. These are souls, and I was called to minister to souls. I am thankful.

Just when I want to take on an assignment from God, the church is shaken. It seems like everywhere I become employed turns into an environment of uncertainty. One of the kindest and personable deacons of the church, Deacon Pinkney, dies. Yes, he may have been up in age, but this didn't take away the caring and thoughtful person he was to me. I don't feel I told him enough that I appreciated his encouragement.

What a blow to the church this feels to be. His daughters that uniquely acknowledged me are hurting, and I feel sympathy for them. Sis Holmes and Sis Logan had lost their mom right before I moved to Maryland, and now, they have lost their father. After visiting my mother in the hospital and seeing her frail body as she fought for her life, this death hits different. By the end of the year, I am back to questioning my existence, and right at the end of the watch night service, my father-in-law announces to the entire church that I am to now begin working with the church mother as an aspiring missionary.

From one thing to another, I am sitting around waiting for things to get better, and that time doesn't seem to be coming fast enough. Internally I am killing myself, hating the fact that I am over thirty years old and my career isn't started yet. I have nothing to show for my years of employment. I am just getting to love KB more and more but far from being a good wife to him in my eyes.

Hating myself, I do nothing but make myself sick. Constantly throwing up and weak, I realize I have caught the flu and really can't do anything but stay in bed all day. I don't want to give up, but I don't feel I have it in me to do anything else. Unexpectedly, I have to conclude that I do not have the flu but that I am pregnant again. How did I not know it? How could I not tell? This is my fourth child; I should know by now!

Wait. This is my fourth child. Am I really saying this? My fourth child? I am months into this pregnancy, and my favorite cousin AA is pregnant too, but I am in disbelief. When I married KB, I remember crying because I felt shame that I was not going to be able to give him any children based on what my doctor told me back in Rochester. Here I am now, carrying another child for him. I want to be happy, but we cannot afford another child. I want to be happy, but what doctor am I going to go to with no medical insurance? I want to be happy, but I feel like I am too old to be having another child. How did this happen to us?

Thankfully, in the state of Maryland, being pregnant qualifies me for special insurance to allow me to receive medical treatment for the pregnancy. I had Kennedi and Kendrick at St. Agnes Hospital and wanted to have this baby there too. However, St. Agnes, being a religious hospital, refuses to tie my tubes, so I need to find another place to deliver this baby.

On my quest, I decided I wanted to have my baby at the hospital nearest me that KB said was a really great hospital. The hospital where Dion passed will be the same place we deliver our last baby if all goes well. But with KB and me, all going well is certainly not a guarantee. Looking through the book of providers, I find an OBGYN by the name of Lillian Hunter. I take this as a sign that everything is going to work out as I smile from ear to ear, excited to call and make my first appointment.

Calling Dr. Hunter's office, all I can think is how cool this will be for a doctor with basically the same name as me to deliver my baby. This pregnancy seems to be going by very fast, and I am glad for that. It helps finding out well into the pregnancy that I was pregnant to make the time seem shorter. Even though we have no idea how we are going to take care of this baby and with what finances, maybe this is just the distraction I need. I am going to just trust God like we always do. This state medical insurance is the bare minimum, but I will not complain. I am thankful that I qualify for something. Even though I am thankful for the medical insurance, it broke my heart to hear Dr. Hunter's office say they do not accept my form of medical insurance. I am very disappointed but glad I did find a good doctor.

Of course, with me, things always seem to go from bad to worse. So not only am I sick all the time, vomiting up acid, never finding a comfortable space, but now I have to take these tests. Test to check my sugar levels, test to see the baby, test, test, test. I am tired of being probed. I am tired of being pricked. I am sick and tired of being sick and tired. Of course, I want to know what the baby is. Of course, I want to know if all is well. Of course, I want to be reassured this pregnancy, although very aggressive with morning sickness, afternoon and evening sickness too, is, in the end, a healthy baby.

So it is disturbing to hear the words coming out of my doctor's mouth right now. Today is May 21, 2009. I feel like I am in the *Twilight Zone* once again as I hear him explaining to me that they see a star on the sonogram of the baby. She is a baby girl; however, the star shining bright on her sonogram is telling the doctors that it is a possibility she will have Down's syndrome. In fact, he says it is an eighty to twenty chance. I don't like the odds, and when he reiterates that he is eighty percent sure my daughter will have Down's syndrome, my heart falls. There that is.

Emailing my cousin AA, I ask her to pray for my unborn baby. As I type, telling her the news in an email, I remember I made a vow to the Lord for Him to use me. When I said yes to God, I meant it, so this is just a way for God to get the glory out of my life and open the eyes of an unbeliever to draw them to Christ, all while increasing the faith of believers. God clearly spoke to me and said that my baby girl did have Down's syndrome, and the diagnosis was correct. The doctor did not misspeak, nor did he make a mistake. The doctor was not practicing, and it was untrue that he did not know what he was doing or talking about. He knew what he was doing, and he knew what he was talking about, but God is going to perform a miracle.

My in-laws are out of town, but the church is still on fire. I sing the Paul Morton song "Be Blessed," the part that says, "I'll pray for you, you pray for me, and watch God change things." As I address the church giving hospitality greetings, I inform them of what the doctor has said to me. I also tell them what God said—He is going to perform a miracle. The women of the church come to the front and make a circle around me. All the believers in the church begin to pray for me. I am crazy enough to believe as the words continue to flow from my mouth, "I'll

pray for you, you pray for me, and watch God change things."
God is going to change things.

No, this doesn't feel good, and of course, it doesn't seem fair.
Of course, this is on me. The doctor explained to me that these
cases typically are because of the age of the mother. Someway,
somehow, everything terrible that happens in my life is strictly
because of me. Now I have put my curse of life on my offspring.
I wish I could take away this self-hate, but this is what I see
when I see myself. I am not the happiest of persons right now;
nevertheless, I am a believer. KB told his parents what the doctors said and let them know I was a little shocked, which may
have given off the vibe of me being depressed or down. My
father-in-law, being the man of many encouraging words, did
what he is gifted to do—encourage.

Calling me to check on me, he began in a matter-fact way,
telling me that doctors don't know what they be talking about—
they just be guessing. He wanted to lift my spirits by telling me
how the doctors have told many women this same thing, and
nothing they said was correct. I replied to my father-in-law
that this time things were different because God had spoken
to me.

God spoke to me and said that we were always looking for a
miracle and desiring Him to perform one, but never want to be
the one the miracle takes place with. God said He was going to
heal her. If the baby didn't have Down's syndrome and the doctors were wrong like everyone was saying—well, that left nothing for God to do. But God said they were not wrong. The tests
were very clear, but if we kept taking away His opportunity to
perform, how would we ever see Him work?

God told me to tell everyone that said anything different from what the test and the doctor diagnosed that they were wrong—not the doctor. God was doing this to get the glory. So with all due respect, everyone telling me the results weren't true was incorrect, but God had the final say. All my father-in-law could say was, "A-aa-all right." God said this miracle would be for the believer and unbeliever, and it was proving to be true so far.

I choose not to be a pity party. I choose to move forward with my life. Unable to get a job because I am pregnant, I continue helping KB in any way that I can with the business. This baby boy of mine, Kendrick, keeps my hands full too. The love he shows and gives to my belly is an indication that he and this baby will be close. Kendrick kissing and praying over my big belly makes me smile when there seems to be nothing else to smile about. Watching his favorite television show, he looks over at me and asks, "Can we name the baby Olivia after the pig?" All I can do is smile and tell him yes.

She's coming. We decide to name her Katelynn Olivia, and she will be here shortly, but I have absolutely nothing ready for her. Where will she sleep? What will she sleep in? Who is purchasing the diapers? Where is her car seat? What about a stroller? I have nothing. But Bunch, as she always does, steps in during crunch time and makes sure this baby has the basics before entering this world. I could not have chosen a better sister and best friend. Not because of what she does, but because she chooses to do what she does without an agenda.

True sisterhood.

Now I have been told that I would get a check because of my unborn baby's condition, but instead of getting a monthly check to help take care of her, I just want a healthy baby. Nothing is changed. No updates. No new news. Can I handle a special needs baby? I won't stress myself wondering because I trust God. I imagine my doctor thinks I am a crazy religious person too because I boldly told him that I refuse to abort or prepare for the worse as if this baby having special needs was going to ruin my life. My life is in God's hands, and so is this baby.

My doctor told me that because I have had two C-section deliveries, this last baby would be too. While he is in there, I want him to tie my tubes so that I will never go through this again. This has been the most difficult pregnancy of all my children. The sickness, the sensitivity, the complications, and the dehydration sometimes make me feel like I am being punished. My doctor gave me the due date of September 18th, but I explained to him I did not want to share my birthday. This little girl truly wanted to be a mini-me already, and she was not out of the womb yet.

It had become somewhat of a tradition to get over to Red Lobster around my birthday because that was when they did the all-you-can-eat shrimp special. I explained all of this to my doctor, and he agreed to let me get the all-you-can-eat shrimp and scheduled my operation for the 22nd of September. This baby and I will have our own birthdays, no matter how close they may be. And most importantly, I get to eat all the shrimp I want with Bunch before I deliver.

I cannot count how many times I have been in the hospital with this baby. I am just ready for her to be out. All my cousins who were pregnant this year pretty much have had their babies, and I am still pregnant. Adrienne had her baby girl. Crissy had her baby boy. Mia had her baby too, but me... Still pregnant.

Because the doctors haven't told me anything different, we are unsure if God has worked the miracle yet. As of now, nothing has changed, and I still give God glory. I would not allow what the future holds to stop me from living in the present and being there for my children right now. Taking all three of them to the library down the street from our home, I want to spend time with them before I am cooped up in the house to have the baby.

After spending a while there in the library, a white woman with red hair walks up to me to tell me how well-behaved my children are. I say thank you to her, but she lingers. With a smile, she asks if I mind if we pray together. My eyes light up because prayer is my language. I love to pray and am ready and willing to pray.

Taking my hand, she begins to pray, "Dear Lord, we thank you for this woman and her beautiful children. Even the child that she is carrying. We thank you now for a healthy baby girl. We give you the glory for healing her from the condition the doctors diagnosed..." My one eye begins to squint open to see what is going on. How did she know my situation and what the doctors said about the baby's condition? As she finishes her prayer giving God thanks for us, "...making it through the delivery in Jesus' name. Amen." Saying amen, the little preacher Kendrick was excited. As I tended to him and turned back around, she was gone. I looked towards the door and around the library, and she was completely gone. Did this really just happen to me?

I can't wait to get home to tell KB what just happened. I am more confident than ever that God has completed the healing of this baby, and He sent an angel to confirm. I cannot make this type of stuff up. God had to do things this way just to prove He could do anything...but fail. I am ready now. I may not have everything in place the way that I want, but I am ready. The stage has been set, and now that God has all our attention, it is time for Him to receive His glory.

KB once again is right there by my side at Greater Baltimore Medical Center (GMBC) to see his last baby come into the world. Things seem fine, and everything is in order. The epidural is working, and I don't feel a thing. The anesthesiologist is standing over my head with KB sitting next to me. I begin to smell something burning like. I hear my doctor saying I have a lot of scared tissue that they are trying to get past. Very much alert, I feel my chest tightening. I feel like my organs are being pushed through my throat. I cannot explain what I am feeling, so I just faintly say, "I can't breathe." The anesthesiologist immediately gives me more medicine, and the feeling subsides, but I feel uncomfortable. Something seems wrong.

KB, grabbing my hand, says everything is going to be okay. I begin to pray, and now I am thinking about my life. This past summer has been one to remember. Being unemployed, I have been engulfed in the business of the church. Sending the pastor's bio, emailing people for our upcoming church anniversary, collecting orders for the Friday church dinner sales, all while still being hated by some because I am married to the pastor's son.

Yes, this has been a summer to remember. I had plans to take my KB to Canada for his birthday since we were going up there for my baby sister's college graduation ceremony but ended up at my older sister's wedding instead. This roller coaster life of mine is just like that—always expect the unexpected. The EEO complaint against my last job ruled in my favor, and it has been over a year I haven't been employed with no income. My house is in danger of foreclosure, my car in danger of repossession. I am planning a surprise birthday party for my mom with my siblings. But I am now on this table in the operating room, and things don't feel right.

My doctor, with a voice of desperation, instructs someone to get the doctor that is on call for assistance. There is difficulty getting the baby out and I am bleeding more than expected. He sends out another request saying he needs the doctor to come and help deliver the baby. I can tell KB was praying. Thinking about all that I have been through to have this baby, I can't believe that God would get me all the way here, and now everything is in chaos.

Looking at the fluorescent lights, I feel the tear roll down my cheek. As I feel KB squeezing my hand, I hear the other doctor come into the room. Ready to deliver the baby, Dr. Lillian Hunter walks into the operating room and gets Katelynn Olivia Hunt out of me. Through all that is happening, God remembered my desire to have Dr. Hunter deliver my baby. What an inspirational message this is. You may have been rejected by man, but when God is in it, He has the final say.

We made it through only to hear my doctor say, "I almost lost you both in there." Looking at my baby girl, I see no sign of Down's syndrome, just like God said he would do. Of course, the doctor says we will have to wait a while and see to confirm, but the confirmation for me is already seen. God healed my baby.

CHAPTER 20

# Bills

All year we have been planning a birthday party for my mom, who is turning sixty years old. She is well-deserving of it. Even with no money, I am determined to make sure she is celebrated. But just like anything else in my life, there has to be some sort of confusion with it. After Mommy's hospital scare and being on life support, she told us what God told her to do, and we had no problem with her going back to her childhood church. But this new rule that has been put in place has me second-guessing. This party is supposed to be a surprise, but Mommy began telling me how the bishop just instructed everyone to no longer have birthday parties to celebrate their birthday. The only birth that should be celebrated is Jesus' birth.

And it is things like this that make people run from the church. What is the real reason why? What is the purpose behind this? We, her children, have a right to celebrate our Mom regardless of what her bishop says, but Mommy said no. She said her bishop has told them not to, and even though she may not understand it all, she will be adherent. So the plans have been canceled. We almost lost our mom and wanted to celebrate her life, but the plans went void. We wanted Mommy to be celebrated because she deserved it after all of the people's lives she has sown into, but it all came to a halt. Church. I cannot roll my eyes any harder.

*Know this:* You only get one mother. Love her, especially when she is a one-of-a-kind great one. Love her!

It is time for me to go back into the workforce. I do not like being home and have never been a home person. The financial struggles are making me feel so down, and I really need to add an income to this home. With Obama being president, black people everywhere feel that this is our come-up, but I feel like I am still drowning. Receiving a connection and having an interview set up, I now attempt to go through the process of getting a security clearance. My credit is terrible, my finances are all wacky, my history is well...my history, but I need this. I really need this break.

Hey. Who wouldn't want to work for the first black president of the United States of America? What a proud moment. What a moment in history to never be forgotten. What a time to look at yourself and reexamine your condition and determine you can achieve your goals and dreams. Life will get better. Black people do have a place in this world, and we are making a mark in history that will never be erased. But does any of this really make my situation any better? Will a black president make my situations be resolved? There is so much hate and racism with the president being black. Will he even do anything for the black people? Should you ever put your confidence in a politician anyway?

Like I do with everything else, I put it in the Lord's hand and trust that God will work it out. If it is His will that I get a clearance, I will. And I do. But I still have no job. Until I do. Saying the right thing to the right person at the right time with God right by my side, I am happy to see God moving on my behalf. If it was not for Elder Larry Gray. The funniest, most laid-back retired military man himself. God used him, and I was blessed. Not just me but my sister-in-law and cousin too. It means something when someone helps you and never throws it in your face, genuinely wanting to help you because they see you need this. God put that in him, and he helped me. It is not easy answering all these questions going through all these hoops. Family, neighbors, and friends interviewed to get a thorough background check done on me. But it is all worth it.

Now working, finances are still in question. Being unemployed for so long caused many bills to pile up. We are so deep in the red I don't see when or how we are going to get out of debt. We have four children, a house, a car, insurances, utility bills, childcare, and so much more that is eating up every check we receive. Week after week, month after month, we seem to be robbing Peter to pay Paul. KB, with the new name of Global Restorations, is still generating income for the house, but we are still in debt. My car loan is through Wacky-O bank. This being like the fourth bank my car loan was sold to, something about this bank is uncomfortable. Every month the same young lady is calling me asking me where my payment is. I say the same thing every month, give me a few days, and it will be there—and it is.

Every month I am paying, but I am late. I have no control over that right now, but I am trying. Driving from work to day-care to church to home, I utilize the time in the car to talk to God. I need help. I need assistance. I need these bills to be paid down so I can breathe. As the collection department for my car loan calls, I take a deep breath and answer. I contemplate doing like others do and let it go to the voice mail; instead, I answer. I can act like I don't see the call, but I answer. I have no money or additional information I can give, yet I answer.

I can tell this collections rep is having a bad day, and I do not want her bad day to trickle over to me. As she asks why I haven't paid my car note on time, I truthfully answer and say that I have been unemployed and short on funds to keep the loan current. I tell her that my husband is looking to make a payment by the end of the week. Not pleased with that answer, she decides to grill me with questions. What am I spending my money on? Why am I never able to pay on time? Can I afford the car? Trying to respectfully answer her questions, I say to her that I didn't dodge her call, I answered.

I answered because I know the bill is due, and I want to stay in communication, but to be talked down to and belittled shouldn't be something I would have to go through. I express to her that everyone goes through a hard time at no fault of their own sometimes, and she should take that into consideration before so forcefully speaking to someone. I really want to pay my bill, I just can't today, but the money will be there by the end of the week, I explain to her.

She is not happy listening to me tell her she is being rude for no reason. It bothers her when I say that I should not have to go through this when I want to cooperate and pay my bill. She replies to me in vulgar language, "Pay your darn bill on time, and you won't have to go through any of this." Shocked, I say to her to be careful how she talks to me because I am a woman of

God. She sharply replies to me, "Church people gotta pay their bills too!"

I am appalled and choose to not continue the conversation with her, requesting to speak to her supervisor. She, refusing to put a manager on the line, lets me know that she will put my car in for a repossession. I know she can't just put my car up for a repossession and said such. The threat was unnecessary, especially since I am paying at the end of the week.

Telling her that our conversation is over and one day she could be me and she will wish she had spoken to me better than this, she keeps talking over me and refuses to remain professional. I am so offended and feel mistreated. I can't wait to talk to her supervisor to tell her all about the level of unprofessionalism I just received. Instead, the call is ended with threats. What could I have done better? What could I have said? All I know is that this is not how it should be. So I pray and ask God to give me peace, to forgive me for the anger I feel, and help me to show compassion and love even to those who mistreat me.

Moving forward, all I can think about is the day when I no longer worry about explaining to the bill collectors why my bills are not being paid on time. I can't wait until I have more than enough money to just buy a car and not have any payments. I dream and wish, wish and dream. With tears in my eyes, I hate this struggle, and it doesn't seem fair at all.

Now I feel like I am being kicked while I am already down as it is a few days later, and here we have an aggressive man and woman who come on to my property to tell me they have a repossession order on my vehicle. My mouth drops to the floor as I remember what the disorderly customer service representative said to me on the phone when she refused to put her manager on the line. She did it. She really did it. She actually put a rush order in to repossess my car, and they are here to take it.

Unbelievable. As my car is being latched on to the towing truck, KB is angrily explaining to the repo company that this should not be happening. The man, being so kind and understanding, allowed KB to talk but still took the car. Meanwhile, I am on the phone trying to reach the bank. KB takes over when I finally get to the supervisor. We had been told that since the car had previously been placed in repossession, this second order would have to be paid in full, and the account must be current, or we could not receive the car back.

God gave me that car. I know what the rule is, but God gave me that car. I know the car is already on the tow truck, but God gave me that car. I know I don't have the money to make the account current, but God gave me that car.

The supervisor, totally astonished and taken by surprise when hearing the events that had taken place, put us on hold. I am so fed up I cannot shed another tear. KB and I both know that we do not have the money to make the account current. We only had enough to make the one payment. What are we going to say when people ask what happened to our car? How am I going to get around now? Why is this happening?

The supervisor comes back on the line, and I am ready to give up. My chest tight and full of disappointment, I hear the supervisor say that all we need to do is pay the towing fees and make the payment, and we can get our car back. I know I misunderstood because we have come to the end of the road, and the car is no longer in our possession. It is now back in the hands of the bank, and we are just left with the bill, so I know I didn't just hear that I can go get my car.

The supervisor, apologizing for the way I was treated, confirms that there should not have been a repossession order on my car and tells me to go get my vehicle back. KB and I look at each other, wondering what in the world just happened, and we both can just say, "Only God." Only God can do this. Only God can change these things around. Only God can open the door that had been closed in our face. Only God.

Getting my car back, I asked God to help me to forgive the woman who took me through this. I asked God to help me continue to learn how to be a better steward over my finances that I never get in this place again. I ask God to help me remember this moment and never forget what I had to go through to be humbled. I ask God to show the woman who took me through this that He is God and has the final say.

Oh yes, He does have the final say. As I become better and better with my finances and doing the right things to keep pressing towards financial freedom, I receive another call about my car. I answer like I always do because I never want anyone to feel like I am trying to avoid paying my bills. It has been months, and I have not had to speak to that woman again, so if this is her, I have had time to get myself together so that I can have a cordial conversation with her.

Instead, I am met with a pleasant voice. A voice I had never heard before. This kind woman is calling to inform me that Wacky-O bank has gone out of business, and she has received my file and will be my new agent. Confused, I ask her to explain again. She goes into detail, telling me that the bank went under and my account was bought out. Not only did the bank close and go out of business, but the employees were laid off and not hired to this new bank.

My mind immediately goes to the woman who just treated me so mean months ago and is now unexpectedly laid off in the same position I was in, as I had explained to her back then. Things can happen so quickly and out of your control. With all my heart and mind, I believe God is allowing that woman to remember everything she said to me and how she treated me at this very moment. Stay humble.

*Know this:* Things don't always come your way to tear you down. Sometimes God allows them for you to grow, learn, and become a better you through it all. You can live through it.

I have great employment now, with nice money coming in. I am so thankful for my job, loving everyone on the job. I show appreciation and kindness to everyone. I am in an environment I have never been in before. I am giving support that literally makes a world a difference. All while still representing Christ.

My job has so many perks and benefits that I have never experienced before, and I am thankful. My lead and others call me all the time and ask me how I am doing and because I know what it feels like to be unemployed, I am overly thankful for this job. I am finally in a career, making a difference, doing something I can be proud of but can't really talk about. Making more money now than I have ever made in my entire life, I see an opportunity for KB and me to do great things.

We have been wondering from paycheck to paycheck how we were going to catch up. With all the money I made and KB running too, we still were so far behind and struggling to catch up. Sitting at my desk one day, I received a phone call from a nice lady, and she asked me how I liked my job. I began telling her how I loved how nice everyone had been to me. I loved the benefits and the comradery. I began telling her how I was offered another job with higher pay, but it didn't feel right, and I didn't take it. I needed the money, but for some reason, God wouldn't allow me to accept it. I told her I thought I made the right decision staying where I was, and I knew God was going to bless me.

Little did I know the woman I was talking to was not an HR personnel. She wasn't some random admin that was calling me, but she was one of the partners of the company. She was so impressed with my candid opinion about the company while not knowing who she was. She was the woman that signed my checks, and I just told her how I had received another job offer. I was so shocked and embarrassed that I didn't know who she was. She told my team lead that she was so encouraged by our conversation, especially because I didn't know who she was and my trust and love for God. And she gave me an increase in my salary.

Yep, just like that. I got a raise. Not that long on the job, and just by being myself, I was blessed. They offered tickets to the Baltimore Ravens' games for free to each employee. We were able to choose what game we wanted to go to by signing up. I never signed up but thought it was an awesome thing for the company to do. The games were on Sunday, and Sundays all day belonged to the Lord in my house.

Word got out and around about the bubbly employee that loves God and the company so much, and the head owner wanted to know who I was. He saw that I had never signed up for a game and wanted to know why. I explained to him that I was saved and a woman of God and that I would not miss church on a Sunday to go to a game. He, too, was impressed with my spirit—so I thought.

A few weeks later, I received an email directly from him, asking me to come to the headquarters. I loved this job and began to pray. I knew most of the people I worked with were cursing non-church attending drinkers and lovers of the world. I did not hold it against them, but I did not join them to try to fit in either. As I got to the main office, the head boss was there. I said to him, "Hi Mike!" with my bubble voice, and he just smiled at me. He said to me he understood and respected my values and religious stance. He commended me for just being me.

Then he said he had tickets to the "Battle of the Beltway" game that would be on a Thursday night, and he didn't want anyone else to get the tickets but me because that was the only home game that was not on a Sunday for the season, and he wanted me to experience going to the Ravens' game. Before I knew it, I grabbed his face and kissed him on the cheeks. He immediately turned red, and the rest of the people there belted out with laughter.

I am blessed. We had four tickets to some of the best seats in the stadium, and I attended my first NFL game. The Ravens won against the Washington Redskins. I love the people, the environment, and the money—so clearly, something has to give.

Because a lot of the people I work with are or come from the same background, I had to adapt to their way of working. To do this, I had to be adopted and led the way by those who knew the ropes already. So God gave me Harriett. She didn't mind taking me up under her wings and giving me insight. She made sure whoever knew her knew me. Whoever took care of her was to take care of me. Whoever wanted to act funny towards me had to deal with her. A big sister, a sweetheart, a friend. She embraced and respected my sincere love for God, my honesty, and my consistency in representing Christ.

Introducing me to so many, she made sure our head boss, the captain, knew who I was. Harriett told me that he was going through some things and that I needed to pray for him; I immediately got his name added to the prayer list at the church. When things started getting rough on the job and he called me into his office, I shared with him that I was praying for him. He didn't really believe me until I pulled a program out of my purse and showed him his name. He was shocked and amazed.

Many people say they are going to pray for you or are praying for you, but it has become just a phrase to say instead of an actual action. He saw that I said what I meant and I meant what I said, and we, from that point on, were closer than ever. Every moment we had a free minute, I would talk to him about the Lord. I told him to ask God to give him a mind to live holy and do right. He would get the words out wrong, but I knew, and more importantly, God knew what he was saying when he would say, "Lord, get my mind right!"

As my supervisor lead, he always made sure I was involved with any special projects going on. He covered me when opposing team members attempted to get rid of me for no reason at all. He saw my worth spiritually and naturally. As he was promoted and preparing to go to the next phase of his life, I was proud of him and happy to share a part in his success.

It came to a point in time where he had to make a huge decision. With promotion and retiring, he had to decide how he was going to continue to stay in the workforce. It was a major decision to make, and I began to go before God on his behalf. My desire was that he remained my lead. I loved working with him and didn't want that to end. He helped me find favor with others that he answered to and gave me an opportunity to create job stability.

I let him know I was praying and that I knew God would lead him down the right path. He was a good man, one that was full of integrity and compassion about everything that he did. We grew to be like brother and sister to each other because of our authentic bond. I was so appreciative of our relationship just as he was, and he expressed his genuineness by saying to me it didn't matter where he went in his career, he was taking me with him. I never forgot those words. Knowing how intelligent he was and all the ideas and creativity in his head, I knew he was going places, and I wanted to be right there with him, supporting him in prayer and in business.

He chose to leave. I was shocked and saddened, but he chose to leave. There was a moment everyone knew without a doubt that he was coming back as a retired worker. But he chose to leave. A lot of people were a bit upset with him, but he chose to leave. After his retirement ceremony and a luncheon to say goodbye, that was it. Harriett was gone, and now so is Kevin. Harriett moved down south with her husband, and now it is feeling a bit lonesome. I don't feel as protected and covered on the job as I used to.

Worried about job security, I do all I can to fit in and keep making myself valuable and an asset. But as we all know in life, if the devil can't hit you one way, he will try to hit you another. I have never made this amount of money in my entire life, but it still seems to not be enough to make ends meet. Each week, we are struggling just to have enough gas money for me to get to work. I made just enough money for Baltimore City Schools to tell me my children had to pay for lunch. Not only do we need to have gas money every day, but we need to have lunch money for the kids.

We don't know where the money is going to come from. We are not spending frivolously; we just don't have enough. The one thing we won't stop doing is giving tithe and offering to the church. Being the pastor's children, it would seem easy to just get it from our father, but instead, we say nothing, and we try to make ends meet on our own. We see how many people the church and the pastor have to help on the regular while they are in their own struggle too. We keep our financial issues to ourselves while they help everyone else. We know if they knew what we needed, they would come to the rescue the best that they could.

We are under pressure trying to keep our home. Our mortgage has been sold over and over again to multiple banks. We realized we had been put in a dilemma back when we purchased the home. We were preapproved for a loan at a high interest rate that would do nothing but cause us to drown trying to pay off the house. Economic history, the Great Recession, when the Federal Reserve made money policies to increase rates of homeownership while loosening the line of credit, increasing the number of high-risk mortgages, creating a home ownership nightmare. As homeowners, we were unable to pay our mortgage, while the value of our home dropped, leaving us with a debt burden that was greater than what our house was worth.

Now the new mortgage company could no longer hold on. Thanks to Obama, I was able to get into HARP, a loan modification program to try and get our home refinanced to lower our monthly payments. The rules were strict, so we documented everything, paying faithfully each month until the trial period was over to get a lower mortgage. After making the last trial payment, we were told we missed one and had been kicked out of the refinancing program. I cried.

I had paperwork to prove we had made every payment on time and we did all we were supposed to do, but we received the letter in the mail that the house was now up for foreclosure. We begged and pleaded with the bank explaining our situation and asking for a review to prove we had done everything right, and the response was foreclosure. The only way to save my home was to file for bankruptcy; however, making that move would put me in danger of losing my clearance, meaning I would lose my job. I cried.

Unsure of what else to do, I went to work and talked things over with my manager. My job decided to work with me and try to keep me employed but with no guarantees while I file. I look for a bankruptcy lawyer in Baltimore and set up an appointment. The lawyer tells me I need to bring with me $2000 to cover the cost. If I had that amount of money, I would pay the stupid mortgage! KB and I, out of options, have to get the money together. I keep calling the bank, emailing the bank, and trying to reach out to as many people as possible to help me, but everyone keeps directing me back to the bank's attorneys that said it was out of their hands and the house was on the foreclosure list. I cry.

I took off from work early to meet with the bankruptcy attorney. All day, I sat at my desk checking my personal email and staying on hold with the bank, checking to see if my loan had been placed back into the loan modification program. During my break, as I searched online, I saw that my home was scheduled to go up for auction on August 5, 2010, at 11:16 a.m. I was unable to get new news from the bank; all they would say was they were unable to help me, so I hung up. I looked online with tears in my eyes, seeing my house listed along with so many other properties up for auction, and left my job to get to the lawyer's office before they closed. The reality was the next day, at 11:16 a.m., we would not have a home. I cried.

The entire way driving back to Baltimore from my job, my stomach was in knots. KB was talking to me on the phone, but there was nothing but sadness. I was even more upset because I had to be the one to file, and I had to do it by myself. As I parked on the street in front of the lawyer's office, I sat there. Enough tears. Now it was time to talk to my Daddy. No deep prayer. No articulated words. No sound at all. Just a simple mouth movement saying, "Abba, help me!"

Feeling like a letdown, humiliated, and ashamed, I walked into the lawyer's office, embarrassed that it had come to this. If

I had been able to help my husband sooner, we would not have been in this situation. The lawyer, trying to ease my mind, told me people file bankruptcy all the time, and it wasn't a big deal, but I knew that my job was at risk. As he was doing small talk, I sat there in a fog, not responding. He asked the address to my home again while also signaling me to hand over the $2000. All the paperwork had been printed and prepared for me to sign. He was trying to get the property information to get the exact court and time for the auction. I gave him my address again and handed him the envelope with the money. He asked me one more time what my address was, and I said it again. He looked up at me and then looked at the computer again. Looked at me, then at the computer again.

I was unsure of what the problem was, so I stared back at him, waiting for him to say something. Finally, he looked me in the eyes and said, "Your home is not listed." My stomach dropped. I knew that the house wasn't set to be placed up for auction for one more day. I had become upset days before because it looked like people had already started bidding on it but was told I had until the 5th. My heart sunk, feeling betrayed that my house was sold before time. The lawyer looked at me and said, "Your house was not sold. The bank removed it from the auction list." I cried.

It only took me forty minutes to get from my job to the lawyer. The last thing I did before I left my desk was look at the auction list. In that short period of time, the bank finally called, and the bank attorneys had my home removed due to the errors that were made in our account. The bank apologized to me and got in a hurry to clean up my account so that I would not lose my job. I cried.

# DIARY 5

# Racism, Just Be You

Racism. All these years later still exists. We said, "Yes, we can" and "Black Lives Matter," but racism is an evil that continues to persist throughout the land. When will we learn that when hate is in control, hate will grow?

On January 20, 2009, we witnessed the first black man to hold the highest office in the land. President Barak Hussein Obama, the 44th president of the United States of America. Thinking back on how we stayed up all night in November 2008 excited to vote and feeling some sense of accomplishment. We had a black president, so things were going to change, right? He was going to make sure that everything that held black people back for so long was corrected, right? Why would we believe that a black man as president would change the black experience to where we would not deal with racism anymore? So excited in the moment, we had no plan. We had no blueprint for the future. We just lived in that moment. We held our heads high as can be. We fooled ourselves.

Why is it that so many choose to hate rather than love? Why is it that black people are always at the wrong end, being hated more than loved? Will this ever end? Being black is not easy. Being black makes your life a bit harder than it should be. So much so that some don't desire to be black anymore. Talking against our blackness, creating division and strife.

Racism is real. Racism exists. Racism is dangerous. Dealing with reality means at some point and time in your life, you will have to face it head-on. It hurts. It makes you become skeptical about everything. You no longer trust anything or anyone. You hear about racism and read about it in history books, but when you encounter it yourself, it will change you. If you are not careful, it will make you bitter. You will begin to think about revenge. You put away everything that you have learned that is politically correct, and now you are "woke."

Then you are a part of the division, and you will easily become part of the hate. You no longer just have a problem; you are part of the problem. You don't support a solution; you instigate more challenges. A blind man can see that black people are treated unfairly and deserve better. Instead of making better happen, we tend to begin to hate each other and bicker between ourselves and never rightfully unify to make proper changes.

I've noticed that other communities see that about black people and use that as an opportunity to promote their agenda. What if black people stuck to fairness and equality for black people and achieved that first? Instead, people with hidden agendas and deep-rooted propaganda take the platform of justice for black people and promote justice for everything else, and the black voice is drowned out. And racism continues.

I have some good white folks that have made major impacts in my life. It was through them I gained awesome opportunities. Knowing them introduced me to a world I never knew. I got to see things I had never seen before. I got to go places I had never gone before. When most black people get this opportunity, the one thing that hurts the most is what they don't do. And that is once you've got your foot in the door, keep the door cracked open to pull another in with you.

Racism is an ugly beast, and spiritually, it is nothing but sin—something that displeases God and is going to send many of all colors straight to hell. You will experience it in the grocery store, and you will be exposed to it even in business. It doesn't matter who you are or where you are. Racism exists. So be you.

No one said that life as you would be easy. No one said that everyone would like you and you would be appreciated like you feel you deserve. But no matter what, you've got to be you. You must realize that everyone is made up of the good, the bad, and the ugly. No one is perfect. No one is going to do everything right. Every decision made may not necessarily be the right one at the time. Everything you feel may not be correct or appropriate, but be you. Give yourself a chance to make changes to become that correct and appropriate person. It's called growth.

Where did self-hate come from anyway? Why are we so easy to hate ourselves and dislike what we are and who we are? Why are we constantly trying to fit in and feel part of something?

Self-hate is such a destructive and extinctive behavior. It leads me to believe at some point in life, someone made the decision that who or what I am no longer deserves to be here, and there was an all-out attempt to completely remove my existence. But why?

Many times, people see you, will describe you, and cause you to fall in line with their description. Sometimes their assessment of you can be off, which will cause a discrepancy. Society bases who you are according to its needs.

I am an angry black woman to someone who doesn't want to address my reservations and reactions to their behavior. I am a good mother to some who appreciate me taking the time to raise my children with morals and values in place for them to be reputable human beings in society. I am a hard worker to those who know they can count on me to get a job done when no one else wants to do it.

Can't forget I am anointed when someone wants me to sing before they preach a message. I am not anointed when I don't agree with what they say that is wrong. I am a good wife to those who respect the uniqueness of the union between KB and me. I am a big mistake and not raised right to those who think so low of me and say I am not good enough for KB.

I am too deep in the church for those who want to keep doing things that satisfy their flesh instead of operating in the spirit. I am not deep enough for those who disagree that some church traditions that are not biblical may not need to continue. I am arrogant to some who can't break my concentration on being the best me I can be. I am mean to those who haven't gotten the picture that I am not a fan of tolerating foolishness.

I'm not black enough when I don't want to march or use my social media to speak on political issues of today. I am one to be jealous of those who spend more time watching my life instead of working on their own. I am too old to those who are young enough to be my children, and I am not old enough to those who are old enough to be my parents.

I am an encouragement to those who want better for themselves and can appreciate the constructive criticism. I am too direct and to the point to those that want me to sugarcoat. I am a strong woman to those who know my story and the things I've had to endure. I am a weak woman to those who feel I should have never allowed things to happen to me in my life. Need I say more? I can.

At the end of the day, all the points of view and optics are out of your control... Just be *you*!

# CHAPTER 21

# The Struggle is Real, God's Favor is Too!

Then comes the government sequestration.

My contract and program were cut, and here I am, back at home, waiting to be called to return to work or find something new. Finances are shaky as ever because we're still in the red trying to make our way to the black. This struggle seems to never end. How will we survive? How can we make it through?

All I know to do is trust God. All I know to do is pray. All I can fall back on is what God has done for us this far and believe that if we made it through everything else, we could make it through this. So far, we have been one hundred percent successful in surviving hard times, and we want to keep those stats.

Yeah, we've been here before. KB and I, asking God once again for divine intervention. It was just back in 2008 when I lost my job because of racial discrimination, and we had to go through a struggle. The year before, we had just purchased our new home, got a new car, and I was at a new job, and within a year, it felt like everything I gained I was losing. I didn't want to lose my house back then, and I remember KB and me praying and asking God to intervene on our behalf—and He did.

As we prayed, we believed. With threats of the lights being shut off, the house going into foreclosure, the car being repossessed, we prayed, and we believed. We did what we had been taught to do and continued giving our tithe and offerings to the church. We wrote checks and asked for them to be held until the end of the week so that we would not miss an offering opportunity to give. We simply believe what the Bible says, "Give, and it shall be given back to you," and we need all we can get at this point. Being faithful to God so that God will reward us and cover us is a no-brainer. But it is a struggle.

We had borrowed so much in times past that we vowed not to borrow anymore. Every son or daughter, regardless of their age, should be able to go to their parents for help when they are in need. It doesn't mean that the parents will resolve everything and get them out of every bind, but at least they know where they can go. I see many people doing wrong and committing crimes because they feel they have no one to turn to for help. This is why it is so important to teach our children at a young age financial literacy, credit responsibility, and good stewardship.

It is nothing for my father-in-law to end a church service by asking the deacons to bring a pan out and ask for a community collection to help someone in the church. As much as we have given financially and in other ways, it should always be an open option to go to the church for help. We know better. KB is a trustee, and he can see who and how much his dad is helping, on top of seeing the financial bind the church is already in. Asking the church for help is something we decided not to do.

Sometimes, although the struggle may be real, the struggle is necessary. Not knowing when I would be back at work, I applied for the unemployment. We saw that times were about to be tough for us, so we had to make decisions that would benefit us for survival. Even being unemployed wasn't enough for my children to get free lunch at school. They still had to pay a reduced lunch amount. Every day, even with it being a reduced amount, we didn't have enough for each child. We had to come up with another solution.

KB would go to the dollar store with $5 and come out with lunch for the week. A loaf of bread, a pack of lunch meat, a pack of plain UTZ chips, and juices. Instead of paying five dollars a day, we had to be wise and go this route to pay five dollars for the week. We did not receive social services, and we did not get a benefit card to get food stamps. It became a habit to go to Dollar Tree and purchase a few packs of Tyson chicken with three thighs in it to fry, along with getting a few cans of string beans and a big grape soda, and that was dinner. KB made sure we were going to eat and be taken care of. He also made it clear that we did not have to look like what we were going through. Holding our heads high, trusting God unsure of what was next, we just believed God would see us through.

*Know this:* Every struggle isn't meant to last forever, but you should remember the struggle and the feelings you felt going through to appreciate life more after the struggle is over.

Thank God my father-in-law started a food co-op at the church that he asked me to manage. Going to the food bank site and ordering food to give out to those in need included giving food to my family and me. We never went hungry. God provided.

Everyone thinks that your life has no struggles. Everyone thinks that you are supposed to have it all together, and there be no lows in life. But if there were no lows, if there were no times you needed to be rescued, what would we need the Lord Jesus for? He is our present help in the time of trouble. Yes, when in a bind like this, we look for God to show up, and He does.

It was God who one day allowed KB and me, while looking through our mail and papers trying to find a document for his uncle Donald, to notice one single sheet of paper slid onto the floor in a majestic way. It caught my attention, and I was drawn to it to pick it up and actually read it instead of discarding it. The letter was from Genworth Insurance company. When I read the letter, I was astonished to learn that if I became unemployed at any time, this insurance would cover my mortgage for up to six months while I looked for another job.

It didn't seem real, and I had never heard of it, and I was wondering, *Is this junk mail or something someone is trying to sell to us?* I gave the letter to KB, and he read it too. We were both college grads and very articulate, but we were puzzled, not sure if what we were comprehending was accurate. We didn't know this company and never purchased any additional insurance.

We stared at each other, wondering what to say next, and then we began to call each other's names. If we were reading correctly, we had insurance that would pay our mortgage for us. It was too late in the evening to call the company to verify, but we agreed first thing in the morning, we would give them a call. KB declared if, in fact, what we were thinking was true, he was going to strip all the way down to nothing and run all around this house.

This house. The house that we have had to fight for more times than we expected, but each time we represented Christ first and conducted ourselves as children of God, and He has seen us through every time. This house. This house that on any random morning, you would hear KB or me crying out on the sofa praying to our Father. This house that has marks of anointed oil on walls and doors throughout where we have pleaded the blood of Jesus numerous times from the bottom to the top, front to back, and on every side.

This house seemed really quiet, and the morning came quicker than ever on this day. As I called and gave my information, the representative on the line confirmed that due to the sequestration causing me to be unemployed, our mortgage would be paid, and we did not have to worry about it. Tears were flowing as KB kept his word and began to take his clothes off and run. I followed him. Apparently, when we purchased the house, we also purchased unemployment insurance too and didn't know it. And just like that, six months not to worry about how the mortgage would be paid. Only God.

These things keep happening to me. God keeps providing for me. I am thankful. I also need a job. Working in the field I am blessed to be cleared to work in, I know if I get back to work, finances will be fine for our family. The loans for the house and the car keep moving from one bank to another, and we keep making new arrangements to be able to keep up with the bills. Thank God KB is a man that takes care of his family.

It is his strength starting a hauling and cleaning company that keeps us from totally drowning. But when the work and the business dry up, our faith cannot. I get so sick and tired of KB bringing people's trash to our home. Living room sets, crock pots, lights, exercising machines, you name it. He is a live and in living color Roc—a garbage man that thinks nothing is garbage. Our dryer broke down, and we needed to go to the laundry mat to dry clothes, but not for long because on one of KBs hauling jobs, he was able to get a dryer that was still in working condition.

He was trying to teach me to be thankful for the things he found, but my pride wouldn't let me. I didn't want hand-me-downs. I wanted my own. God had to show me to be thankful in my current state so that he could take me to my next. My basement became overcrowded with things we had purchased and things he was able to get from jobs throughout the years. We were able to bless others with things he would find also. We were provided for. That was God.

Yes, the struggle is real, but you don't have to do anything wrong to make it through the struggle. Trust God. KB uttered out as if he was talking to another human being, "God, I need a couple thousand dollars to help get us through this drought." And that was all he said. Father's day was coming around, and I didn't have much money to get a gift, but he was deserving of something—my father-in-law too. I decided to drive up to the old, faithful Dollar Tree to see what was in there that the kids could put together as a gift. It is the thought that counts.

I wanted to just run to the store and back and didn't care what I looked like at the time. I had been cleaning the house and getting the kids ready for church, so I was in lounging clothes. I remembered I needed to get the load out of the wash and put another in the dryer before I went to the store. I had been given some coupons to purchase some laundry detergent and had about ten to fifteen bottles sitting on top of the dryer. I was determined to get as many clothes cleaned as possible because the pileup was getting ridiculous.

Going down to the basement, I began to smell smoke. I walked into the laundry room and saw smoke coming from the dryer. When I opened the dryer, it was on fire. I was trying to get the brand new bottles of laundry detergent from on top of it, but it was too hot. I was not going to be able to put the fire out, so I had to run. I ran upstairs and got the children out of the house. I called 911, and I called KB. KB was out on another job and came speeding home to us.

The firemen came, and I told them to go to the basement where the fire was. The door was open, and all they needed to do was go in. Instead, they got their ladders. I was so frustrated not knowing that all they were doing was their protocol. The door was open, but they broke windows anyway. I said the fire was in the laundry room, but they broke down the basement door and the bathroom windows. I was sad.

They explained they needed to do what they did to make sure the fire didn't travel anywhere else. They wet up the entire basement. All of our clothes, furniture, shoes, and so many other belongings were ruined. All I could think about was how we were going to get all that stuff out of the basement. Thankful the entire house didn't burn down, we humbly just asked God, "How are You going to get the glory out of this?"

I kept my mouth closed as much as I could, but I wanted to fuss at KB for the dryer and all the other stuff that was ruined. I wanted to be big mad because the smoke went through the entire house and left that burnt smell. Then my neighbors came over to the house. The neighbor across the street battled with the next-door neighbor as to who would take the kids while we dealt with the aftermath. The next-door neighbors won, grilling food and giving the kids popsicles, saying a fire could be very traumatic to children.

One thing both neighbors had in common was that they were both commercial real-estate realtors. As KB and I were scratching our heads trying to figure out where we were going to get the money from to get everything fixed up, they said to us, "Call your insurance company." We have been behind in our mortgage and have so many financial issues. We didn't want the insurance to try to cancel us or accumulate any additional bills, so we declined. They insisted we call, explaining that was what the insurance was for. There was no reason why we should not call, and they all but dialed the number for us to make sure we got an adjuster out to the house as soon as possible.

As I was trying to find the State Farm number to call, there were people walking up to us saying they were from different organizations and wanting to know if we needed to find shelter or a hotel to stay. Everything was so overwhelming we didn't know what to do. The Salvation Army came and gave us vouchers for money to go to Walmart and purchase clothes. They also provided us with a place to stay for the night. We didn't know we couldn't go back into the home. The gas and electricity were shut off, and we had to wait for it to get turned back on, so the fire detectives told us we needed to go to a hotel for the night. They boarded up our home, and we left.

The next day we called our insurance company, and they told us they would take care of everything. All the things that were in our basement had to be cataloged and accounted for as ruined property. Yes, the things that KB was able to get from his jobs that were in our basement our insurance covered and replaced. KB's uncle Donald came down from Jersey and began getting the details and renovated our basement the way KB always wanted. KB had asked God for finances to carry us through, and God not only carried us through but upgraded us. New dryer, new basement, new house items. God did that.

So yes, the struggle is real, but so are the blessings. Everything bad isn't always for our demise. God allowed that fire to happen to show us He is God, and He can send resources from the north, south, east, and west. All we have to do is ask and believe. KB asked, we believed, and look at God.

We didn't have to lie, cheat, beg, or steal. We didn't have to be out of godly character. We didn't have to do wrong, and God took care of us. Many times when we can't see, God wants us to sit back and wait on him so He can clear our vision. When we are in His will, things like this just don't happen by chance of luck. With God, there is no such thing as luck. We are blessed. Even in the struggle, we are blessed because God will always provide.

I want a job, and I need a job. I prayed for a job, and I believe a job is on the way. At one point, I had been gone for so long from the employment scene I didn't know how I was going to get back. It got to where I was almost willing to take anything, even out of the sector I had become accustomed to. I had spoken to one of my old colleagues, and he mentioned to me that my old boss was looking for me and wanted me to give him a call.

Captain Reynolds, now retired Major Reynolds, and I had lost contact with each other when he chose to retire instead of remaining in the position he was in as my boss. Shortly after he left, I was transferred from one contract to another and then to this sequestration and never heard from him until this point. He said he was trying to track me down because he was starting a business, and he wanted to hire me.

I know many people starting businesses, but I can't afford to live off someone's dream. He reminded me of the promise he made me when he found out that I was honestly praying for him and had my church family praying for him with his name printed on the church program prayer list. It meant so much to him because he saw I cared; he said wherever he went, he was going to take me with him. I wanted him to keep his word. I explained my financial situation and the struggle that I was in, and he asked me to hold tight and give him time to get some contracts together to get me on board. Months went by, and no job.

My car decided that it no longer wanted to act right. We took it to the service garage, and they told us it would cost thousands of dollars to repair my BMW 5 Series. We already couldn't keep up with the monthly payments of the car, and I just wanted to throw the car away, but then we would have no vehicle. KB and I decided to go to the dealership and see what we could get. I had no job, just an offer, and no clear indication when I would be working again. KB had his hauling and cleaning, but there was nothing official on record as income.

We went to the dealership anyway and met a lady named Kim. She was the only female salesperson working there. She took KB and me into her office and wanted to get us in a new car. We were honest with her and told her we needed her help. I asked Kevin to write me a letter as proof of income of the job we were hoping I would get at some point, and he did. With that letter in hand, no money in our pockets, and a BMW that did not work, we left the dealership with a new car.

We couldn't believe it ourselves. Somehow Kim worked those numbers along with the trade-in, and we drove off with a new car. Who goes to a BMW dealership with no job, no income, no money down, and drives off with a new BMW X3? We knew we were going to have to hustle and get some business for KB's company to pay the car note, but at least we had a working vehicle. Only God.

Funds are depleting, we are still in the red, and it doesn't look good for us, but because we have seen God come through for us before, we believe He will again. So we stay on track, serving in the church, serving in the neighborhood, doing whatever God calls us to do so He can continue to get the glory out of our lives. No, it is not always easy. We see others excelling and seeming to accomplish things we desire, but we know we must just wait our turn. God is going to do it when we least expect it.

It was at an evening service during one of those winter storms on a Sunday night that God showed up again to prove He was in control. KB had been invited by Bishop Luther C. Moore Sr. to preach at Community Church of Christ. The organist Andre Nance went over with us to play behind KB as he preached. It was in the thick of his message when my phone rang. I looked down at the caller ID and couldn't believe the name coming across the screen. It was Major Kevin Reynolds.

I grabbed my phone and walked out of the service to answer. On the other end, he was so chipper and happy. I was happy to hear his voice as he said to me, "Lillian, are you ready to go to work?" I could not believe what I was hearing. I quickly said yes, and he was more excited than I was. Hanging up with him, I went back into the service and couldn't help but give God praise. KB was preaching and was at the tune-up part of his message. The church was up, Andre was backing him on the organ, and I couldn't hold my peace. I began to run around the church withholding nothing. KB thought I was getting excited at the word he was preaching—but I was overjoyed at what God had done.

I began giving God praise and crying out to God, so thankful for what had just happened to me. After months of waiting, I was finally able to see light at the end of the tunnel. This job offer was starting at $90k a year with full top-of-the-line benefits. For years now, KB and I have been without decent medical insurance. I am finally about to build back up a 401k plan and savings. Excited to be in the tithe line giving the ten percent God requires from me and more. We can't help but say it again, yes, the struggle is real, but the favor of God is too.

While in a struggle, God will sometimes make it look like you are going through with ease. People on the outside looking in are trying to figure out how you survive. Many think you have no struggle, so they want to put their cares on you to carry along with your own. We took in many who needed a place to live, needed a support system, needed someone to be there for them—even when we didn't have it because we knew the struggle was real.

Here's where we grew into Kenny and Lil. This is our struggle. This is our life. This is our testimony. This is our family, and it is time we own it, embrace it, and live it to the fullest. Against all odds, God favored us. He put KB and me together for a reason, and we know this. Down through the years, we have sat back and listened to the lows and the triumphs his parents had to endure, and it was an encouragement to hear. We know the stories about going to social services to get the food stamps, the post office job and Mr. Sissero, the catering adventures, and even witnessed struggles right there in the church. But now, God was giving us our very own testimonies of encouragement. First-hand encounters to confirm God's ability to do anything but fail.

It's time. It is time we have our own family discussions, family trips, holiday dinners, and create memories for our children. We had to grow up and make our own tradition, tell our own stories to our children, live our own life and appreciate that God put us together to go through and grow through as one. Our children need to know the struggle is real, but so is the favor of God.

# CHAPTER 22

# Zion

Yes, I had a son out of wedlock. No, things did not work out between his father and me. No, I did not steal him or keep him away from his family by moving to Baltimore. As a young mother at the time, I did what God instructed me to do, believing and knowing it was what was best for the both of us—even if I didn't fully understand how. In the beginning, it was just Zion and me. With me married now, he is a big brother and the first to come through the upraising of Kenneth and Lillian Hunt. It's no longer all about him, but it all did begin with him.

Many battles to fight. Many things to explain and even more to try and understand. But my firstborn is special. He was the one who saved my life. He broke the mode. He kept me alive. So now I owe it to him to somehow try to keep his life from ruins, but who said that would be easy?

The firstborn is the trial and error child. The firstborn is the one the parents grow up with. The firstborn is the on-the-job training and hands-on experience for the parents. The firstborn goes through parental growth and will experience the good and the bad with the parents to hopefully make them better for the next child to come.

Throughout this marriage, there has always been that spoken but unspoken elephant in the room. KB made it very clear to Michael that we would never sue for child support or take anything from him, but he could give whatever he wanted to his son. KB could never replace Michael as the father who gave birth but be an additional father who, under these circumstances, would manage what happened under his roof. KB set the tone and the guidelines; there would only be one head of household, and that would be him, but that would not stop Michael from having a relationship as a father to his own son. It should have been both KB and Michael supporting one another in raising a special child united, but it wasn't.

*Know this:* Children out of wedlock change the family dynamics—nowadays, it is the new normal, but it should not be.

What about Zion? What does Zion think? What should he be expecting? How should he feel? Every child wants to be loved and have the impression of being part of something. Every child wants to feel wanted and be happy. Many times, as adults, our behaviors and responses will cause a child to hurt, but we don't see that until well after the fact.

Zion walks around so happy and proud that he has two dads until he is told he only has one. Zion feels blessed able to receive love, protection, provision, and comfort from a man that did not conceive him, with expectations that if a man that did not bring him into this world will love him like this, it can only mean double for him because surely his real father would do the same or more. Instead, there is disappointment.

The rigorous phone calls and disturbing conversations in attempt to force me to go along with my child not accepting my in-laws as his grandparents were, to say the least, sad. I am constantly reminded there is an entire family in New York that is his blood, and my son does not need anyone pretending to be his family. What hurts the most is Poppy, Suga Momma, and Aunty took Zion as their blood with no hesitation—they didn't pretend and didn't have to. They treated him as the first grandchild withholding nothing. At the same time, Zion never received phone calls, letters, inquiries, invitations, smoke signals, junk mail, voice mail, email, express mail, or anything from the family that so dearly wanted to be recognized.

The division, the lack of communication, the bitterness, the pure hate make it hard. I choose not to tell Zion the realities about his dad in hopes that one day his father will get it together and be the super great dad his son thinks that he is. I choose to accept being described as the bad parent, the parent that made life bad for everyone, the parent that took Zion from a great life. But I refuse to allow my son to reject the love that he is rightfully receiving and deserving of by the family we have been blessed to create and be a part of. In keeping silent, I made my son believe the lies he was told every time he went upstate. This was my mistake. A mistake I do regret.

Zion just wants to have a happy, normal family and get his way as much as he can. We know as children they learn very easily and quickly how to go between parents to get their demands met. But never should it have been placed in his mind that one family cancels out the other. He can be happy with his mother and a father and siblings all under one roof and be happy with his actual dad too.

To love, respect, appreciate, embrace, honor, and obey KB doesn't mean to hate, reject, despise, ignore, and banish Michael. To care for, enjoy, and relate to Michael doesn't mean to burden, be problematic, and elusive to KB. I hate watching Zion act as if being defiant to KB brings him closer to Michael. No, it doesn't stop KB from loving him and being there for our son if he wanted the love or not, but it hurts.

It hurts to see Zion stop calling KB "dad" and start referring to him as my husband. It hurts to see Zion become jealous of the other children as they are being born because their last name is Hunt, but his is not. The seed was planted that they seem to get better treatment, and that made Zion feel that he was treated less than. Instead of me negating it, I tried to embrace, understand, and navigate through it. I was wrong.

I wish I knew better and understood what he was thinking and how he was feeling as things were happening. Maybe if I had been more prepared and understood how he was processing things, I would have been better at responding. Zion knew Michael was his father. Michael wasn't completely absent from his first two years of life. When I moved to Maryland, we were states away, and that made frequent visits more difficult. Zion didn't understand it. I couldn't explain it. Having KB as his bonus dad was a blessing, but when the seed was sown that KB was a replacement, I can only imagine what could be going through this little boy's head now, *If Mommy can replace Daddy with a new dad, she is having new children that will replace me.* I was devastated.

My son would reject the love and affection as a response to not allow himself to be replaced, not knowing that there was never a replacement, just additions and growth, change that was good, not bad. The adolescent mischievousness, which was a way to fight against the thoughts of being left behind along with a child just being a child, created more discipline that created more distance. KB stood up to the challenge and delivered, but Michael did not.

Birthdays and holidays came and went, and if it wasn't an over-the-top expensive gift, it was nothing sent and received from New York. Never anything in between. KB had to be the disciplinarian dad, which gave Michael the opportunity to paint himself as the understanding, loving dad. Michael and my communication have diminished to almost nothing. The only reason I continue to tolerate hearing his voice is for our son. I don't want my son to lose the connection with his dad. I don't want him to grow up and regret not having a relationship with him. I make sure that what I feel and my past with his father don't become a bad seed planted to create a bias and animosity. I stay silent.

Zion has never seen or heard KB or I behave ungodlily. He wasn't old enough to comprehend me in an unsaved life before marriage. All he sees with us is ministry, church, and Christlike behavior because that is who we are; that is what we are behind closed doors and in the public eye. We hold no secrets to who we used to be but raising him in the church according to the Word of God is our standard.

He sees us struggle to provide, but he never went without. Zion was taught to work, hustle, and survive using his own skills and not waiting on someone to take care of him from the age of three. He had to be groomed into a man that could stand on his own two feet. KB did that for him; KB loved him even if the love was not returned. Before and after the other children came, as the firstborn, he was able to enjoy all the perks of being the one and only then the oldest. Going places no one else has gone, doing things no one else has done. But being the oldest also requires no lingering time in growing up. Others are coming behind you, so you can't afford to be immature. Your growth cannot be stunted.

I did my best to shelter my son from the things that happened in the past. My hurt and disappointment and my mistakes too. I try my best to keep him focused on his future and not worry about what he thinks he missed or left behind. I remind him constantly that his effort to succeed will show that the choices I made to remove us from everything we knew was worth it. I encourage him, push him, stand up for him, discipline him, love him, help him, nurture him and always be there for him so that failure will not be an option since so many would love to see us fail. Maybe I should not have focused so much on what others would think and focus on the both of us growing. At the end of the day, he had to grow.

But who would want to grow if growing means you are being moved out of your position? Growing up means having to accept reality and that everything is not always as it seems. Growing up means accepting hard truths. Growing up means some things you try to hide forever eventually will come to light. We all must grow at some point.

Going up north for short periods of time, Zion would have to be deprogrammed when he returned. It seemed as if everything we put in place for order and structure was scrutinized, rejected, and ignored. Not being on the same page with parenting pitted us against each other. We were advised to not allow Zion to go to New York for family visits, but I declined that advice because I never wanted to be a legit reason why my son did not have his father in his life. Of course, this would not end well.

After Zion's last trip to Da Roc, he came home, and we expected, as normal, for him to be distant to KB. For some strange reason, this time, he was flip at the lip with me instead. His harsh tone towards me and aggressive responses almost caused him to have a major concussion. Instead of him respecting, appreciating, and acknowledging me as the one that has always been there from day one, I was now regarded as the reason behind all the chaos in the first place. I silently own it.

I was hurt and not fully understanding but just attributed it to something I had to take. I was glad he wasn't being wayward to KB, so I took it and made the decision if he was going to come home and disrespect the ones that were taking care of him, his trips to New York would be far and few in between. So here we are. After raising my son on my own, then marrying a man who took on the responsibility of teaching him how to be a man, work, show honor and respect, we come to a place of no return.

One hot Saturday in August, we had a back-to-school church event, having a blast all day giving out book bags and school supplies while serving snacks and drinks. Everything seemed fine all day. Zion even had fun making cotton candy and serving it to the younger children. He is always a great help when I am doing major events and need muscle.

It was another successful event, and KB and I, having done so much running around to make sure everything went well, could do nothing but fall asleep on the sofa as soon as we got home. We didn't even make it to the bedroom. We crashed so hard, getting some much-needed and well-deserved rest. KB had to go out and serve a few summonses later, and I had to prepare for Sunday's service, so this nap was priceless. Until we were unexpectedly awakened.

I heard tumbling and running down the steps rapidly, and I jumped up. KB, feeling my aggressive movement, jumped up and off the couch, standing. We look to see Zion running out of the front door. KB ran after him to see what was going on and was met by police officers who had driven up on our grass and were all in our front yard.

I was still trying to process what day it was. I didn't understand anything at this point. I thought I was dreaming when I heard KB ask, "What's going on here? Zion, what did you do?" Running out the door, I saw an officer with his hand on his gun still in the holster, asking KB to back away from Zion.

Over about five to seven officers outside asked us to go back into the house. I refused to go in the house and leave my son outside without knowing what was going on and what he did. An officer explained to me they had an emergency child abuse call they were responding to. Zion had called the police. The officer asked me if there were other children in the home, and when I replied, "I have four children," he said they needed to come out on the porch. Then, he asked if there was a relative or some place they could stay—they could not go back in the home because we would be under investigation, and they would be put in foster care until the investigation was over.

All this, hitting me at one time, I didn't know what to say. I was shocked, confused, and did not know how to react. I simply said, "These are my children, no one is being abused, and not one of my children is leaving this house going to a relative or into foster care or anywhere else." I turned and looked at Zion standing at the end of the driveway and asked him, "Do you know who we are? Do you know who we live for and who we serve? We are God's chosen children; the last thing you want to do is come up against God!" It came out of my mouth so quickly, and I couldn't believe I was even saying this to my own child.

KB was in the house with the other officers being questioned. The officers said that Zion called 911 and said that his mother's husband was abusing him and he was hiding in the bathroom. They came so quickly because they were led to believe Zion was in fear for his life. When they pulled up and saw KB running out of the house after Zion, it made the story even more believable, which is why they had their hands on their guns. At that moment, all I could think about was how bad this could have gone so quickly if any of those officers were quick trigger-happy cops.

At this point, I was boiling with fury, listening to KB tell the officers, "Yeah, I beat his behind, and I will do it again. I do it so y'all won't have to!" He went on to say, "I'm a man of God. I don't abuse my children, but I discipline them according to what the Word says!" The officers stood quietly as KB began preaching to them what the Bible says. I was standing at the front door but went back out to the porch with the rest of my children, trying to make this make sense. A young black male officer was standing there with me, and he could see on my face the distress as I looked over at my son and shook my head. These officers immediately could tell this was not a legit domestic violence or child abuse call, so they were at ease but still had to do their job.

At that moment, while we were in the thick of things telling the police no one was abused in this home, Kendrick loudly speaks out and says, "Mommy, is Zion gonna get a beating for calling the police?" I just closed my eyes. Slowly opening them, the young black cop said to me as he laughed, "You might want to get him to keep his mouth closed so this doesn't escalate any worse." Only Kendrick!

After KB finished preaching to the officers inside, one came to me that was with my son and said Zion was claiming he had bruises. If there were any bruises, he explained, Zion would have to be taken to Johns Hopkins, where he would be photographed and treated, and Child Protective Services would place him in foster care. He said Zion mentioned that he wanted to call his dad because his dad said he would come and pick him up. Puzzled, I needed the cop to repeat what he just said. One moment. Let me let that sink in.

KB, with his closing remarks, was asking the cops to move their vehicles off his lawn and out of the way so he could go deliver a summons, not comprehending that they were there to arrest him. The officers, not knowing what to do, just stood there. The officer said to me that my husband would be charged with child abuse and would most likely be held without bail if Johns Hopkins confirmed bruises on my son's body. I did not know KB had given Zion a whipping earlier that morning before they got to the church, but that's what it was, a whipping, not abuse.

In speaking to Zion, the officers were able to gather that my son was under the assumption that he could call the police and say he was being abused, and then he would be able to go and live in New York with his father. Zion did not realize making this claim would also cause his siblings to be put in foster care. An investigation like this could cause me to lose my security clearance and my job, removing major income for the family. He did not realize these actions would cause KB to be arrested and have a criminal record, or did he?

I told the officers he had no bruises and he was not going to Johns Hopkins. They explained to Zion that he needed to decide. Was he going to retract his story of being abused, or would he stick with it getting his father arrested, siblings removed from the home into foster care, and his parents under investigation? Zion chose to stick with his story at the expense of my husband and children, my beautiful family, and everything I had worked hard for. I could not understand. I became the black mother—the black momma bear!

"Where? Where?" I asked. "Show me the bruises." In front of all these police officers, I insisted my son dropped his pants and showed me the bruises now! The officers, noticing that I had changed from a patient, unclear-of-what-was-going-on mom to a black momma that is about to whip everyone in her sight, interjected and told me to take him into the bathroom to verify the bruises instead of making him strip in front of them.

While in the bathroom with my voice at level one thousand, I was demanding to see these bruises and get an explanation as to what was going on. Seeing not one bruise on his body, I told him he better showed me something before I made a bruise for everyone to see. So now it was sinking in. A plan to completely dismantle and destroy my family was something a thirteen-year-old did not come up with on his own. I didn't have a moment, but I needed one because it was sinking in.

Zion told me that when he went up to New York to spend time with his father, the conversation came up about him being disciplined and what kind of discipline my son had been subjected to. When Zion told Michael that KB gave him whippings, Michael did not take the time to find out why. He didn't call KB, nor did he call me to talk to another adult. He did not explain to Zion that there would always be consequences to his actions. He did not reiterate that KB loved him and was raising him, and discipline was part of the rearing of a child.

Instead, my son began to tell me how his father told him no one had the right to put their hands on him, telling him that KB was not his father and what he was doing was child abuse, and I was allowing it. Michael told Zion the next time KB put his hands on him, Zion was to get a phone, hide, and call the police and then call him and he would come and pick him up. He promised Zion that the police would take him and keep him safe until he got there.

Zion went on to tell me he called his father as planned, and when he called Michael to tell him he called the police, and he needed Michael to come and get him, Michael replied that he was on a photoshoot job at a wedding and couldn't talk at the moment. Could not talk at the moment! He told Zion that when the police come, they would take him to foster care and when he got there, Zion had to call him so he could come and pick him up. The anger I felt—no other option but death came to mind for Michael.

It was then. It was this day. It was this moment; I had to face a truth and tell the truth. It had all sunk in. I had to tell Zion when he was born, his father never signed his birth certificate. I had to tell Zion there was no way Michael could come near him without my permission because he refused to claim Zion when he was first born, so he had no rights or parental authority. He had to learn his daddy that he thought so highly of never wanted to accept or claim him as his child. He had to see that KB had more rights than Michael did—not because KB took it, but because Michael never wanted it.

Zion, hearing his father never signed his birth certificate and realizing the only reason why Michael was still in his life was that I, as the only documented parent he has, allowed it, was an eye-opener for him. He had to be fully informed that the only person who claimed him, took care of him, and always came through for him from birth was me and me alone! How dare Michael use the emotions of my son to disrupt my home and try to put my husband behind bars. Even with all this, I still could not tell Zion everything about his father that he adored so much and listened to at the expense of my hurt. I hurt in silence.

Zion no longer wanted to go through with this foolishness, but the damage was done. The police gave him a speech on being grateful for parents that cared about him and told him calling the police to make a false report was a criminal offense. Instead of taking his dad out in handcuffs, they had the right to arrest him. I was too upset to cry. No one was arrested. They expressed this was a waste of time, and there were children really being abused and other emergencies they could have been reporting to instead of being here. The police left, KB left, and my home was silent. I wondered if Michael was even worried about what was happening to his son...or was he more concerned about photos at a wedding? I wanted to take a trip to Da Roc and slam heads.

KB called Michael and told him to cease and desist. Michael cowered down as if he didn't know where KB's demands were coming from. KB didn't care that he was playing stupid; KB was the head of this house, and another man's influence was not going to be accepted. I took blame. KB should not have to deal with this. He deserved better. Zion did too. There would be no more phone calls or visitations. Enough was enough.

He didn't want to take part in the raising, upbringing, rearing, and instilling of morals of Zion, but he wanted to single-handedly destroy any good thing happening in Zion's life that he didn't have control over or was a part of. I never wanted Zion to know that his father didn't want to claim him. He wouldn't have ever found out from me if this hadn't happened. Still, I tried to cover his father because that was his father.

The bitterness and the unsettling lingered right up to his graduation. All these years, Zion would sneak and call his family to stay in contact, continuing the toxic relationship full of false information and assumptions. While I have forgiven and moved on, I did not forget, but yet my one and only desire that was there from the beginning was for my son to be successful so no one would be able to say I failed as a parent. I didn't put into account his success wasn't just on me being a good parent, but on him wanting to be a good successful son.

I have been talked about, mistreated, disrespected, and counted out, all trying to support my son. I have been the loudest parent, patient parent, concerned parent, providing all I could for my son. I know he doesn't like everything or agree with everything, but I am his mother, and I will do what I can while I can. I was profiled for him. The assumption was made that I was a statistic, a homeless single black mother working at a fast-food chain with no education and no experience to properly guide my son.

Supporting and fighting with everything in me, I go up against some of Maryland's most prominent and well-respected political figures just for Zion to be considered for the Naval Academy. I have to make it clear I am a homeowner with my husband standing by my side. I work for the United States Department of Defense, I have multiple degrees, and I am surrounded by the same military my son wants to join. I negated every stereotype they tried to attach to me. He still didn't get in.

At the top of his class, he graduated as valedictorian, he got numerous college offers and congressional support as well as city council support, but he didn't get in. He got accepted to KB's alma mater University of Maryland Eastern Shore (UMES), so he can go there to start his adult life and build a career. My boss offered to get him security clearance and be sure he was taken care of, making well over $60k right out of high school. I applied for financial aid for him; I went to the city board meetings; I volunteered to be a parent liaison. I did all I could, but it wasn't enough. I am sorry.

I worked hard to get my son to this point, and I deserve to celebrate my son's success because it is mine too. It hurt to hear the blunt rebellion and irrational decisions being made after all the hard work and sacrifices that I have made. KB, as any husband who loves his wife would, is tired of me exhausting myself and it not being appreciated. Many children think everything parents do they are supposed to do, but that is not the case. Some of us do more.

KB knew I never told Zion things that went on between his father and me that caused me to move to Baltimore. All these years, I took the blame so that I would not have to relive the pain of my past. All that did was made me live in pain today. KB was tired of the entitlement attitude, the lack of respect, and the ignorance. He told Zion how his father raped me. He told him how he had a knife to me and forced me to have sex with him. I didn't have him arrested. I didn't report it. I took it. I blamed myself.

KB told Zion how I left Da Roc to get away from him and his manipulating and controlling ways. I didn't leave to hurt his father; I left so that his father would not hurt me. I never bothered his father for child support, never interfered in his relationships or his life. I just wanted to get far enough away from him as I could so he would never do what he did to me again. Never exposed him or dragged his name through the mud. All while I was being fought against to give Zion a chance at a life free from abuse, free from the negativity, free from the hurt. We couldn't co-parent together like nothing ever happened. But I forgave and tried to live the rest of my life. Now Zion knows.

After the family that did come to Zion's graduation gave us the cold shoulder and rejected our extended hand of peace, I was ready to break, but I remembered everything I did, it was for my son. My son, in his cap and gown, wanted a picture with his family. So I stood there with KB on one side and Michael on the other. A picture with the man who forced himself on me, but I couldn't tell anyone because who would believe me back then? Here I was at a moment of success in my life, and I had to share it and breathe the same air as the man who wanted to end mine.

A photo I should be proud of, but a bitter taste was there because I knew this man never contributed, never supported, never helped, but he was the father. I took a photo with him and the child whose birth certificate still remains fatherless. To the very end, I do all to hold in the truth for my son's sake so he can keep the positive image in his mind of his father, all while I am villainized. He never apologized for what he did to me that still haunts me. But for Zion, I choke on my tears and accept it. At the end of the day, I'm Mom. I am to blame.

# CHAPTER 23

# Ministry

My life may not be all that I want it to be, but I know there are some things that I do not want, based on what I see in other marriages around me. So many in the church and out of the church cannot seem to be faithful. Hearing and seeing the behaviors pushes me to be more and more open with KB and praying and believing he is being open and honest with me. Choosing to love KB was a choice I made because God ordained for it to be so. Choosing to let go of the love I had for Mr. Marc-Train was a choice to make so that the love I had with KB would not be contaminated.

Communication is dead between Mr. MarcTrain and me. There is no need or reason for us to talk. What has been said and done is finished. There is nothing between us to keep ties any longer. There is nothing to bring us together. We have no children together. All financial ties have ended. There are no more vehicles or property or objects being withheld. There is nothing that we share. Except.

Mom. With all the closure that took place the way that it did, there was never an ending with Mr. MarcTrain's mom. I never spoke with her. I didn't get to truly explain myself. When speaking before KB and I got married, she was only in defense of her son. She felt obligated to stand up for him when it seemed like he was being mistreated. I made it clear to her then how much I love her son and would never want to hurt him in any way. I have professed my love for her son to her so many times in many ways via telephone conversations, letters, and cards. I meant every word, and he knew it, and so did she.

But now. With a new life. A new family. A new situation. Where has that left Mr. MarcTrain's mom and me? I feel the time of no communication between us has been long enough, and I should reach out to her. It was not her that I was in love with and endangering my marriage by holding on to that love. She was not trying to end my marriage. She didn't deserve to be isolated and pushed away because things didn't go well between her son and me. She has always shown me that she cared for me. Being Mom to me is something she doesn't have to be, but she has been. Why the sudden urge to reach out to her, I do not understand, but I want to. I don't want things to stir up between Mr. MarcTrain and KB, but I want to reach her. There is nothing more for me to say or entertain with Mr. MarcTrain, and leaving him out of this, I need and want to talk to Mom.

Calling her number over and over, I am getting no answer. I am worried and troubled because what other way can I reach her besides Mr. MarcTrain? Is it worth it to reach out to him to contact her? Should this door be opened? Would KB approve of this? Why do I suddenly need to speak with her so badly?

Finally, a reply! We haven't spoken in so long, so we have so much to catch up on. I give details about the children. How many? How old? Boy and girl? So excited to tell her how my life is going and what I have been up to. She listens to me go on and on with excitement. I realize who she is to me. She is a mom to me that every woman needs that will sit and listen and just be an ear for you. She doesn't try to tell me what to do, nor am I in competition with anyone for her attention. She is just Mom.

I have the best mother in the world. A woman who is the epitome of strength to me. She wears many hats, and I have never met another woman in this entire world that could ever compare or come close to Irene Brumfield Nowlin. She is the original Mrs. She is the best confidant. She is the prayer warrior. She is the nurse. She is the critic. She is the straight shooter. She made me strong. She helped me heal. She guides me in parenting. She makes me laugh. She can make me upset too. She is fragile, while her vitality is solid. She is easy to love. She is my mother from birth through life and beyond. So Mr. Marc-Train's mom could never compare, yet she is just Mom.

Getting back in communication with Mom has been a blessing for me. I can say things to her and speak freely with her in a way I am unable to do with anyone else. I don't have to worry about sharing things with her and them being repeated incorrectly or assumptions made negatively. We all need someone who is there to listen, not fix anything, just listen. Not take sides, judge, or voice their opinion all the time; just listen. I already have this with my own mom, but for some reason, the desire is there to have this with her too. I can't explain it, but I know it is a mother-daughter relationship that was meant to be. It seems, though, that when I begin to speak and talk about my life, the conversation shifts to the goodness of the Lord every time. Regaining communication with her is a joy, and I realize after months of conversing why.

She told me she was looking for a new job, and I wanted to help her. Taking her résumé and sharing it, all while praying, I believed that God would open a door for her. But now, I just don't need God to open a door, but to also heal her. It has hit me like a ton of bricks to find out she has, of all things, cancer. The tears swelled in my eyes, knowing how horrible this disease is that has killed so many.

Now that I have found a mother figure that I can confide in, talk to, and appreciate, all while being loved, she is stricken with cancer. It is so selfish of me to think about how unfair this is to me and what I desired for us while she is the one going through it.

I want to reach out to Mr. MarcTrain to let him know that I would appreciate him keeping me abreast of anything that is going on with her in the event she is not able to reach out to me—is that too much? Yes, me being selfish. Why would this man want to communicate with me about his sick mother? Just because she has adopted me as a daughter doesn't mean that he is okay with it. Just because she and I are happy to speak with one another doesn't mean that he is. She said she would make sure I was contacted if anything was to ever happen to her.

As she grows worse and is admitted into the hospital, I am wondering how to say something to KB. I made the vow that I would not keep any secrets from him. It doesn't matter the significance; my husband will know everything. But how will he take it? How will he respond? Is it really worth bringing up, or should I just pray from a distance?

Pause. I remember who I am married to. I remember the marriage I am in is not by chance but created by God. I remember that this marriage has already been tried and proven to withstand anything the enemy tries to bring our way. So I open up, and I tell him. Nervous, I tell him. I am not doing anything wrong, there is nothing for him to be upset about and no legit reason to be nervous, but I am.

*Know this:* Ministry is ministry. When you are true to a ministry life, it shows.

Knowing she is in the hospital, I tell KB, and his response is the KB response to be expected, "Let's go pray for her." Our marriage is bigger than us—it is ministry. Going up to Mercy Hospital, I pray that Mr. MarcTrain is not around. My concern is on her, but I don't want there to be any confusion. I know my husband is going because he cares for anyone I care for, just as I care for anyone he cares for. Together we go. Together we love. Together we are strong.

Walking into her hospital room made everything real. Her cancer is real. My relationship with her is real. My need for her in my life as "that mom" is real. She is talking to her sister on the phone that lives down in New Orleans when KB and I walk in and disrupt the call. She says to her sister that she must call her back because Lillian is here. Evidently, her sister asks the question who Lillian is because the next thing she says is, "The one that is supposed to be my daughter-in-law—and she's my daughter anyway!" I smile. She smiles back, acknowledging KB as the son she has gained as well. How these dynamics have come together is one thing that shows God can do anything.

Now KB and I have an Aunty in New Orleans who has accepted us into the family regardless of the history behind our acquaintance. Inviting us to come down whenever we are ready brightened KB's eyes because he has always said he wanted to take me there to experience the culture.

Mr. MarcTrain's mom has become a special woman to me. I care hard for her, and I want the best for her. More importantly, the more we talk, the more I ask God to completely heal her. I desire for all her discomfort to be removed. Cancer is ugly. Cancer is deadly. Cancer makes me sad. But God is beauty. God brings life. God will make us glad because He is bigger than cancer.

*Side note:* Many must cope with loved ones being attacked by this deadly disease. We all deal differently. Cancer seems to suck all the hope, determination, and faith out of people sometimes. There is no easy way to manage. Sometimes you want to have a positive word and message to get you through to the next chapter of life, to the next paragraph of experience, but I've got nothing. I hate cancer!

Inviting her to church was, of course, our plan of action. She, without hesitation, agrees. We realize how small the world is when she tells us how she was once a member of a church we are connected to. She explains how the pastor inappropriately brought a bed into the church for a demonstration, and after that, she left and never went back.

Coming and visiting Mount Hebron was special. She stood as a visitor and let everyone know that I was her daughter (play daughter) that invited her to church. Enjoying the services, she continued to visit and even went to New Jersey with the church for a service, riding the bus and hanging with us as if she had been a part of the church and part of our family forever. She fit right in.

But all good things come to an end. Treatment after treatment. Hospital visit after visit, there seems to be no end to this disease. When she starts looking like she is feeling a little better, her sister down in New Orleans takes ill and becomes sick too. They both want to be there for one another, loving and supporting each other. No matter where they lived, how far the distance from one another, they are there for each other.

Here I am. The play daughter/niece, genuinely concerned for them both, but understanding my place and the complex dynamics of this bond. My job is to pray. My husband right by me, we pray. We believe in the Healer, so we go to Him in prayer.

Cancer is ugly, and it destroys many families. It does not care about what family you came from, what city or state you were raised in, or what your profession may be. Cancer doesn't care how many children you have or how long you have been married. Cancer doesn't care if you haven't had the chance to walk down the aisle or have a baby. Cancer couldn't care any less about your hobby, career, or your future plans. Cancer is ugly, but cancer will not win. We win when we choose to support and love in spite of.

My husband and I with Mr. MarcTrain's mom and aunt. What would be his reaction to his family's acceptance of the woman who chose someone else over him along with the man that took his place? How can he easily deal with this strange arrangement? Part of me wants nothing to do with it, keeping all ties broken, but Mom promised if anything was to ever happen to her, Mr. MarcTrain would do whatever he could to contact me and let me know. After all, I am her daughter.

Cancer. *Dear Abba, Father. I thank You in advance for never having to heal me from cancer. Thank You for keeping cancer far from my body and organs. Thank You for the shield that protects me from any detection of cancer ever coming into my body. I thank You for me never having to say I was healed from cancer but instead always be able to say thank You for never allowing cancer in.*

Call me selfish, insensitive, unreasonable; all I know is I can go to my Father and be specific, and He, like the kind father He is, will answer. I have been here and have become very familiar with facing cancer kill too many times, and I don't desire for that to be my story. I just don't want that for my ending. Not my last chapter.

I saw that naturally, I wanted Mom in my life for what I thought was about a relationship between her and me. God showed me differently. It was about speaking life into her. It was about ministry. It was about giving her a place where a real man of God could lay hands on her, and she should recover. I didn't have to be in a conversation with her every day and every week. I didn't have to invite her over to the house for every big event, even though Brother Tony Cotton would have loved that. I didn't have to be at the mall, shopping with her, or she and I going on trips and out to eat together. My assignment was spiritual. I accepted that and focused more on being the one that called her name out in prayer rather than calling her on the phone. I wanted to fulfill my purpose that God may be glorified.

Nothing in my life can be just a simple, insignificant, minor, inconsequential circumstance. It is not just by chance or opportunity events happen to me. There has to be more, a deeper meaning and purpose behind it all. As I seek understanding, I realize I have to stay faithful. I have to keep feeding my hunger to be more like Christ. I must stay busy with the works of Christ that I may please Him. I can't allow anything or anyone to hinder my destiny. Ministry.

*Know this:* Being true to ministry demonstrates your trueness to God. I'm not a part-time disciple; ministry truly is my life.

I feel cut off from family and friends. The deeper and closer I get to God, the more disconnected it seems I become. Everything and everyone cannot fit in this life of ministry that was designed for me. Everyone cannot have a say in what God has chosen for me. I am not able to be what everyone else wants me to be and who God has appointed me to be. I must choose. I choose ministry.

Going to classes at the C. H. Mason Bible College in the basement of The Good Shepherd COGIC, I not only get deeper into the Word of God, but I gain new acquaintances. It is important for me to finish these classes because I feel the pull on my life, and I need to properly be prepared for what is to come. I was told to take these classes to become a Deaconess Missionary.

I pass all my classes and enjoy the fellowship. But throughout my class time, during the day, and in my dreams, I keep getting the same message that there is more. There is more to taking these classes. It is not about becoming a Deaconess Missionary. It is not about passing the classes because you are being taught by who becomes your favorite teacher in the world, Pastor Isaac Joy. It is not about a title or opportunity. There truly is more.

God is doing something in me that even I cannot fully explain in words. So I cry. I cry as I hear over and over, "I'm not making no more missionaries," belted out over the pulpit, which makes me wonder why I am even taking the classes. I cry as I see others notice the anointing in my life and become literally and spiritually jealous of me. I cry as I am skipped over to minister but always called on to do the work no one else wants to do. I cry as I am only seen as the one that can sing a solo but never taken seriously with God's Word. I cry as I see my children being mistreated and picked on every time God uses me to carry out a spiritual assignment.

I cry as people pretend to care about me and act as if they are nurturing me, but they don't know I overheard their real intentions and thoughts about me. I cry as I feel cut off from others that say they are in ministry because their behaviors don't line up with what they profess. I cry because I feel like not even my own family on any side truly understands and supports what is happening to me as much as my aunty Myrl.

I cry as I see my best friend, who was all I had, go further and further away as I go deeper and deeper in the Lord. I wonder what I did. I wonder how I can stop this from happening. I need my best friend. I have no one else. Everything and everyone else dropping from my circle, I may cry, but somehow, I am able to handle it, but this, not this, this hurt. I hear the rumors; I feel the distance; I see the bad connections. I try to make excuses; I try to make it make sense.

It felt like 1993 all over again, balling my eyes out, pulling off Morgan State University campus, leaving my best friend going back to Da Roc alone without her. This loss hurts more than I can explain. See, I am a person of habit. I am a person of routine. I am a person of loyalty and commitment. I am not a switch-up kind of person. Being switched up on makes my stomach turn. To know all my deepest, darkest, vulnerable components and then become inseparable to a group of people we know mean no good because we discussed it many times made me feel betrayed.

I can't put my finger on why, so I cry. I put on like I am okay because, at this point, any sign of weakness on my part I feel will destroy me. I can remember her voice saying to me after I spoke one evening at a service, "I can see me having to carry your bags as your adjutant when you go out to preach." I didn't think anything of it then, but now I am wondering, *Is that why?* To have my best friend just be my sister and my best friend is all I want. I don't need anyone to be an adjutant and carry my bags. I see less and less of my bestie until I see her no more. No more phone calls, no more visits or family gatherings. I know the pastor is my father, but I never thought we would deal with another father figure separating us again now that we are grown women. His chastisement and harsh communication as pastor always make people take it out on me, the pastor's daughter-in-law.

How is this even happening? It has already been made clear that I will not be allowed to have that sister relationship with my sister-in-law because of jealousy. I don't have that closeness with my mother-in-law either. I have Holmes as my cheerleader and supporter, but I must be careful because I don't want to harm or be harmed by anyone being members of the church my father-in-law pastors. Mr. MarcTrain's mom is not the replacement, so what do I do. I have no one outside of my husband anymore, and with this cutting so deep, I feel I never will again.

God knows what is better for me better than I do. He knew the importance of starving my communication habits until they died. He knew that the only way He could get my full attention was to weed out any possible distraction. I have nothing more to do now, just serve. With my husband, I serve. I make sure he gets down to the church with the boys and cleans the sanctuary. I serve. I cook and feed him and anyone else who is hungry. I serve. I make sure my husband is always available to the church and his father. I serve. I wait as he picks up and drops off members all over the city. I serve.

I couldn't believe my father-in-law made me the Purity Lady for the church, teaching the teenagers when I had a baby out of wedlock, but I serve. He said no better person to teach them, and he was right. I serve. Preparing the back-to-school event every year and making sure the kids have toys for Christmas, I serve. Creating and designing programs, setting up a church computer, being the church financial secretary, I serve. Whatever my hands find to do, or whatever my father-in-law summons me to do, I serve. I get snapped at, yelled at, and sometimes feel unappreciated, but I serve. Teaching Sunday school, being in Young Women's Christian Council, on the praise and worship team, in the choir, part of the missionary board, I serve. Serving got selfishness out of me. Serving made me humble. Serving removed all pride. Serving made me stronger for ministry.

Ministry. Doing work in the church and serving in departments is one level of ministry, but God had more. There are souls out there that need to be reached. I could be one of those souls had it not been for God. I wasn't in the classes to get a license to be a Deaconess or Evangelist missionary; I was in the classes to solidify my learning as the scripture says, "Study to shew thyself approved unto God, a workman that needeth not to be ashamed, rightly dividing the word of truth" (2 Timothy 2:15). All this time, I was caught up in noise being made about titles, authority, opportunity, and notoriety, but God opened my eyes for me to see this was about souls.

Pastor could say all he wanted that he wasn't making any more missionaries. He had every right to say what he wanted as the pastor, but he never made the first missionary God did. I had to understand no one can make you what God has already done. I appreciated my father-in-law, my pastor, for this. It showed God in true form; He was in control. By there being no hopes and dreams of becoming, my mind was focused on the work, and as I went, I became. Without title, without attention, or anyone making mention, I became.

Ministry means a lot to me and KB. Soul business is our sole business. My father-in-law created teams and charged us to go out and witness. We were already doing plenty within the four walls of the church; it was time to go beyond. Together, KB and I would leave the children at home, and we would go to the infamous Mondawmin mall. With tracks in hand, we stood outside one of the main entrances, trying to reach as many souls as possible.

My gift made room for me. I can tell so many the good news without being in front of an audience and a podium. I didn't need to hear a lot of amens; I just needed the ears to hear what

I was saying about Jesus. In the cold and in the warmth, we constantly went out and became a regular fixture at the mall. Many would gather around as I would sing a song, and after the singing would get their attention, KB would say a word to grab them. Sing and grab—all about the souls.

Singing. A gift God gave to me that I take seriously. I was singing, "I love You, I love You, I love You, Lord, today, because You cared for me in such a special way." While I would sing at the mall, there was a man that would linger around being used by the devil who would heckle me. As I would say I love You, he would say, "I hate you," and back and forth, we would go through the entire song. Some of the passer-byes would tell him to cut it out and fuss at him, and he would stop. KB would say something to him, and he would calm down, but I knew my voice was ministry. The anointing in my voice broke down strong walls. The anointing destroyed yokes. I sang to a few like I was singing to millions, giving my all and my best every time.

It was necessary. All of it, for ministry. Using my voice to speak and sing the gospel of Jesus Christ made it all worth it. The ups and downs, the loss, the hurt, the tears. It was all for ministry. I teach with conviction, and I sing with passion because of all I have been through. So I testify in song. When I sing, I'm sure to make it personal. I never sing a song just as the original maker, but I take it as my own.

I am not an entertainer; I take my worship seriously. I realize that I could have had my voice snatched from me back when I would sing in clubs or at house parties. I know I am being effective as someone tells me that I tell too much of my business in a song. That is the reason so many can't get with church now.

Everyone wants to hide their business, but I choose to let my life be ministry. All of it. The good, the bad, and the ugly. It's all about ministry. After singing to God came prayer...prayer warrior is my ministry.

# CHAPTER 24

# In Law, In Flaw

I have turned from opening my mouth to say what is on my mind to opening my mouth and asking God to help me. A hard lesson to learn for a strong-willed person, but I had to accept that God is my defense. How did this come about, you ask? Plenty of humbling moments. Every moment, not so pretty, but teachable.

It is a very uncomfortable feeling sensing that you are the topic of a not-so-favorable conversation. I wonder how I am suddenly the burden, the outcast, and the one that just doesn't fit in. At one point, I was the one everyone talked about as a welcomed addition, a blessing, anointed, gifted, and talented. I came that way from the schooling, morals, and values instilled in me throughout childhood from my parents.

I have always had a level of confidence, but sometimes when you are made to feel unworthy of the love you are receiving, you start to believe that you have a negative self-image. When you start feeling like people are being distant to you and you don't understand why you look within to see what you have done, you wonder what changed. You start to realize that maybe people never looked at you as an entity with potential but as a threat.

Marrying into a family, you begin to see that while we are all human, we all don't do things the same. That doesn't make one right and the other wrong; it makes us different. A marriage is an opportunity to put those unique differences together and make an even more unique implementation of family. It takes everyone knowing that they don't have it all together and that we need one another to become better. As soon as one feels that they are merely there to be helped and can offer nothing when they know and see different, the flaws begin.

In-laws. This is part of marriage. Mothers-in-law, fathers-in-law, sisters, and brothers-in-law. There are many layers to the in-law aspect of marriage that can make or break a relationship. This is a very sensitive matter, and if not handled correctly, can be very damaging. KB and I must learn just like anyone else; there's no way of getting around it.

What's odd is your in-laws also being your pastor and first lady. One of the very first places you should always be able to run to for guidance and direction in marriage is to your spiritual leaders. But what if they are your in-laws? Can you express what you need to and go through the growing phases of a marriage without the lines being crossed? Is there any objectivity, or will there be private scrutiny? If you've never experienced it, how can you properly go through it and be correct all the time? This is new for me, for KB, for my parents, and of course for his parents, our spiritual leaders, so obviously, no one will get everything right.

In ministry, my husband is always the go-to all-hands-on deck guy for his father and the church as he should be. But what happens when he has family responsibility and obligation? My husband has been raised to be a man and to take care of his family first. His father taught him that. He is to go according to what the Bible says. A man leaves his mother and father and cleaves to his own wife. The problematical part about that is when the lines are blurred between family and ministry.

I see my in-laws three to four times a week because of church, not because of family. The family portion only came when controlled by one side and not properly gathered by both. This causes my involvement or noninvolvement in church to be measured as family interaction, which should never be. Everything about my life and my world is surrounded by the church and my husband's family. My family at a distance in Da Roc, I never really get to see as much of, so KB's family tends to be more influential and prominent. I started to feel like I was only the go-to person when something needed to be done, but outside of that, I was just that...outside. I don't like the picking and choosing when I get to be treated as important to others or not. I choose to back off.

KB has a responsibility to be the head of this household. We are his top priority. If anything goes wrong, I don't look for his father or any other man to rectify anything—it's all him. Although I don't have a close relationship with my father, even if I did, I don't look for him to manage my home; that's KB's job. My uncle Bill who is always a father to me, doesn't have any say or rights in my home either. Just KB, that's all. KB had to know that. KB had to learn that. KB had to own that. KB became and did just that.

Control. Everyone cannot have control. Everyone should not have control, especially over another's life. Every holiday, every event, every vacation cannot be dictated based on desires that may not be the same for everyone. As a self-sufficient person, going into a family that has controlling traits can be difficult. The controlling isn't always negative but may sometimes become overbearing.

I had to learn controlling individuals don't always mean harm or don't believe in you or trust your capability, but they like to monitor and keep things stable according to their desires. It is a need to feel safe and on top of things with so many unsure and unstable surroundings. I had to accept I could not fight the family trait of being controlling, but I had to express to my husband how it made me feel so that we could find a way to cope.

You never want anyone to feel offended when you choose to do something your way instead of what they suggest, but when they are conditioned to be in control all of the time, you are bound to offend and be offended. You don't mean to, but you do. I cope. You don't want your spouse to feel like they are about to be in the middle of something that could go wrong really quickly, so I cope. You never want your spouse to feel like they have to choose a side, so I cope. You laugh, you enjoy, and you make the best of moments, but after a while, it starts to make you feel marginalized. But I must cope.

You may have an overly sensitive in-law that will make every decision about them. It makes the entire family feel like they must come to the rescue and defend the helpless one. But when you are the one that made the not-so-favorable decision, you have now become the villain, and your in-laws are victims. I cope.

When there are no boundaries, there is chaos. When there are boundaries, but it is not made clear and detailed to everyone, there is another level of chaos to deal with. KB has the utmost respect for his parents, and I love that about him. Those are his parents, the ones who raised him, the ones who provided for him, the ones who made it possible for him to live the life he has lived. Everyone should have that same utmost respect for their parents. When you become an in-law and join that family, you have the same respect, but also remember that your parents aren't diminished because there is now another set of parents. Your in-laws can't take credit for who or what you are or are not, but they can encourage and be motivation to keep striving for better.

Because my relationship with my father is so scarred, I appreciated and gladly welcomed my father-in-law as my poppy. I didn't take the place of my sister-in-law. We weren't now in competition for his attention. He didn't need to treat her badly to make me feel welcomed into the family; he was just a dad. My relationship differed from hers and from KB's, but he is Poppy to us all. I didn't need him to be my husband; his son has that spot, but my dad—yes. He is encouraging; he can make you feel like you can accomplish anything; he is a great support. To talk with him about the Lord on the phone for hours, get prayed for, and help make plans to do different things for ministry is awesome. I always wanted that, needed that, and appreciated it, but then I got hurt.

There have to be boundaries. Some decisions are not up for a family council and debate. We take the advice and make the choice we feel is best. That should not put us in a category as know-it-alls where we no longer need advice because we chose to do differently. KB defending and speaking up for his wife is not being disrespectful; it's him setting boundaries. KB making sure my momma doesn't interfere with him raising our son isn't him disregarding the reverence due to her; it's him setting boundaries. This is not rejection; this is living, growing, decision making, and sometimes we get it right, and sometimes we get it wrong. But there must be boundaries.

On the outside, looking in, all is peachy. I am an asset; I am a blessing; I am a benefit and key component that some families with this dynamic don't have. But when you have abilities, and you have skills, and you have wherewithal and stick-to-itiveness, sometimes that is also seen as a vulnerability. It is a welcomed advantage as long as it doesn't make anyone of importance seem less than. Oftentimes, what you are and what you can do intimidate others. One of the biggest mistakes a family can make is comparing one person to another. My skills and capabilities should not be measured by someone else's. That includes dumbing myself down or building myself up more than I should be.

To support me doesn't mean not to support someone else. To appreciate what I bring to the table doesn't mean everyone else lacks purpose. Accomplishments shouldn't be diminished to appease others' status. To be wrong about something doesn't make you a terrible person; it makes you human. None of us get it right all the time. Parents do get some things wrong, but that doesn't make them terrible people. That doesn't make them ones to be hated for life. It makes them normal. My in-laws are normal. So am I.

Being an in-law doesn't mean that you are taking something away; it means that you are adding something. It means that you are joining something. It means that you are multiplying something. When the feeling changes from a gain to a loss, it shows in the behaviors and the treatment of in-laws.

*Know this:* Noticing something that isn't right with a person isn't always made known for you to exploit their error. Sometimes God allows you to learn what to do by showing you what not to do.

Boundaries. Setting boundaries doesn't mean that you've removed yourself from the family. To eliminate conflict, I learned that I don't always have to stand my ground; I just choose my environments wisely so there will be no need for me to. I stand with and support my husband at all times, but it was hard for him to stand and support me like he sees his father do for his mother, especially when it was his father he needed to stand against.

It was one crazy Tuesday night, one that I would never forget. I was so taken aback by it that I had to write about it in my diary. I had a hard day at work and wasn't feeling well at all. I almost fell asleep driving home from work. I knew I had to go to church because we had Bible study, but I really wanted to just get under my covers and rest. My house was out of order, and I needed to cook dinner for my family. My husband had car issues, so we had to deal with that. I had Christmas gifts that needed to be wrapped and at this point, getting some rest was out of the question. If I had laid down and fallen asleep, I would not have gotten back up to go to church.

We got to church late, and when I got there, my pastor, my father-in-law, called me to the front at the side of the pulpit. He began railing at me, fussing at me for not getting a report done before a meeting he was having later in the week. As the church financial secretary, each month, I completed the reports and would have if I had the time. I explained I didn't have a chance yet, and that was unacceptable to him.

Reading my diary, I see how my responses were very unbothered at his urgency. I didn't feel well, and I didn't appreciate how he was talking to me. It got worse. The back and forth. Him telling me of all the days and times I had the opportunity to get the report done. I had to reply, explaining that I am a whole wife. I am an active participant in the ministry. I have a whole job. My weekend was taken up making pans of mac 'n' cheese for a dinner we had at the church. I worked all week, cooked all weekend, did my daughter's hair, and prepared for church, then had church on that Sunday, where I was never able to just sit back and spectate. After service, I served the people, and of course, this is Mt. Hebron, we had an evening service.

The conflict was he felt I had time to get the report done, and I felt differently. I accepted what he felt, but that was not good enough. There needed to be more. I had nothing more to give at this point. The entire Bible study class can hear him talking to me. They clearly are not paying attention to the teacher. They see him towering over me. I wanted to walk away, but I immediately thought about how disrespectful that would look. So I stood there. Trying to be as respectful as possible, I stood there. I offered to do the report right at that moment, and he didn't want me to work while the class was happening, but he could yell at me during the class, though.

I explained I wanted to get the report done, but I had to do it in a way where it was balanced and convenient for me, not anyone else, and on Tuesday or Thursday were the times that I was able to work on it because that was when I was here at the church. He felt I should come to the church during off church days and hours to do the work, but I disagreed. Just because my husband had a key to the church and we could get in whenever we wanted or needed didn't mean that our time and life schedule could accommodate that. He said, "No work is to be done during church time," although that was how and when I had done the work up until now.

The conversation got louder as he got more aggravated. The report was due only once per month, he exclaimed, so it wasn't hard for me to get it done; I just needed to fit it in. I began to say to him, "I am doing work for the church on top of my other responsibilities. The last time I said what I had to do for my family, you went and said something to Kenny as if I had said something very wrong because I had to feed my children in between services, and I know I hadn't said anything wrong because that is what you preach here—that a woman's first responsibility is to take care of her home. I do what I do for the church because I want to help. I have the skill and capability to do so. I fully support this church and don't feel that I should have to further inconvenience myself when what could be done can be done while I am here on a Tuesday or Thursday night."

I was looking up to him as he stood over me from the pulpit, looking down at me with a stand of intimidation, eyes glaring as if I was prey and he was getting ready to attack for the kill. Full of fury, he came down and sat on the side of the pulpit, where he became louder with the conversation. I could feel out the corner of my eye that the Bible study was being distracted. I was trying to figure out how I could get out of this, how I could walk away. *Lord, please give me a way of escape.* He went in to say, "I don't care what I told Kenny, just like I'm going to tell you, and I will tell Kenny again." At this point, being loud and inappropriate, I felt like I couldn't take anymore—the bomb was getting to drop; this was not going to end pretty, and I didn't even understand how I got here. I should have stayed home.

Feeling sick to my stomach, wondering why I ever even pressed my way to church, I felt like there would be no resolution, and this man was showing me that he clearly didn't respect me or what I had to do for my home or the church. Words were forming in my head, but none of them seemed respectful, none of them seemed like peaceful words, nothing but venom ready to fly out like fire to defend myself as I felt I was not in a conversation with my leader, my pastor, my husband's father, my father, my father-in-law, the grandfather of my children, the man I look up to and have such great and high respect and dependence on.

Defense mode came on, and I was ready to attack back. Asking the Holy Ghost to intercede on my behalf, I saw out of the corner of my eye walking towards me...my covering. As he came closer, he said, "Hey, hey, this conversation is loud. Pop, don't you think you need to take this in the office?" He replied, "Kenny, I am telling your wife that when I say I need something done, it needs to be done." "Pop, I know, but come on, let's take this in the office," KB replies.

"That is what I am saying, Kenny. He is not trying to hear what anyone else has to say on the matter; he wants it his way or no way, and you can't tell me to do something according to your time when it is me that is doing it, so it needs to be according to my time. There isn't even a will to compromise." He replied, "Compromise. I don't compromise with no one."

Trying to stay respectful, but at the same time I have had enough, I said, "Well, maybe that was the wrong choice of words, but what I am saying is I have been doing the reports and delivering what you request because I know what to do and how to do it. You don't know how to use the computer; if you did, you could do the reports yourself." Kenny again tried to end the conversation asking his father to take this into the office because the people could hear us, and with ferocity and wrath, his father said, "I don't care!" I couldn't take anymore as I heard myself saying, "See Kenny, he doesn't care, and he is wrong!"

I remember walking back to my seat to sit in the rest of the Bible study in shock. I was so humiliated and embarrassed. I wanted to walk out of the church and never show my face again, but I sat there. I knew walking away would have looked disrespectful, so I had to take it. I was even more hurt because when my covering came to cover me, my father-in-law chose not to respect my husband not only as a man intervening for his wife but as a son he could talk to any kind of way he deemed appropriate. What broke me was when KB tried to calm him down later, and he would not even hear him out. He kept saying to

KB, "That's *your* wife." That hit me hard, and it hit my husband even harder. From that day forward, I question every time I am mentioned as a daughter. A boundary was set.

My diary goes on to express: "

> *My emotions are all over the place, yet there is a peace that is within me. A peace that won't allow me to shed not one tear. A peace that will allow me to become angry, but sin not. A peace that I don't quite understand, yet I am thankful to God for it. Who talks to a woman in this manner in front of the congregation while Bible study is going on and thinks that this is okay?*
>
> *"With my husband standing there, you still deem it appropriate to talk to someone's wife as if she didn't deserve respect. Knowing good and well if a man was talking to his wife in the tone and aggressive manner that you talked to me, you would not have that, yet you put my husband in a position where he knew he needed to step up and handle business just like you would if it was your wife, all at the same time recognizing that you are his father, his pastor, the man he looks up to. I never wanted my husband to be in a position like this. I spoke a message on Sunday...didn't quite finish it, but I know it was for me, "Shut the door." Some things must come to an end, and no better time than now..."*

Whew...what a diary entry. What hurt, what pain. I ended the entry saying:

"So the Lord woke me up early this morning to go before Him in prayer. I was wide awake. Went out to the living room and covered myself with a blanket and began to sing and pray. Praying and singing...then I began to ask the Lord, "Why?" Why am I always the one that has to be tough and take things that I shouldn't have to go through? All I ever wanted was a happy family, and I can't get that on either side. Yes, my immediate family, husband, and children. In our home, there is peace; there is love and contentment. But as soon as one additional factor comes into the picture, the atmosphere changes. The Lord let me know this morning that this test is not for me to be made strong, but it is for me to hurt, to feel pain, that I might learn to depend on him. So with that being said, finally... I cried... I cried almost the entire way to work, every now and then belting out a moan here and there. I was trying my hardest to keep my composure while dropping my son off to school. He asked me if I was okay, and all I could say was that I would be fine. I needed to release this hurt, release this pain. I only wish I had my husband to hold me to cry on his shoulder, to wipe away my tears. Then, the Lord revealed to me that He allowed the tears to flow like a broken levy while my husband was not around to show me that He was there; He was the lifter up of my head; He was my comforter, my strength and redeemer. Look to Him..."

My husband showed so much strength and restrain. Flesh would say, "Why didn't he fight for me?" But the spirit said, "Because we were as sheep counted up for the slaughter, we will be rewarded. We may have been cast down but not destroyed."

KB and I communicate and understand that for us to grow together, we need to set boundaries. We need to set realistic expectations. We need to refrain from conflict engagement and not allow there to be any public drama. I refuse to put my husband in a position where he feels he is going to have to choose between his parents and me, so I distance myself, so there is no reason for there to be a conflict. I never want my husband to ever feel less than a man because of me. I no longer have a desire to be an exemplary daughter that my in-laws can be proud of. My duty is to my husband, and that is my focus. Everything else is secondary, even church work.

I felt banished, downgraded, and ostracized. It didn't feel good, but for my husband to be at peace, I had to be okay with whatever I was dealt. I had to put on that I was okay so he wouldn't worry about his father and me. I realized that I was not my husband, nor was I my sister-in-law, so taking that type of talking was not for me. I would never get used to it. I would never accept it. But before I became disrespectful, I would take being sidelined.

Afraid of what might be said, I scaled back on being around. I tried to take everyone's viewpoint into consideration. I didn't play victim to my husband or anyone else because I didn't want to be looked at as dragging anyone's name or reputation down. I didn't feel I got the same in return, but I wanted to make sure I was representing my husband correctly.

Having difficulties with in-laws doesn't mean anyone in particular is toxic. I realize we are different. I make an effort to understand the importance we all play in the family and respect that. I see that I cannot take everything personally, even if it is meant to be personal. I choose to encourage my husband to stay attached to his parents and family and do not ever feel he has to lose them to fully have me.

I missed out on being an aunt to my nieces and nephews. I missed out on being a more involved sister and sister-in-law to my side of the family. I sacrificed it all for ministry and gave every ounce of me to this life here in Bmore. I felt that it was the right thing to do, but in-laws matter and have a place with balance. Having in-laws overly involved in every part of your life is just as bad as having in-laws that are no part of your life at all.

I didn't get invited to the brunch and girl's day out. I was left out of the cruise trips for daughters. I wasn't picked up and whisked off to the mall for a day of window shopping or shopping sprees. It was just me. My flaws were made more apparent than anything else. To anyone looking on, obviously, I had to be wrong because certainly, my reputation doesn't stand a chance against anyone else's. I had to be the issue. I had to be the flaw.

# CHAPTER 25

# Writing, Therapy in Black and White

So I am a writer now. Mommy gave me a diary book as a wedding gift, and it was time to release the writing. Being unemployed for so long, at one point, I had time at home to do just that—release. I have been so hurt and disappointed in my life, past and present, so I write. I feel I have been taken for granted, so I write. I have no other outlet. I go to church, and I feel the stares and the glares, so I write. Throughout the years, there have been so many negative incidents that I no longer have a desire to be around any of the same people who initially seemed to be supportive of me. I get sick to my stomach and want to vomit every time I go to church or be around family, so I write.

Writing down all that has happened in my past, I pray I come across something that can help me with what I feel right now. I have been lied on, talked about, left out, and treated as a house guest who overstayed their welcome. I complete my writing to keep myself poised. I complete my writing to give me my own voice. Black and white therapy is priceless.

In doing all this writing, I had no idea what to do next until Nakeia. Meeting over food, we became the best phone pals, but it was when I found out she was an editor that I knew we were meant to be. Nakeia agreeing to edit my writing was a treat for her and me. Writing and being able to let out all that had been bundled up in me for years was more therapeutic than I knew.

As I went through learning about getting things copywritten, ISBN numbers, submitting my work to the library of congress, getting the correct typesetting, and completely nervous about what people would think about my life, Nakeia was right there. Reading my chapters as I wrote them, she became like a fan. She was supposed to be editing, but she was reading the book as a book reader, not an editor. Engulfed in the characters, she was able to get the full detail of my life.

Nakeia was all the way on the west coast, which made our time zones different. It would be past my bedtime and into the early mornings, and we would be on the phone going through reading the book over and over as my life was being made to black and white. My friend-turned-editor encouraged me all the way. When I didn't know how to stop or where to stop, when I didn't want to write, God put it in me to do. Mom said it would be the diary of a pastor's daughter-in-law, but I had to first tell how I got there. *The Covering.*

From one chapter to the next, Nakeia inspired me to remain transparent, and I couldn't help but be real. No need to make anything up because my life on its dullest day was full of energy. The sorrows, the joys, the pain, and the lessons learned. I always thought my life was a mess and embarrassing until God told me to write. Writing helped me understand that so many can relate to my life because they, too, have gone through some of the same things.

*Know this:* Writing a book is awesome therapy, but that doesn't rule out other forms of therapy.

All for ministry. I started to understand that being an open book invites others in to understand there is no need to try and be perfect. There is a disconnect within churches where many don't feel they fit in because they are looking at the current product and not what once was. God told me to write to close the gap. I was to tell all to show that although everything in my life may look perfect right now, it is far from perfect. So I write. Writing becomes ministry.

Nakeia and Nakeia only is my editor, but I wanted to run my writing by my husband's aunt to get her take on my grammar since she is an English professor. I sent the script to my siblings as well to get a jump on the reading. I didn't want anyone to think I was going to embarrass them or humiliate my family. This book is about me and my triumphs. No need for me to write anything in anger or with malicious intent. There is no healing in doing that. KB's aunt was shockingly surprised at my transparency. She even asked me if, now that I had written *The Covering* and got it all out of my system, there was still a need to publish it for others to read.

I didn't understand the question. I thought the book was good, so why ask me to consider not publishing? She explained that I went into a lot of detail in the book and was very forthcoming about many private and personal events in my life. She went on to say, one day, my girls would be old enough to read this book, and she didn't think it was something they should read or know about their mother. I replied, "They are the reason I wrote the book." They came from me; they are my daughters; they are a part of me; therefore, they are like me and will very well most likely experience some things like me. If no one else shares their life with them, the last person to keep life a secret should be me.

Here lies the problem with families and people in general now. So many want to wear a mask of always having things together and never having anything out of place and are only fooling themselves. Family secrets and internal competitions have had families at odds for generations. Me, I choose to be different. I choose to break the mode. I choose to not be confounded by the useless traditions, lowered ceilings, and brick walls.

She may have been embarrassed of what I had gone through, but my daughters will appreciate their mother never hid anything from them, and who she is today came through a lot of hard times and suffering to be respected. I came a long way, and I don't ever want my girls to think I was always well put together all the time. They need to read about me in my mess to respect me in my triumph. They can value who I am today because of what they know I have survived. Everyone won't understand that, but at this point, who cares?

My favorite cousin Kevin Berry did the artwork for the cover, and all I needed was a print company to get books printed. United Book Press, Inc., over in Woodlawn, Maryland, took my book for printing, but now I needed the money to pay. At the beginning of this venture, I was not working, and I had no money to fund this project. I knew that once the book came out, I could make money from it, but to make money, you must spend money. Harriett, knowing my passion and eager to read the book herself, began inquiring and pushing me to get the book out.

With her free spirit and giving heart, we came to an agreement for her to fund the printing but for me to pay her back. She knew the bind I was in, not working and needing an income. She was willing to take a risk on me selling this book to pay off what she invested. I could not believe she was doing this, but it was happening. Because of her and Nakeia, my life in black and white was coming out for the entire world to see.

Now I needed someone to market the book and get me some media coverage. Timea Gaines stepped up to the challenge and began promoting the book and doing a countdown to the release. When the case of books came to the house, opening the box and smelling the books made it real. All over social media, I was letting everyone know about my book release party and book signing events. People showed up, and I was selling books left and right. In church, on my new job, on Amazon, I'm everywhere. Timea made plans for me to go back home to Da Roc for a book signing event. My brother's good friend Monsanto, who is like a brother to me also, owned a restaurant and gave the okay for me to hold the book signing at Arnette Cafe.

With everything planned and underway, I couldn't have asked for anything more. People were getting the book and reading it within a day. Down south, up north, east coast, west coast, and everywhere in between, the reviews kept coming with a thumbs up. I wrote a book and my life became a target of display. I wrote because people needed to see they were not the only person going through the phases of life they were dealing with. I needed to face things from the past for my marriage to not fall apart.

February, I got the call while in church from Major Reynolds that I got the job. March, my book was released, and then came April. Everything was going as planned. I was sidetracked by the excitement and didn't focus on blocking any ways the devil would try to creep in and disturb this moment. I knew there was jealousy and gossip behind the book, but I didn't care. I knew it was going to help many, so I stayed focused. Brand new on my job, I immediately made friends, and everyone was more like family. In no time, as I began introducing myself and telling everyone what I did, they purchased my book too.

On my job. With my book just coming out. The Monday after Resurrection Sunday, April 21, 2014, KB called me while I was at my desk. He said to me with distress in his voice that Dr. Levy just called him and said that he has end-stage renal failure. Pause. I made KB go to the doctor because he wasn't eating his normal portion sizes and other signs that he was coming down with something. Coming down with something that antibiotics can fix, something that a steroid would clear up, something that a change in daily habits can fix—not end-stage renal failure.

He began telling me Dr. Levy said he would have to get on dialysis for the rest of his life. KB's cousin Lenny is on dialysis and goes multiple times a week for treatment, and that's all KB could think about—he didn't want that life. In shock, I didn't think KB heard correctly, and I needed to talk to Dr. Levy myself. I asked him what he was supposed to do, and he said the doctor wanted him to come at the end of the week. The end of the week was too long for me. I needed to understand what he had been told now.

KB, working at the Baltimore City Community College, had to be at work not knowing what all this meant. I called his doctor, and Dr. Levy confirmed to me what KB said. I needed to understand why he would tell KB this over the phone and not let me know. Why would you say something so life-changing and then say, "See me Friday"? He was so apologetic and expressed that he should have told me first or with KB to handle this better. He was trying to reach a specialist and said he would call me back. I emailed my support sister Harriett and told her to pray for me *now*!

I didn't get a call back until Tuesday afternoon. On my drive home from work, Dr. Levy called and said the specialist wanted KB to come in immediately. We needed to get over to GMBC Hospital emergency as soon as we could. I called KB's parents and told them. I knew this was going to be hard for KB to accept. Tuesday night was Bible study night. Wednesday night, he was supposed to be a guest speaker at another church. I told him we had to go to the hospital. We went. He had his Bible with him with expectations that he would be examined, told the diagnosis was wrong, and we would go home. He had to stay. So I stayed.

KB had kidney failure. According to his medical records, his blood work shows his kidneys had not been functioning for seven years, and we were never told anything. I immediately went back to when God worked an Easter miracle in my life for Zion and believed that He would do it again for my husband.

The doctor explained to us that there are multiple ways to do dialysis, and KB had to choose which one he wanted to do. He chose peritoneal dialysis, which would enable him to continue to work and still have a normal life. We cried. Then faith kicked in.

KB needed a kidney transplant, but until then, he needed to have surgery to put the line in for his dialysis treatments. With the family dynamics being what they were, things were already tense. KB taking ill didn't make matters any better. Dr. Levy pulled me into the hallway to speak with me and gave me the one-on-one pep talk. He said to me that he had dealt with situations like this many times, and I needed to follow his instructions.

He said the only way that KB would survive this was if I was strong. He explained that KB would give up and not want to fight if it seemed too much for me to handle. He said that if KB felt like he was bringing the family sorrow and sadness, he would choose to give up instead of bringing difficulty to the family. Dr. Levy said KB needed to be celebrated. He said KB needed to want to live and have a reason to live. It was almost KB's fortieth birthday, and I wanted to do a surprise party for him. Dr. Levy told me to do it, "Don't wait, don't stall, do it."

Every day, I had the same routine waking up at five in the morning at the hospital. I would leave there while KB was sleeping and drive to the house where Zion was taking care of the kids. I would get them all up to get ready for school, and I would shower and change to go right back up to the hospital to meet the doctors for rounds. I was so proud of Zion for stepping up and being responsible. I needed him to take charge, and he did. Regardless of what he had done before, when it was time, he was up for the challenge.

My in-laws were very short with me, and things seemed to get worse and worse. I decided I had to be in tune with God to survive this. I knew this was nothing but an opportunity for God to get the glory out of our lives, so I always had to conduct myself like so. I thought maybe this crisis would bring us back closer, but only if within the right parameters. I knew KB was used to be the one sleeping on the uncomfortable chair in GBMC. That's what he did for Dion when she was sick in this same hospital; now, years later, he was in the bed, and I was in the chair.

KB has always been the one trying to take care of everyone. He was always wanting to make sure everyone was okay and trying to do whatever he could. This time it was him. His first time ever in his entire life having to be hospitalized. He was worried about everyone worrying about him. He was trying to do all he could to make everyone else comfortable about him being in discomfort. That was KB's heart. That was who KB was. He didn't deserve to be going through this and then add on top of this, being concerned about everyone else's wellbeing.

As his wife, I looked at him and told him I needed him to focus on himself. We had children at home that need their father. We had a whole life to live, so he needed to focus on getting out of here. I saw just what Dr. Levy was saying to me. I told everyone there would be no sadness coming to this hospital room. Anyone sad stayed home. We would not make KB feel like he had to comfort anyone. He was the one going through, and we were either going to be here for him or not be here at all. My standards weren't taken well, as his mom became very upset, saying to KB and me that I couldn't tell her how to grieve. I said he wasn't dead, so there was no reason to grieve anyway.

From that point, I was alone. Somehow it turned into stress for the parents watching their son go through rather than the real stress of the son concerned about his future. It bothered me that everyone was making what we were going through about them going through. It was time for KB to have surgery to get the line put in to start dialysis. His father and uncle were there at the hospital. When the time came for them to wheel him back to the operating room, they left to get something to eat. No one asked if I wanted anything—they just left.

No one thought about if I needed someone to stay with me for support; they just left. Everyone was going through, and this was hard for everyone, but I was the only one there. As I kissed KB before going into the surgery waiting room, my mind went into twilight. We were a young couple with young children. I wanted KB to see his kids graduate. I want KB to see his kids get married and have grandchildren. I didn't want to be a widow.

I sat in the waiting room and looked around. It was other families there sitting with each other and supporting each other, and I was the only one in there alone. They had a loved one in surgery, but they also had support with them while they waited. I had nothing. What did I do to deserve this? While sitting there, a code blue came over the loudspeaker. We all looked up, and each family began talking to one another. We were all hoping the same thing—that it wasn't our loved one having the code blue.

I had no shoulder to cry on, no hand to hold. I was about to break, and my phone received a text message. It was my aunt Marilyn. I started crying as I texted her. She wanted an update, and I began telling her how I was all alone in the waiting room. She asked where KB's family was and became bothered when I told her they all left. She told me I was not alone. She confirmed what I already knew, God was with me, and that was more than an entire family being there. It still hurt.

I told her I would keep her posted, and as the Lord began to comfort me sitting there alone, I felt her prayers over me, and I noticed strength came into my being. Now was not the time for me to give up or become weak. In my weakness, I felt God making me strong. As I looked down at my phone, Dr. Levy came and sat next to me. He began to tell me KB did well in the surgery and was going into recovery. My head just fell onto his shoulder, and I wept.

I had to have Timea put out a cancellation on my book release. The concern was postponing would cause the book to lose momentum, but I didn't care. My husband meant more to me than the book. I didn't want to be a widow, so not doing book signing events did not matter to me. In the hospital, KB could not get out of bed for forty-eight hours as he received his first treatments of dialysis after surgery. I was there the entire time as his doctor, and I made plans for us to get trained on how to do dialysis after we left the hospital.

Being in bed unable to move for two days was more impactful on the body for KB than he knew. When it was time to get up, he could barely move. He was only able to hold on to the wall while I held him up and bathed him like a child. He was so helpless. He looked so down. I bathed him with joy. I bathed him with excitement. I bathed him, knowing that I could be mourning him. That was how I looked at everything. I would rather put in all this work taking care of him instead of him being dead and gone.

I was not a widow. I was not a great communicator either when my mind was set to do one thing. Family and friends alike felt that I was not keeping in contact and keeping everyone updated. I was trying to take care of KB and trying to run updates to everyone, and it wasn't working for me. I had no help until the frat stepped in. They made sure I was okay. They made sure all their bruhs stayed informed, so I didn't have to call each one back. They stayed up at the hospital with me, and never did I worry about being by myself because they were there. My family couldn't be there is all the way in Da Roc; KB's family picked and chose when and how they were going to be there, but the fraternity was there.

I had to write. This was my therapy. This was my conversation. This was my getaway. More and more people were purchasing the book. My own father unannounced came down to Bmore to get the book. He said he was coming to check on KB, but his focus was getting the book to see what I said regarding him. I was getting email after email from so many about the book, and it brought excitement and joy to KB and me.

My job sent me a laptop and told me to work from home and take care of my husband as long as I needed. Kevin had flowers delivered to the hospital, and when KB came home, he came over to visit. I remembered what the doctor said, so I planned a surprise birthday party for KB that was hard to do. I didn't have the support of his family. Trying to go through my sister-in-law for everything seemed so petty, and I was over it. The enemy was in my mind saying, "Leave and have his family come take care of him." I was tired of hearing people say how they were praying for his parents and praying for their strength. No, pray for his strength. Pray for my strength. I was the one taking care of him. I knew what Satan was doing, so I had to breathe deep and resist the devil.

At his party, KB's uncles, aunts, frat, and church family and friends surprised him. I booked the Luna Del Sea Bistro Restaurant and was so happy he was surprised. Going home that night as he did his dialysis treatment, he expressed how happy he was but how down he felt at the same time because of the demeanor of his parents. I felt like it was my fault and really wished he was married to someone else, not me, so his family could be better. I wouldn't say anything to him, but we are one, so when he hurts, and I hurt. So I write.

I posted on social media that KB needed a kidney. I said that this was going to be a faith walk, and by faith, we were going to get through this. There was such an outpouring of love and support. But one message stood out. A young lady reached out to me and said that she had been praying and asked God to give her an assignment—a purpose. She said that after she prayed that prayer, she got on Facebook and saw my post about KB needing a kidney. She was the same blood type that KB needed. She read that I said we were going to make it through this by faith, and her name was Faith.

KB and I had gone down to the University of Maryland, where KB selected that he didn't care whose kidney he received as long as he was on the list. KB and I became closer and closer as I took care of him hand and foot. Sitting with him during his treatments and trying to adjust his meal plans to be healthier. Faith kept in contact with me as if she had known me all my life. I had never met her, but the fact that she wanted to give my husband one of her kidneys made me instantly love her.

KB and I went through training at a DaVita Dialysis Center in Woodlawn, MD. God favored us, and we had a black nurse trainer who couldn't help but talk about the Lord with us. She was honest with us and said that most people, especially couples, came in very optimistic and supportive of this training. She said that after a while, the patient began to come on their own because the spouse was unable to handle the severity of kidney failure. She told us how a lot of marriages didn't make it through something like this. All I could think about was how much I truly loved KB and did not want to live without him. Week after week, I was right there, and the office was amazed because generally, at some point, the support ends. If KB and I were going to stay together or not, I was not going to leave him to have to do this on his own.

KB went back to work after I went to his office to make sure the place was sanitized enough for him to do dialysis treatments there. He was starting to feel stronger and more confident. As Faith went through the screening to make sure she was a good match, we did nothing but trust God. Her own parents weren't all that happy that she was doing this, but we believed that it was nobody but God that could orchestrate such a thing.

We were getting spiritual insight from many people. We were getting advice from many others. KB and I would sit up at night and during treatments and talk about how so many have opinions about getting a transplant, but we only saw it one way. However God wanted to heal, that was what we wanted. We would not be picky or choosy. We would let God have his way.

We had to remind people this wasn't about me; this wasn't about KB's parents, family, or friends; this was about KB. He is only forty years old and still has a whole lot of life ahead of him. This was about him surviving. This was about him extending his life here on earth to remain being a son, a brother, a grand-son, nephew, cousin, and somewhere down the line a husband and father and one day, grandfather. So I stayed quiet. I used my therapy, and I wrote.

# Bonus Chapter

I swallowed it. What I had to accept as KB's wife, not even being concerned about was tough, but I swallowed it. My husband was near death, and I had to take hits like I had done wrong. The cold shoulder, the unease, and intense gatherings were just odd and uncomfortable for my children and me. KB, wanting everyone to get along, tried his best to be the peacemaker, but it seemed things only got worse.

I knew we needed to focus on his health, so I chose to make myself be invisible. I didn't want anything to be said or done to me, especially now while KB was sick, to make him feel like he would need to speak up for and defend me from anything being said. I choose to make myself even more distant. I started hearing things being said in church that made me question if it was being referred to me. KB heard them too, but again only wanted peace. God told me to stay quiet, so I did.

The back-to-school event this year was a blast. I was able to get sponsors who helped me pay for all the things I got to make the event a memorable one. Instead of supporting me and the church event, some made plans to do another event on the same day so people wouldn't show up to support what is an annual church function, but I didn't care. My job paid for us to get donkeys for the inner-city children to ride on. We had inflatable mountain climbing moonbounces and so much school supplies, more than ever before. It was like God had opened the flood gates for me to be a blessing like it was going to be my last time. I gave it all I had like I always did, and despite other events and no shows, it was a huge turnout and the best back-to-school event ever done. I was amazed at its success, and so was the rest of the community. I found peace in doing things God could get the glory from.

Just as we are getting the hang of dialysis and preparing for a kidney transplant, KB was saying the Lord was speaking to him, dealing with him on some things. I shared with him that I was willing to hold on and support him however I could and do my duties as a wife, but it was getting really hard. I had never fasted and prayed as much in my life. It really got intense the day that we were in a Sunday morning service, and the oddest statement was made.

In the middle of my father-in-law preaching, as he had the crowd on their feet, including me, he turned to KB to address him directly. He said to him, "Son, God didn't give you to nobody else in this room but me and your momma!" I was confused. I was humiliated. I was at a loss for words. After service, some came to me and asked me what that meant. I told them they needed to ask the person who said it, not me. Person after person was coming up to me as I was trying to hightail it to the car so I wouldn't have to speak to anyone asking what that statement meant. I sat in the car while KB was still in the church, and I wept. I guess it wasn't God who gave me my husband. I cried.

I needed to understand what God was doing and why. That night after evening service, a very special woman came up to me as I was crossing the street to do my regular routine of getting in the car immediately after service. She caught me and said she was very unhappy with what transpired in service today. She said that she was going to say something to the pastor and get him straight for doing that to me because he was out of order. She said that she wasn't afraid to confront him. She couldn't understand what made him say what he said.

I looked at her, knowing she wasn't meddling but only wanted to show me support. I had no words for her. I was hurt myself. But her willingness to confront him for me did something to me. Finally, someone was willing to do something. Finally, someone was bold enough to say, "Now, that's enough." I looked at her and began hearing words come out of my mouth that I hadn't put together or planned to say.

I said to her, "Say or do nothing in defense of me. What you all are witnessing firsthand is God anointing me. This is happening because God is preparing me for greater and better; this isn't to embarrass me; this is to reward me!" I paused. This was my voice I heard, but these were not my words. I didn't know where that came from, but I knew it was me speaking. The last time that happened to me was when KB asked if I loved him enough to marry him. When that came to my mind, I knew it was God. He was telling me to love through it all. Because I didn't fight back, because I stayed humble, God was pouring out his anointing on me and was going to reward me. Wow. With great expectations, I stayed in the zone I was in and waited on God.

After returning to work, life begins to fall back into place. My manager Kevin shot me an email and said to me that he was so thankful and glad that we were working together again. Everyone had nothing but kind words to say about me, and I was a good fit where I was working. He said he wanted to give me a raise. He said the raise would be a $10k raise. I wanted to scream. Ten thousand dollars more than what I was already making made my heart start beating fast. He said to me I deserved it.

I called KB and began whisper yelling on the phone, "Gloraaayyyy, Hallleluiahhhh." KB didn't even know or care what I was praising God for; he just started praising God with me. I told him Kevin just gave me a $10k raise effective immediately. I cried. I thought about the conversation I had with the woman at church. I thought about the discussion I had with KB on the matters that were being done to me. I thought about how God told me to be quiet, and I did. Had I stepped out and took matters into my own hands, had KB stepped up and said something, had we done anything wrong, we would have forfeited this blessing. I cried.

I went to church that Sunday and testified during service how God had blessed me with a $10k raise. I worshiped God at the top of my lungs, and I didn't care who didn't like me or who didn't want to hear me. God deserved this and more. After service, as usual on a Sunday, we went downstairs to eat dinner that I had cooked. We would sit down in the dining hall of the church with the group of ladies we called "The View." Mother Hinton, Mother Duppins, Mother Holmes, Mother Logan, and

Mother Keemer. Whatever I cooked, I made sure I always had enough for them as well.

God had placed me on a Daniel's fast, so I was eating salad, but everyone else was eating collard greens, fried chicken, and mac 'n' cheese. While I was eating my lettuce, I decided to text Kevin and tell him how I gave God praises for my raise, and I thanked him again for hiring me. Truth was, I was hired in February, got medical benefits in March, and KB was diagnosed in April. Timing.

Kevin replied that he was thankful for me just as much as I was thankful for the job. He said I had been a spiritual encouragement and blessing on the job to everyone. Then he added, "Oh, by the way, it's not a $10k raise; it is a $15k raise!" I could not believe what I was reading. KB and I began to run around the entire dining hall. In service that evening, I testified again, and I could feel I was making the devil mad!

The next day at work, Kevin took me out to lunch and asked me how it felt to have a six-figure income. I told him I gave God all the glory, and his response to me was there was more where that came from. Later, that day I received an email from Kevin. He was saying to me that he was following up on what we had discussed, but unfortunately, he was not going to be able to give me a $15k raise. "I knew it was too good to be true," was what came into my head. But as I kept reading, the email said instead of $15k, I would be receiving $20k starting with this upcoming check. I cried.

I called KB, and I had no words. God wanted to see if I would praise Him in what felt like a strange land because of what I had been experiencing. He wanted to see if I would hold back and be in my feelings. I showed God I was committed to Him, and He showed me He was committed to His word. Going home from work that night, I was driving down 295, giving thanks, and then I heard something say, "Nobody gets a $20k raise. That's a person's salary, not a raise." I nodded my head in agreement. Then I heard something say, "God gave you that raise because your husband is getting ready to die, and you need money to take care of your family as a widow!" I yelled out, "The blood of Jesus!"

Satan was trying to torment me; I had to rebuke him with the blood. It's true Satan will do everything in his power to make you feel like you are failing even when God is blessing you. The First Lady's tea event for my mother-in-law during the church anniversary was approaching. I had been absent from events to keep my distance, but I promised my husband I would extend my hand and go, so I did.

In her closing remarks, she gave thanks to everyone and was showing her appreciation. She said how thankful she was for her son; she was thankful for her grandchildren; she was truly thankful for her daughter, who was like a best friend. Then she wanted to give thanks to her special daughter, who had done so much. It wasn't me, but everyone noticed how everyone in the family was acknowledged; even my children were mentioned, but I was not.

KB was so upset and could not stop expressing his disappointment. He kept saying, "How can you mention the kids but not mention the woman who gave birth to them? I had gotten used to the behavior by then, but KB was just catching on. I learned to grow through it. KB wanted to sit down and finally discuss it. I was done talking, and I chose to let God handle it. I had done all I could. I even went to other family members for help, and all they could say was this was what they have always had to deal with. They gave me a place of refuge and an opportunity to vent, but this was something for God to handle, not me.

Discussions didn't go well. Things got worse. Statements were made that were untrue. Comments were made that did not make things better. When KB was told I wasn't raised right, it was the most insulting comment made, and I knew there was no resolve in this. When I heard, "If your wife wants to leave the church, let her leave," I was done. I may have been rejected, but God had other plans for me. I didn't want to leave, but I did want to be respected. Where was I going if I left? This was my church home—the only one I had here. This was my family—the only one I had here. Exactly where would I go? Where could I go? This hurt. The next day my father-in-law called KB and apologized to him. I loved my in-laws. Never stopped loving them and never will. But I was done.

If getting verbal confirmation of the displeasure for who I was wasn't enough, my baby girl Katelynn took ill, and the doctors were concerned that it was her kidneys. In the hospital for days, I started feeling like things were going bad for me and spiraling out of control. God touched me in prayer and reminding me that I was that olive being crushed and made into anointed oil. Katelynn being sick and in the hospital allowed me to stay home, and therefore, I was able to be away from the family for a while.

As she got better, so did my schedule. I missed another Sunday to go to Memphis, Tennessee, for a book club that read my book. KB was planning to come too, but on a different flight at a different time, so I was at the airport alone. It was so many people on the flight, so the boarding area was crowded. I put one of my books in my purse for casual reading while on the plane. While I sat there waiting for the time to board, I looked up and couldn't believe who I saw. After all these years. All this time going by. After I had just written a book about my life, I ran into Mr. MarcTrain's mom.

I was so happy to see her. We hadn't talked in a while after she made it through cancer. She looked so good, and we both thought it was crazy that we were both getting on a flight to go to Memphis. When I told her why I was going, she insisted on getting my book so that she could read it. I knew I had a casual copy in my purse, so I autographed it and gave it to her. We decided to sit next to each other on the plane, and we caught up with what was going on in our lives.

This was my first time in a long time seeing her and not being concerned about her son, just happy to see her. My thoughts did go to, *What if he reads my book? Would he be upset with me for sharing so much of our relationship?* At this point, it didn't matter. The book was written and done. I was on my second one now. As she began to read the book, I closed my eyes and pretended to be asleep. I couldn't believe I was a real author. Just like at this book club in Memphis, I had another book club invitation in North Carolina thanks to Harriette and all the beautiful women of Fuquay-Varina, North Carolina. It was exciting talking about the book and then telling how I just ran into Mr. MarcTrain's mom at the airport. You just can't make this stuff up.

I didn't plan it, but it was a blessing to take a few Sundays off away in a different church setting. I wasn't looking for a new church home or looking for reasons to not be in place, but God knew what I needed. I had had to deal with many different moods, attitudes, and personalities at church and had to learn they were spirits. I knew everyone wasn't happy with KB's decision to get a kidney transplant. Some wanted us to wait and see if dialysis would get his kidneys working again. KB and I were moving too fast. Were we?

I knew my husband. I knew he felt less of a man having to do dialysis. I knew he felt that he was not strong because he was always exhausted. I knew he felt handicapped because he was limited. He didn't want anyone to see this side of him because he had never shown weakness. He didn't allow any conversation about this because he didn't want anyone feeling sorry for him. He didn't want anyone telling him he shouldn't feel the way he felt because he was the only person in his unique skin, built the way he was, and entitled to cope how he saw fit. I could never explain this in detail because he was my husband, and I covered him. Nonetheless, I seemed to have taken on the reputation of the one who was influencing KB incorrectly and pushing the transplant.

Week after week, in every prayer during service, it was prayed that his kidneys be revived instead of the surgery. KB became frustrated, and I tried to explain to him that because people were not in his shoes, they would never fully understand; they just wanted what they thought was best for him.

He was tired of it, and I didn't know what to do to help him but stay by his side and support him like I had. His body was going through so much and now his mind and, spiritually, he felt he was being attacked. We needed everyone to comprehend that we were not in a place of "lack of faith"; we were actually just trusting God to take this wherever He desires as long as we survived it.

People that didn't even talk to us, who had been more than rude and pestiferous, seemed to have more spiritual insight than we did. My husband came to me one Sunday in between service and said how he was told a young lady who had been nothing but a vexing and troublesome spirit to us our entire marriage expressed that she needed to pray for him. He was being instructed to let her pray. He was upset because he couldn't understand how that gesture could even be taken seriously after all that this individual had done to our children and us throughout the years. Here he was with more than we both ever imagined having to go through right now, but yet he was presented with this request; a request that was more like a directive, a no option order.

Because we wanted God to be God, we did not deny any prayer, but KB didn't know that he was going to be put on the spot. In the middle of the next service, called to the front and told to kneel at the altar, the one who had caused hurt in times past was handed the anointed oil to now lay hands on to heal. Knowing full well if other players were in this scenario, there would never be a day that someone with this negative history against your spouse would be allowed to lay hands. God told you to pray for someone, do it. You don't need to make a scene or get everyone's attention. Just pray. We didn't understand it, and with all the other things we were facing, we didn't try. We cried. We let God know that we were confused. We let God know that we didn't feel like we could take any more. And God did what He always did: He comforted.

Before I knew it, book sales were picking up even more. It was closer to the holidays, and people were purchasing my book, The Covering, as a Christmas gift. I was receiving emails from people from all walks of life, from a bishop to seasoned mothers to young girls to single men. Married men and women reading this book and talking about the effects that it had on them. Reading emails and listening to people tell me that this book should be a movie made me feel good. Hearing different people from different backgrounds all say they could relate to this book made me feel like I accomplished what I set out to do. It gave me great pleasure time after time hearing everyone say how they could not put the book down after reading the first chapter; they needed to go on to the next to see what happened. I was humbled.

But as things get good, the devil is always busy trying to make things go bad. KB was told at his job that they were cutting his position. It was right before Thanksgiving, and his job was laying him off. He went to the head and asked if they really thought it was right and fair to lay a man off right before the holidays. That made them retract and tell KB that his last day would be the last week of the year, but he didn't have to come back to work.

I realized then how much God loved us. I didn't get the $20k raise because my husband was going to die like the enemy tried to make me believe. I got the raise to help cover costs as my husband was getting laid off. That really didn't bother us because the kidney transplant surgery had been set, and the date was coming up. God had been speaking to KB, and it was time for him to make some moves.

The holidays came and went, and it was getting closer and closer to the time. Faith was excited, and so were we. I was making the most passionate love to KB to give him reasons to fight while on that operating table to keep on living. I needed him to remember what he was getting better for.

We went to meet with the surgeon for the preoperation visit, and KB and I did the same thing as we shook his hand. We held it a little longer and were praying for his hand as we greeted him. We couldn't do anything but laugh.

This entire ordeal had done nothing but make KB and I take a closer look at our relationship, our relationship with God, and where we were to go from here. KB deserved to have someone wait on him and foot and take care of him just as he had done Dion when she was sick. While it was humbling for him to go through, it showed the both of us how strong and how deep our love was. After all we had been through and even still facing, we were still together.

January 22, 2015. We got up early and prepared to get to the hospital. While my full trust and confidence were in God, I was still in need of prayer. To KB, I tried to remain strong, but internally I was a wreck. Faith was truly going through with this. She had five children of her own that could one day need a kidney, but she was giving it to my husband. I was so thankful that her husband gave her permission to follow the leading of the Lord.

Now we were here. Now it was time. Now, as they wheeled Faith away, I knew it was time for me to say my "see you later" to KB.

The way he kissed me and held on to me made me feel like he was doing it just in case this was our last time. I cried. If there was ever any doubt before, I knew for sure that I wanted this man in my life. I let go of his hand to let the nurse do the final preparation, but I stayed right there. I knew others were trying to make this moment significant for his parents. They had never gone through one of their children being in this situation. It was hard. Imagine though. KB. He was a forty-year-old man. He hadn't seen his children graduate high school like his parents had. He hadn't seen his children get married like his parents had. He hasn't been blessed with grandchildren like his parents had. While many wanted to say how hard this was on everyone, it wasn't harder on anyone than it was for KB.

KB was my husband, and that was who I made my vow and commitment to, so that was who was my concern. No one else—just KB. I didn't want to break down, so I didn't think about myself. If something was to happen to KB, I would be a widow. My in-laws would still have each other, but I would be alone. My children would not have a father. Everyone else neglected to see how much this impacted us more than it did anyone else. It didn't matter because I trusted God, and this faith walk was one that God would get all the glory from.

My mom was not risking me being alone this time. She made it to Baltimore and was right there with me at the hospital while I waited. No, the family didn't sit all together, and we didn't hold conversations with one another, but one thing I knew we all did was pray. When the doctor came out to give me an update after hours of sitting, he told me that the surgery was successful. The surgeon said that the surgery was so successful that KB began urinating on the operating table right after the kidney was connected. Most times, the donated organ is sleep and takes days to wake up. But God wanted to show that this was His doing, not mine, not KB's or Faith's, not the surgeon's or anyone else's. He gets all the glory.

Twelve years ago, on this very date, Dion passed. KB's life was changed forever, and he would become a widower at a young age. Marrying me a few months after, three years later, I gave birth to a male child on this very same date, representing life and another generation of Hunts. And now, everyone else had left the hospital after hearing it was successful. Mom went to my home to be with the kids and celebrate Kendrick's birthday. Faith's parents waited for her to get into her recovery room, and then they left.

Everyone was gone, and here came Clinton. Right as he was coming to check on me, they told me I could go back and see KB. Clinton came with me, and we were the first to see my baby in recovery. My eyes got watery as I thanked God for what He had done. KB, opening his eyes, told me he loved me as I kissed his forehead. Then he sought Clinton and began telling him how he needed to be saved. He blurted out to Clinton that he would be starting a ministry soon, and he wanted Clinton to be a part of it. Without hesitation, Clinton agreed.

KB looked back at me and said that he was so hungry and he really wanted something to eat. He made me get a nurse and ask for them to bring him something to eat. He didn't like the food and really shouldn't have been eating it, but that's my KB...

He would not have it no other way. While eating, he went right back into discussing ministry.

KB and I have been together all this time and have gone through so much. God made him my covering, and like any marriage, Satan will challenge your stability and validity. He will complex your union and make you question if it should be. Not only should KB and I be together, but our assignment is together. Soul business is our sole business, and that will not change. We have purpose together, which is greater than any force trying to pull us apart.

We aren't perfect; our marriage isn't perfect; our relationships with in-laws, children, and friends are not perfect. But God's divine will for our life is. There is so much more. There is so much to do. So much to witness. So much to become a testimony. KB's parents, my in-laws, are my parents too. They taught us the importance of unity and sticking together. They taught us how to weather the storm. They taught us how to love and forgive to heal. Yes, we are humans. Humans make mistakes, but we must give grace because you never know when the shoe will be on the other foot.

I'm about to be a pastor's wife.

# DIARY 6

# KB & I Say Goodbye

In 2013, KB and I went on a vacation with another married couple. We went to Hawaii and spent over seven days there. We needed the break and time away from everything and everyone. This couple had just gone through their marriage almost being completely destroyed because of infidelity. As KB and I hung out with them and had critical and helpful dialog, it helped me to see there were some things I needed to be honest about with my own marriage. Helping them and encouraging them was good, but my marriage was my priority.

It was time to stop looking to blame others for what was or what was not. Our marriage and life decisions belonged to us. We were the ones who stood before God and made vows, no one else. It was time to take ownership of our own flaws and then appreciate the things we had been spared. It was time to cut the cord on excuses and be real. It was time for a divorce.

Divorce. I finally made the decision I was going to get a divorce, but not from my husband. Divorce is described with the definition meaning to separate or dissociate (something) from something else. Yeah. It was time for us to start divorcing some things in our life.

Divorce yourself. I am divorced from the hurts of my past that keep me thinking I am not deserving of that happy ending I have worked so hard for. Divorce yourself. I am divorced from the first lie ever told to me that I believed about myself, which had me thinking less of who God made me to be. It sounded so true, so I believed it—now I have divorced it. We have all made mistakes and are flawed. I will no longer allow those who sat front and center while I made my mistakes continue to sit at the table with me bringing my past up to shame, hurt, or demean me. I am divorced from my past; I am not the same person anymore.

Divorce yourself. I am divorced from the people who feel they know me better than I know myself and want me to be what they feel I should be instead of living my own destiny. I am divorced from the jealousy of people around me that see the gifts and talents in me and hate that they are unable to see their own gifts. I am divorced from lowering my level of greatness because it supposedly offends someone else. I am no longer responsible for your lack of becoming because I decided to grow. I'm not slowing down so you can catch up. And with that, say what you want, but I am divorced. From the desire to respond to every attack against my character. I will no longer attempt to defend or address every negative comment directed at me. I am excusing negativity from my life; you have lost your place and opportunity to dwell in my presence.

Divorce yourself. I am divorced from the idea that I am second because that is how I have been described. I never was second. That was designed to make me feel like I wasn't good enough to be first. I didn't realize it wasn't about when I became, but it was the fact I was chosen to be. I didn't choose to be KB's wife; God did. I'm glad He did and no one else. I'm not the second wife; I am the one and only wife. I don't worry about him being unfaithful or unsatisfied. He will never have to worry about me being unfaithful, and oh God, yes, I am very satisfied. KB is the only man in the world who has ever made melodic symphonies of love with Lillian Mary Nowlin-Hunt, and he is the only man who ever will. No love triangles, mistaken identity, moments of weakness, or sloppy seconds over here. Originals only.

Divorce yourself. I am divorced from the thoughts of being a terrible mother and an awful wife. I am blessed to have a wonderful husband and children, but they are even more blessed to have me. I am doing my best, and that is what they deserve—nothing but the best. I don't have to live up to the baby momma description. I can and will continue to live in peace. Raising my children in church, teaching them to honor and love God, and instill in them the right way to go. What they do when they become of age will be their own decision. I go hard for each one of my children and will continue for the rest of their lives. I carried them in the womb, I gave birth to them, and I have prayed for them to be covered. I owe no man nothing when it comes to my children. Your opinions don't matter. Yup. I'm divorced.

Divorce yourself. I am divorced from being a widow. The fear I had of my husband leaving me to raise our four children alone is a feeling I will never forget. I told God I wanted to grow old with this man, and I believe God hears and will agree to my prayer. He will live to see his children grown and, one day, even have grandchildren. We will become gray together and be there for each other's last breath. I am divorcing myself from any other ending to this wonderful life God has given to me.

Divorce yourself. I am divorced from the idea of always being a victim. I don't make all the right choices. I don't do everything to perfection. Everything is not always on someone else. I have to own my actions and who I am. I have to accept that every time someone does something to me, it doesn't mean they are out to get me. When I do things that are not so favorable to others unintentionally, I have to remember the same can happen to me. I am not a victim. People make mistakes. I make mistakes.

Divorce yourself. I am divorcing the daydreams and wondering what would of, could of, or should have happened. I now see with God in control of my life, I got the best results. I don't need to hear anyone tell me they love me because I love myself, and more importantly, God has shown me He loves me. I have divorced the insinuation that God is not real and His Spirit is not needed. If God had not filled me with His Spirit, I would have ruined my marriage when the opportunity arose. I am divorced from the thought I could ever do this or make it in this marriage without God. Everyone else may have divorced their spouse, but I am divorcing myself from that option.

Divorce yourself. I am divorced from every third party that, in any way, shape, or form, attempts to separate my husband and me. No family, friend, or long past time relations will ever interfere with what God has placed together. I am divorced from the rumors and the lies that we have outlived this far. I am divorced from the fake apologies from those that see we survived the attacks against our union. There is so much purpose in this marriage, and because we put God first through ministry, our marriage is sealed by God. The future, the joy, the satisfaction, the passion, the commitment, the connection, the honesty, the dependability, the faithfulness, the love, the peace, the arguments, the making up—we are sealed by God and divorced from all others.

Divorce yourself. I am divorced from the thoughts that someone else could ever love me more than KB. He was strategically made and designed specifically for me. The way he fits me—yes, in all the ways he fits me, there is no question or doubt in my mind God knew what He was doing when he put us together. With that said, I am divorced from trying to fit in with other couples who are unhappy in their marriage. I am happy. I am thankful. I am satisfied. I don't have to pretend to be happy or make up reasons to be unhappy. This marriage from the beginning has been unique and always will be. I am not going to make up misery for my marriage. What you see is what you get. We are who we are, and we have divorced ourselves from any other image.

Divorce yourself. I am divorced from entertaining anything that doesn't involve my Lord and Savior. God has been too good to me for me to act as if He doesn't belong at the center of my very being. I am not ashamed that I live my life for God, nor will I allow anything or anyone ever to make me feel that way. He gets all the credit for my life being what it is today and the bright future to come. This isn't about religion; this isn't a denomination or family thing. This isn't about a "personal" relationship with Him. This is me accepting my real being—my spiritual being. I am breathing and alive because His Spirit is within me. I embrace my Lord's spirit and am thankful to be a vessel. I'm not compromising that for anyone.

Divorce yourself. I am divorced from trying to fit into someone else's ministry. I don't have to be in the in-crowd. I don't have to be well known. I don't have to be upfront and center. I don't have to kiss up, butter up, and do wrong to advance or gain opportunities. I may never get called to sing, preach, teach, or minister anywhere, but I will still be a vessel of honor for God right in the vineyard He has me in. My life will be the pulpit. My diary writing will be my sermonic solos. My books will be my sermons. I don't have to get invited anywhere. I declare over my own life my gift will make room for me because I am divorced.

Divorce yourself. I am divorced from being "the pastor's daughter-in-law." So what? I married the pastor's son. I had an identity before that, and my identity continued to develop well after. I don't need to be the cookie-cutter daughter because, first of all, this family isn't a crisp cookie-cut family. I'm not going to listen to anyone who tries to divide us, and I will not be minimized to only existing because of who I am married to and what family I married into. I am getting ready to be a pastor's wife now. After watching all that my mother-in-law went through, I could care less about the title. I am divorcing myself from all titles and just want to do the work. People are going to have something to say about what you do and what you don't do. It is best I divorce myself now and save myself the heartache later.

Divorce yourself. I am divorced from long-time grudges. I don't hate anyone, and I feel sorry for those who feel they hate me. I love. I want to continue to love and be loved. What has happened is done; learning from it all is the best thing that I can do. I know I am not perfect, so I cannot expect the people and situations that arise in my life to be perfect either. I forgive and thank God for the opportunity to be forgiven.

Divorce yourself. I am divorced from the stigma of being a black woman. If I say too much, I am loud and untamed. If I say nothing, I am passive and not true to the cause. I am a black woman that loves being black. I love being a woman. I don't have to go with what all other black women are doing, saying, and feeling. I don't have to force other black women to feel like I feel. When I want to command attention, I have that right just as much as anyone else. When I want to be off to myself, I am entitled to that too. I don't have to agree with today's sexy. I am my own sexy. My husband likes it, and I love it. I'm good.

Divorce yourself. I am divorced from poverty! For too long, we have struggled. For too long, we have suffered. We made poor decisions, and we have learned from them. I am now thankful to be a good steward over the resources and finances that come into our lives. I see that giving makes space for God to give to us more than we could imagine, so being stingy or selfish is not an option. One of the best divorces ever—lack, be gone!

Yes. Divorce yourself. I am divorced from feeling like I must pretend to be someone I am not just to fit into a place or group that I had no business being a part of in the first place. Who would ever get to know me if all they see is the masked me? I am divorced from wearing masks—either you love me, or you don't. Either way, I still exist. I am divorcing myself from every negative force that attempts to invade my life and make me miserable forever. I don't deserve that, and you don't either. We are better than that. My thoughts, my opinion, my decisions matter to me, and that means something. It may not mean anything to anyone else, but so what? All of your thoughts and opinions and decisions don't all matter to me either.

Divorce yourself. Learn to not chase anyone that doesn't appreciate your presence. Let them see what it is like to feel your absence. Do not beg anyone to stay in your life. Know your worth. Divorce yourself and learn to appreciate and spend time with those that matter. Accepting what cannot be changed, changing those things you cannot accept, and divorce yourself.

Divorce yourself. To everything and everyone designated to tell me what I could not do or could not become—we are officially divorced. It's time. It is actually past time. We should have done this a long time ago. Get your dignity back. Get your integrity back. Get your peace back. Get your confidence back. Divorce yourself. Realize the things that make you happy—for me, it is my husband, my children, my life that I am developing, the life God gave to me. The very things that God put in place are just what Satan wants you to leave, destroy, end, and get rid of. But now that I see and know better, I can make a better choice. I am getting a divorce, but not from the life God made and intended for me. I am divorcing everything else that never should have been. Goodbye.

...And now, I am a pastor's wife, and the new diary begins.